BRITISH BUILT
AIRCRAFT
GREATER LONDON

BRITISH BUILT AIRCRAFT
AIRCRAFT
GREATER LONDON

Ron Smith

TEMPUS

First published 2002, reprinted 2005

Tempus Publishing Limited
The Mill, Brimscombe Port,
Stroud, Gloucestershire, GL5 2QG
www.tempus-publishing.com

British Library Cataloguing in Publication Data.
A catalogue record for this book is available from the British Library.

ISBN 0 7524 2770 9

Typesetting and origination by Tempus Publishing Limited.
Printed in Great Britain.

Contents

Introduction

Some twenty-five years ago, on the formation of British Aerospace (BAe), the American magazine *Aviation Week and Space Technology* wryly commented that the final phase of development of the Society of British Aircraft Constructors (SBAC) had now taken place. Whereas previously the numerous members of the SBAC had reflected the vigour, diversity and inventive spirit of the British industry, it had, following restructuring in 1960, been reduced to the 'Society of Both Aircraft Companies' (i.e. the British Aircraft Corporation and Hawker Siddeley Aviation Ltd). The formation of BAe was the final act in the process, with the once great industry reduced to the 'Single British Aerospace Company'.

This lighthearted comment contains an important message. British aircraft industry names, which were once well known to the public, have disappeared from the day to day business of manufacturing aeroplanes. Indeed, in many instances, their operating sites have even disappeared from the map, this being nowhere more true than within Greater London. At first sight it seems as if the once vibrant British aircraft industry has contracted virtually to the point of extinction since the Second World War. The entire industry has been reduced to the firms of BAE SYSTEMS, AgustaWestland, Slingsby and Britten-Norman (surviving, as I write, in its latest manifestation: B-N Group), together with sundry microlight and home-built aircraft suppliers.

Many British aircraft manufacturers have disappeared altogether and this fact has provided the inspiration for this survey of the industry. Pondering on the demise of such company names as Sopwith, Hawker, de Havilland, Fairey Aviation and Handley Page, and the loss (in the context of Greater London) of such sites as Hanworth, Heston, Hendon, Croydon and Cricklewood, the idea grew that an effort should be made to record something of Britain's aircraft construction history and heritage.

The first outcome of this desire to document the past glories of the British aircraft industry was a successful entry in the 1994 Pooley's International Dawn to Dusk Flying Competition by the author, with his colleague Colin Dodds. The entry, under the title *Lost Names in British Aviation*, consisted of the record of a flight made on a single day (between dawn and dusk) in a 1936 de Havilland Hornet Moth, over sites in Britain where aircraft had once been built, by companies that no longer exist. The research carried out in support of that competition entry has been greatly extended to provide the basis for this record of British achievement, innovation, failure and success.

This volume is the first in a series, which, when completed, will provide a complete record of aircraft construction in Britain. As soon as one starts to examine the history of the aircraft industry, it is clear that it has developed through a number of distinct phases. These phases can be characterised as: pioneers (1908 to 1914); First World War mass production (1914 to 1918); collapse and re-birth between the wars (1919 to 1939); Second World War mass production (1939 to 1945); post-war (1945 to 1960); and modern times. A discussion of the evolution of the industry covering these six main periods of activity can be found in the next chapter. Whilst this section provides the general background, it also places aircraft manufacture in Greater London into this overall context.

Each volume of this work will focus on a different regional area, documenting activity over the whole period from 1908 until the present day. This will thus provide the first comprehensive review of aircraft construction in Britain, keyed to the places where this enterprise was actually performed. The objective of the whole project is to pay tribute to the heritage of the British aircraft industry, and to create and preserve a record of its lost endeavours. The

Hornet Moth G-AELO is seen here at Pocklington prior to the 1994 Dawn to Dusk competition flight by Colin Dodds and the author. (Author)

major new element presented in this work is to shed some light on the sheer scale of the effort involved in the construction of aircraft during the First World War. This is nowhere more true than in terms of the activity within Greater London.

Content

This series of books, of which Greater London is the first, records British aircraft manufacture in nearly all its manifestations, in the form of a regional survey of the United Kingdom. The scope of the work is deliberately wide, including as many locations as possible where aircraft have been built, whether by their original designers or by contractors. Exclusions are limited to balloons, the majority of gliders and microlight aircraft, and home-built aircraft of foreign design, unless substantially modified in the form flown in the United Kingdom.

Being centred on the various manufacturing sites, the book allows a wider scope than a mere litany of product histories, allowing additional discussion of people, places and events. As a result, the major players of the industry are recorded alongside the wealth of early activity, light aircraft and one-off designs that provide a rich background to the main scene. Such is the scope of this record that the space that can be allocated to any individual firm is necessarily limited. This mainly has the effect of producing a somewhat condensed view of some of the largest and best known companies. This limitation is, hopefully, compensated for by some of the fascinating but lesser known material presented, covering many companies which are likely to be unfamiliar to the reader.

Those interested in the detailed history of the major manufacturers will be able to find many excellent books with which to fill in the detail if they wish. However, the same cannot be said for companies such as Palladium Autocars Ltd, Hewlett & Blondeau Ltd, Wells Aviation Co. Ltd, The Regent Carriage Co. Ltd, Glendower Aircraft Co. Ltd, and the many other lesser known London companies included here.

Considerable research has been required to identify the companies themselves, locate their operating sites, and to illustrate some of their products. Also included are photographs of the often fast disappearing remains of once proud factories and airfields as they return to agriculture, housing, gravel pits and decay.

Structure

These introductory remarks are followed by a discussion of the evolution of the aircraft industry, highlighting the activities that characterise each of the main periods identified above, and tailored to the specific region covered by each volume. The contraction through successive mergers that has given rise to the present shape of the industry is presented, together with a family tree of British Aerospace (which contains all of the aircraft heritage of the present BAE SYSTEMS), and of the helicopter manufacturer AgustaWestland.

The main content of the volume follows; Volume One being a survey of aircraft manufacture in Greater London. The grouping of entries into particular locations within Greater London has been based on their proximity on the map, rather than by formal reference to either administrative districts, or, for example, postcodes. The presentation structure chosen is alphabetical by location, and then generally alphabetical by manufacturer's name at any given site.

Only one variation in this approach has been adopted: where activity at a single site has only involved one firm at any time, or where the evolution of a single major firm has dominated a particular site, the presentation is chronological, rather than alphabetical. Kingston upon Thames is an example of such a variation, its entry comprising the chronological transformation of the Sopwith activity into British Aerospace, via H.G. Hawker Engineering Co. Ltd, Hawker Aircraft Ltd and Hawker Siddeley Aviation Ltd. This is then followed by an alphabetical listing of other companies that operated in the Kingston area.

This volume covers the Greater London contribution to Britain's aircraft manufacturing heritage. When the series is complete, the intention is that it will provide a comprehensive geographic and product history of United Kingdom aircraft construction. I have attempted to cover all sites where aircraft manufacture took place, and to select photographs which provide a balanced mix of example products, locations as they are now and as they were during their heyday, or combinations of these. A number of the photographs are of the sites taken from the air during the 1994 Dawn to Dusk competition.

Information Sources and Acknowledgements

A number of major reference sources were used to create this survey of the British aircraft industry. Chief among these were magazines, such as *Flight, The Aeroplane,* and *Aeroplane Monthly,* and the following books and publications, which provide particularly useful material across the whole spectrum of the industry: Terence Boughton's excellent *History of the British Light Aeroplane*; A.J. Jackson's *British Civil Aircraft since 1919*; the individual company histories published by Putnam; Ken Ellis' *British Homebuilt Aircraft Since 1920*; R. Dallas Brett's *History of British Aviation 1909-14*; Arthur Ord-Hume's encyclopaedic *British Light Aeroplanes – Their Evolution, Development and Perfection 1920-40*; many editions of *Janes' All the World's Aircraft*; a wide range of test pilot autobiographies; and numerous other sources. A comprehensive bibliography is provided at the end of the work.

In setting out to document the British aircraft industry, I wish to give a flavour for the breadth of the endeavour in terms of diversity of both products and places used for aircraft manufacture. It is not my intention to provide a definitive record of every aircraft built, nor an encyclopaedia of production quantities. In some cases, I have found the latter aspect clouded with uncertainty; unless clearly definitive data is available, I have used Bruce Robertson's *British Military Aircraft Serials 1878-1987* as a guide when indicating production quantities. I have not hesitated to highlight areas where conflicting information may be found in readily available references. It is for others to research and clarify these issues.

Particular thanks are due to my colleague Rob Preece for the loan of his original unbound copies of *Flight* covering the period 1911 to 1923, and to Liz and Peter Curtis for access to a complete collection of *Aeroplane Monthly* magazine. Thanks are also due to Chris Ilett for the loan of *Flight* magazines from 1929 and 1930. A further acknowledgement must be made to the Royal Aeronautical Society library; not only are their early copies of *The Aeroplane* bound complete with their advertising pages, but here I also found a copy of R. Borlase Matthews' *Aviation Pocket-Book, 1919-1920* whose Gazetteer of the industry put me on the track of many unfamiliar companies. I am most grateful for the assistance provided by George Jenks (AVRO Heritage Centre) and Barry Abraham (Airfield Research Group).

Acknowledgement is due to those companies still extant (and not today associated with the aircraft industry) who answered my correspondence. Mention must also be made of the information and photographs supplied by Ken Ellis, and by Mr A.H. Fraser-Mitchell (Handley Page Association), Fred Ballam (GKN Westland), Olivia Johnston (Bombardier Aerospace, Belfast) and Del Hoyland (Martin-Baker Aircraft Co. Ltd). I must further acknowledge the access provided to photographic material by my present employer, BAE SYSTEMS. In making this acknowledgement, I should also stress that all opinions expressed herein are entirely my own.

Finally, as indicated earlier, the research for this book was triggered by the successful entry in the 1994 Pooley's International Dawn to Dusk competition. This could not have been made without the support, encouragement, experience and competence of my colleague, Colin Dodds, who flew the aircraft, and the generosity of David Wells, who made his aircraft, G-AELO, available for the competition flight.

Not Yet Found (and Imperfect Knowledge Disclaimer)

In a work of this scope, it is inevitable that mistakes and omissions will be made; for these I apologise, throwing myself upon the mercies of a hopefully sympathetic readership. Any additions and corrections made known to me will be most welcome and will be incorporated in any further edition that the publisher sees fit to print. Wherever possible, the company names used are those that the firms themselves used, for example in their advertising.

In some cases, the amount of information presented is effectively limited to the manufacturer's name. This is an indication that I know nothing else about them. The authorised share capital may also be given of companies when initially registered. This is included because it, hopefully, gives a basic indication of how 'serious' a concern they were. One might, for example, conclude that the Edgware Engineering & Aircraft Co. (share capital £100) was not of the same mould as Cremer Aircraft & Industrial Works Ltd, of Lorn Road, Brixton, which had a share capital of £10,250.

Whilst the original intention was to list companies that built complete aircraft, lack of information about the actual products of some companies means that (particularly in the First World War) the content has certainly strayed into the component supply industry. Although this may stretch the scope of the menu beyond the taste of some, it does at least add richness to the feast.

Some firms which sound like aircraft factories may have only built parts (for example, the Highgate Aircraft Co. Ltd); others, which entered the industry to build parts, ended up building complete machines (for example, R. Cattle which spawned the Central Aircraft Co.); finally, there are those which might have done almost anything (for example, Witton, Witton & Co). Once again, I must trust that any blurring of definitions as to what to include or exclude will be forgiven.

Mention must also be made of aircraft and companies which are definitely known to have existed, but for which I have been quite unable to establish a location. At the time of writing, these are:

The **Buckle** parasol monoplane. Illegally flown, unregistered, in 1929, the Buckle monoplane was constructed by Mr S.L. Buckle for the princely sum of £17. Sopwith Snipe wings, ailerons, rudder, elevator and tailplane were used. A simple rectangular section fuselage was built, and power was supplied by a 45hp six-cylinder Anzani radial. The propeller was obtained from a shed at Brooklands and cut down until the Anzani provided a satisfactory rpm. (Source: *Aeroplane Monthly*, April 1979).

The **Newport Aircraft Co.** A question was asked in Parliament in November 1918 in relation to unpaid wages and bonuses at this company.

In addition, other companies whose addresses are unknown include **Cambrian Aircraft Constructors Ltd**, and **Northwold Aircraft Co. Ltd**.

R. CATTLE

27, Wybert St., Stanhope St., N.W.,

has pleasure in announcing that owing to large increase in his Aircraft business he is now conducting same quite separately under the style of

THE

CENTRAL AIRCRAFT CO.

Palmerston Works, 179, High Road, Kilburn. TELEPHONE: HAMPSTEAD 4728

R. Cattle on announcing the formation of the Central Aircraft Co.

The Evolution of the British Aircraft Industry

This section presents a summary of the overall development of the aircraft industry in Britain, highlighting specifically (in this volume) activities in Greater London. London, with its many small businesses and industrial areas, its political and financial base as the nation's capital city, and, at least until the encroachment of suburbia, its many airfields and flying sites, played a major role in the development of the aircraft industry.

As this volume reveals, the main activities associated with Greater London comprise:

- Pioneer flying and construction at a number of locations.
- Large-scale manufacture during the First World War, backed up by a substantial parts supply industry, and a number of training schools.
- The growth of many large and small concerns building aircraft for the private owner, including, in particular, The de Havilland Aircraft Co. Ltd at Stag Lane, and a great variety of companies at Croydon, Hanworth and Heston.
- Aircraft manufacture by The Fairey Aviation Co. Ltd at Hayes, and by Handley Page Ltd at Cricklewood throughout the lives of those companies.
- The successive manifestations of Sopwith, H.G. Hawker Engineering Co. Ltd, Hawker Aircraft Ltd, Hawker Siddeley Aviation Ltd and British Aerospace plc at Kingston upon Thames.
- The establishment of the head offices and registered addresses of many firms, many of these being either in the City, or in the vicinity of Westminster.

The closure of many airfields as a result of increasing pressure for housing, and the development of Heathrow as an international airport means that the preponderance of activity described in this volume occurs up to the end of the Second World War. Those companies whose production activities did continue in Greater London (e.g. Fairey Aviation, Hawker and its successors, and Handley Page) all established flight test airfields outside the area – at White Waltham, Dunsfold and Radlett, respectively.

1
Pioneers
(1908-1914)

Flying in Europe began in France in 1906, with the flights of Santos Dumont in October and November of that year. By 1908, practical machines were being flown in France by such pioneers as Farman, Voisin and Blériot. The Wright brothers astounded their audiences with the performance and controllability of their craft when it was publicly displayed at Le Mans in the autumn of 1908. The time was now right for Britain's pioneers to take to the air.

A.V. Roe had been experimenting for some time at Brooklands, but his short flights of 8 June 1908 failed to achieve official recognition. S.F. Cody flew at Farnborough in October 1908, J.T.C. Moore-Brabazon flew at Eastchurch at the end of April 1909, and by July 1909 A.V. Roe's triplane was performing well at Lea Marshes. In February 1909, the Short brothers took a licence to manufacture Wright biplanes for the Aero Club, setting up a factory at Leysdown on the Isle of Sheppey. Britain now possessed an aircraft industry.

The pioneering period prior to the First World War was marked by adventure, experiment and innovation – the techniques of building and flying aeroplanes were not yet understood. There was no right or wrong solution to any aspect of design, and consequently almost every possible configuration was attempted and many blind alleys were explored. Potentially good designs were let down by poor detail design, inadequate control arrangements, or heavy, inefficient and unreliable engines.

The pioneer aircraft that have been included in this work are, in the main, those which are known to have flown successfully. In some cases, where the fact of flight is not entirely certain, aircraft have been included which at least have the appearance that they might have flown successfully (e.g. the Fritz Monoplane at Brooklands, 1911). Known freaks have been excluded (e.g. the Aerial Wheel Monoplane which was entered in the 1912 Military Trials at Larkhill).

Great enthusiasm and considerable public interest marked this period. Pioneers were building aircraft in unlikely places and, in the perhaps extreme case of Mr Jezzi at Eastchurch, even camping out in their aeroplane sheds for days at a time to get in the maximum amount of flying. Showmen like Grahame-White, Hucks and H.J.D. Astley toured the country with their machines. The flying meetings at Hendon were enormously popular, and provided a showcase for both machines and men.

The main manufacturing locations prior to the First World War were Brooklands, Eastchurch, Hendon and Shoreham, with Hendon being second only to Brooklands in importance. Other Greater London locations where significant production and/or flying took place during the pioneer period include Barking, Battersea, Camberwell, Cricklewood, Erith, Hackney, Kingston upon Thames and Richmond.

Given the individualistic nature of pioneers in any field, it is perhaps not surprising to find them popping up throughout the London area, sometimes at unfamiliar locations. Thus we find that during this pioneering period many of the founders of the British aircraft industry were already active within the Greater London area, including:

- Frederick Handley Page at Barking, Cricklewood and Hendon.
- Robert Blackburn and Claude Grahame-White at Hendon.
- Geoffrey de Havilland at Fulham.
- A.V. Roe at Putney, Hackney and Wembley.
- T.O.M. Sopwith and H.G. Hawker at Kingston upon Thames.

Hall Aviation Co. on building their own aircraft.

Enthusiasm for flying resulted in the establishment of a number of flying schools, notably at Brooklands and Hendon. The schools, which continued to be active during the First World War, necessarily became adept at the repair, modification and re-building of aeroplanes. As a result, even where their school machines were initially of standard types, many were later modified, adapted, re-engined, etc. to become new variants. A number of schools then branched out to design their own machines based on the experience gained in school flying. Manufacturers whose origins lay in successful flying schools include W.H. Ewen, G.W. Beatty, Hewlett & Blondeau, Hall Aviation Co., London & Provincial, Ruffy Arnall & Baumann, and many others.

L. Howard Flanders at Richmond, British Deperdussin at Upper Holloway, and Warwick Wright Ltd of Battersea made short-lived contributions to aircraft production, but had come and gone before the First World War. Finally, we must not forget the enthusiast experimenters, such as H.S. Dixon and J.D.B. Long at Acton, Everrett Edgcumbe, Chanter, and G.M. Dyott at Hendon, T.W.K. Clarke at Kingston, and Perry-Beadle at Twickenhem.

In all the excitement of this period, with its many bizarre and unsuccessful designs, the seeds of today's configurations, and of the future aircraft industry were sown. Great fruit was to be harvested once these seeds found the fertile ground of warfare.

The RUFFY-BAUMANN

SCHOOL of FLYING

LONDON AERODROME, HENDON, N.W.
'PHONE: KINGSBURY 151.

POINTS

FOR

PROSPECTIVE PUPILS.

1. HIGH-POWERED MACHINES.
2. DUAL CONTROL—THE SAFE SYSTEM.
3. LIMITED LIST OF PUPILS.
4. FIRST-CLASS INSTRUCTORS.

The Saving of Time and Money is as Important as the Saving of Daylight.

RUFFY - BAUMANN
BIPLANES - - - -
DELIVERED - -
FROM STOCK

AEROPLANES

SPARE PARTS
- - AND METAL
FITTINGS SUPPLIED

OFFICES & WORKS:
Kendall's Mews,
George Street,
Portman Sq., W.
'PHONE: MAYFAIR 5046.

AUXILIARY WORKS:
The Burroughs,
Hendon,
N.W.

Ruffy-Baumann on building their own aircraft.

2
First World War Mass Production
(1914-1918)

The First World War saw an exponential growth in aircraft production, in which London-based companies played a major part. The importance of the aeroplane during the First World War and the reasons for the rapid growth in production demand are therefore discussed in some detail below.

The Aircraft as a Machine of War

At the outbreak of the First World War, the utility of the aeroplane had only just begun to be appreciated by the Services. It was then slow, fragile and unarmed; moreover, very few were available. Thus the Royal Flying Corps (RFC) had a total of only sixty-three first line aeroplanes, with a further thirty-nine landplanes and fifty-two seaplanes available to the Royal Naval Air Service (RNAS).

The war developed into static trench warfare, with major actions or 'pushes' preceded by artillery barrages. An early use was found in reconnaissance and artillery observation, and this role became the cornerstone of military aviation. General von Below is quoted by Maurice Baring, in *Flying Corps Headquarters 1914-1918*, as stating in a memorandum: 'The main object of fighting in the air is to enable our photographic registration and photographic reconnaissance to be carried out, and at the same time to prevent that of the enemy.' The use of fighters to prevent reconnaissance operations was therefore a natural development, followed by the application of the aeroplane to bombing operations, anti-submarine patrols and operations against airships.

Changing operational roles and the rapid development of aircraft and armament meant that existing in-service types were rapidly rendered obsolete. Maurice Baring indicates that 'by the time a machine or an engine or the spare parts of both were available in sufficient quantity, the engine or machine or spare parts in question by that time were out of date'. New designs were essential, and had to be rushed into large-scale production. Aircraft were flown intensively, and losses were high through both enemy action and accidents. A large-scale training activity was required to maintain a supply of pilots to the operational squadrons, giving rise to its own losses of both men and machines.

All of this required a rapid expansion of production of all types, a process hampered by the fact that many of the potential workforce were enlisting in the Services. This problem could only be solved by bringing into the production effort industrial enterprises that had no prior experience of aircraft manufacture; the furniture and motor trades were both critical in this respect. Similarly, the work force needed to be augmented, and many women entered the production lines of the munitions factories (including the aircraft industry) for the first time.

Loss Rates

The expansion of production during the First World War was, in truth, an enormous enterprise, and is reflected in much of the content of this book. Because of its significance, it is worth reflecting on some of the facts and figures associated with this accelerated production programme. As background, one needs to appreciate the intensity of air operations, and of

The demands of increased production brought new companies into the aircraft industry. In this case, Sopwith 1½ Strutter aircraft are seen under construction at the Westland Aircraft Works of Petters Ltd, Yeovil. (Westland)

the high rate of loss and material consumption involved, as indicated by the following contemporary data:

> *The average life of an aeroplane at the battlefront is not more than two months. To keep 5,000 aircraft in active commission for one year it is necessary to furnish 30,000. Each machine in the period of its activity will use at least two motors, so that 60,000 motors will be required.* (M. Flaudin, head of the Allied Air Board, quoted in the American magazine *Flying*, September 1917).

These figures seem extraordinary, but closely match the levels actually achieved by the end of the conflict.

Aircraft losses in late 1918 were running at some 200 per month. In fact, aircraft destroyed by the enemy, and in training accidents, together with those that had to be scrapped as being obsolete, represented some 60% of the total constructed during the war. Sadly, training exacted a heavy toll. A question in Parliament during the 1918 Air Estimates debate revealed that during 1917 more men were lost at the training schools than were lost flying on all fronts. W.S. Churchill also spoke in Parliament on 4 April 1917 on the subject of the heavy losses being suffered by the RFC during training.

Data published in 1919 (in *Flight* and elsewhere) indicates that the total Flying Service casualties over the whole period of the war were 6,166 killed, 7,245 wounded and 3,128 missing. Three hundred and thirty British airmen lost their lives in April 1917 – the so-called 'Bloody April'. At this time, the expected operational life of an RFC pilot was no more than 17.5 flying hours. Peter King in *Knights of the Air* indicates that losses in every month of 1918 were equal to the entire strength of the RFC at the start of the First World War.

The demands imposed by these short service lives and high attrition were considerable; how were the resultant production needs to be met?

Expansion of the Production Programme

Production at existing aircraft companies was rapidly expanded, and contracts were placed with established industrial concerns, particularly in the motor car and furniture trades, to boost supply. Many new companies were also founded specifically to meet this growing demand, and to provide a sub-contract infrastructure. The resultant explosion of industrial activity was truly amazing, and has been (in my view) inadequately recorded.

In May 1917, less than three years after the outbreak of the First World War, the position was summarised by the 'British Comptroller of Aeronautic Supplies' in a statement to the Board of Governors of the Aero Club of America. He stated: 'There are 958 firms in England engaged on work for the British Directorate of Aeronautic Supplies, 301 of which are direct contractors and 657 are sub-contractors.' The report further states that 'the total number of hands employed by the fifty firms of most prominence is 66,700. [...] The present British budget for aeronautics in the present year totals $575,000,000.' (Reported in *Flying*, June 1917). These are impressive figures by any standard.

The Aviation Pocket-Book, 1919-1920 listed 148 aeroplane manufacturers and many other suppliers, and commented on the adequacy of its Gazetteer thus:

Products of the Royal Aircraft Factory were, in the main, built under contract by the wider industry. This BE2C was built by the British & Colonial Aeroplane Co., one of the most important contractors of this type. (Via J.S. Smith)

It does not pretend to include the names of all who are accustomed to making aeroplane parts, for many firms were doing so for the period of the war only – in fact there is hardly a motor car or motor car accessory or wood-working firm that was not fully occupied with aviation work at the time of the Armistice. […] Possibly, however, some names are not included that ought to be, since it is not an easy task, when compiling a directory of this nature, to ensure its being absolutely complete.

The author must echo these sentiments in respect of the present work.

Manufacture was split between aircraft manufacturers, with their own design teams, capable of producing original designs; contractors, who built established designs to order; and component suppliers. Within what is now Greater London, the most significant aircraft manufacturing concerns were The Fairey Aviation Co. Ltd at Hayes, Handley Page Ltd at Cricklewood, The Aircraft Manufacturing Co. Ltd (AIRCO) and The Grahame-White Aviation Co. Ltd at Hendon, and The Sopwith Aviation Co. Ltd at Kingston upon Thames. Little is known of many of the speculative/entrepreneurial companies founded in pursuit of this new area of enterprise. A few examples of companies registered during the second half of the First World War are:

- Aircraft Consolidated Ltd, 97 New Bond Street, W1. (September 1918)
- Brentford Aircraft Ltd, The Market Place, Brentford. (April 1918)
- Chiswick Aviation Works Ltd, Chiswick. (November 1917)
- Morley Aviation Co. Ltd, 1 Renfrew Road, SW11. (September 1918)
- Ikaros Aircraft & Manufacturing Ltd, Effingham House, Arundel Street, WC2. (September 1918)
- International Aircraft Works, 12a Emmanuel Avenue, Acton. (January 1918)
- Cremer Aircraft & Industrial Works Ltd, Brixton. (September 1918)
- Whitfield Aviation Ltd, 14 Paternoster Row, EC, and 10 Dane Street, WC. (September 1918)

One curiosity is that individuals and companies continued to build and fly experimental aircraft without official sanction until April 1917. This was stopped by the Aeroplanes (Experimental Manufacture) Order, which stated: 'On or after 1st April 1917, no person shall commence or proceed with the experimental manufacture of any aeroplane or seaplane without a licence from the Minister of Munitions.' This order was eventually suspended in January 1919.

Production Quantities

The achievements of the rapidly expanding industry were remarkable. This is illustrated rather graphically by the following statement made by W.S. Churchill, Minister of Munitions, speaking in Parliament on 25 April 1918, when presenting the Estimates of the Ministry of Munitions:

We are now making in a single week more aeroplanes than were made in the whole of 1914, in a single month more than were made in the whole of 1915, and in a single quarter more than were made in the whole of 1916.

The total British production during the First World War is widely reported as 55,093 airframes (other figures are also quoted, see below), with an additional 3,051 purchased abroad. Very significant production was also undertaken in France and the USA, with American production running at around 12,000 aircraft per year by the end of the war. Data published after the First World War (an official paper dated 1 January 1919 and published as a Parliamentary Paper on 24 April 1919) gave the following figures for British production.

First World War Aircraft Production

Period	Duration (months)	Aircraft built	Aircraft per month
Aug 1914 – May 1915	10	530	53
June 1915 – Feb 1917	21	7,137	340
March 1917 – Dec 1917	10	13,521	1,352
Jan 1918 – Oct 1918	10	26,685	2,669

(Note: This gives a total of 47,873, some 7,200 less than is given by more recent sources).

The expansion in production is also reflected in the number of aircraft on charge with the RFC and RNAS, as follows: August 1914 – 272; January 1917 – 5,496; January 1918 – 11,091; October 1918 (RAF) – 22,171. These figures, from the same source as the production numbers, show that in four years the aircraft establishment of the flying services had been increased more than eighty-fold, with the production rate increasing more than fifty-fold.

To provide a comparison with UK production, one should acknowledge that this enormous acceleration in the field of aviation was evident among all combatants. In other countries, the following production quantities have been quoted: France – 67,982 aircraft and 85,317 engines; Germany – 47,637 aircraft and 40,449 engines; Italy – about 20,000 aircraft and 38,000 engines; and USA – about 15,000 aircraft and 41,000 engines. This gives a wartime total in excess of 200,000 aeroplanes, and approaching a quarter of a million engines.

Production Difficulties

Significant production difficulties were encountered (and re-encountered in the Second World War) due to the difficulty of building up production among a large number of dispersed and sometimes inexperienced sub-contractors. The requirement to accelerate production was hampered by the steady depletion of the workforce as more and more were called up for service in France. Near continuous industrial unrest resulted due to the heavy demands on the individual, and the Defence of the Realm Act was much used to maintain stability in the munitions industries. There is also a suspicion that the parent firms resented the loss of production to sub-contractors, and did not always go out of their way to assist them.

Engine suppliers had great difficulty maintaining pace with airframe manufacture. Early in 1915 a serious shortage of 90hp RAF engines occurred, leaving Armstrong Whitworth with no less than 100 engineless BE2 machines hanging three or four deep from the ceiling. Similarly, in January 1918, no less than 400 SE5As were waiting for engines. The lower than expected performance of the Siddeley Puma proved to be a problem for the DH4. Martinsyde F3 production was reduced because of the need for Rolls-Royce Falcon engines to power the Bristol Fighter. The lack of availability of Falcon engines resulted in the Bristol Fighter being flown (with variable success) with 300hp Hispano Suiza, Siddeley Puma and Sunbeam Arab engines. Production of the FE2D was also constrained by the shortage of supply of its Rolls-Royce Eagle engine. The 200hp Hispano-Suiza engine fitted to the Sopwith Dolphin suffered from frequent connecting-rod failures. The supply of engines was further hampered by the need to create a new industry to supply magnetos, the manufacture of which, until the outbreak of the First World War, had been the almost exclusive province of German industry.

At the end of the First World War, engine orders were running at around 65,000 per year, more than 8,500 of these orders being for the disastrous ABC Dragonfly. F. Warren Merriam comments, 'There is no doubt that at this late stage in the War, our aero engines were becoming less and less reliable.' Shortages affected nearly every type. Standardisation was absent: in early 1918, Mr Pemberton Billing pointed out that forty-four different types of engine were in use. Ironically, the attempt to standardise on the Dragonfly also was an ignominious failure. In 1918, with vast numbers of engines on order from thirteen contractors, the Dragonfly was achieving a typical engine life of only two and a half hours before failure.

Scarcity of Resources

The needs of aircraft production resulted in a tremendous drain on resources, and even had an impact on the agricultural landscape through the demand for flax to supply the need for aircraft linen. In July 1917, Dr Addison, Minister of Munitions, gave a specific indication of the strategic requirements of the aircraft industry:

> *The fact that no fewer than 1,000 factories are engaged on some process or other connected with the construction and equipment of the flying machine proves the magnitude of the work we have in hand. The needs of the aeroplane programme are enormous, almost passing belief. For our present programme of construction, more spruce is required than the present annual output of the United States, more mahogany than Honduras can supply – and Honduras is accustomed to supply the requirements of the World. Besides this, all the linen of the type required made in Ireland, the home of the linen industry, and the whole of the alloyed steel that England can produce can be used. As for flax, the Government has actually to provide the seed from which to grow the plant essential for its purposes.*

The Government requested in late 1917 that farmers carry out a census of ash trees, where potential supply problems were causing some concern. In supporting this request it was stated that 'the Government requirements for the next 12 months [i.e. 1918] are expected to exceed 200,000 trees'. In all, about one third of the volume of timber standing at the outbreak of war was felled, much being used in aircraft manufacture. When the Forestry Commission was established in November 1919, its remit was to ensure that a three-year reserve supply of native-grown timber was available for any future conflict. This measure was a direct conse-quence of the highly successful German submarine campaign. Wood was a valuable strategic material, but because Britain had insufficient supplies to meet her wartime needs, large volumes of wood had to be imported by sea. Not only did this take up space that could have been used to import food and munitions of war, but also many lives were lost in the process. Much of the wood grown by the Forestry Commission was spruce and other conifers, which, as well as being more productive than native hardwoods, was suitable for use in aircraft construction. The requirement that the Forestry Commission should plant trees to provide a strategic timber reserve was not removed until 1958.

Flax seed was supplied free to growers, who were further encouraged with significant subsidies and guaranteed prices. The scheme was administered by the Flax Production Branch of the Board of Agriculture. Further financial assistance to growers was offered in July 1918 as a result of the Flax Companies (Financial Assistance) Bill. So successful were these measures that by the time of the Armistice, production of aircraft fabric was running at seven million yards (nearly 4,000 miles) per month. By April 1919, the Ministry of Munitions had in stock and available for disposal no less than 31,970,725 yards of linen. In mid-1919, the total surplus (by now 40,000,000 yards, or nearly 23,000 miles of fabric, in sixteen varieties and widths of 25-72ins) was sold to one individual, Mr J.L. Martin, for about £4,000,000.

Overall, perhaps the most striking feature of the First World War mass production effort was that the entire enterprise, involving more than a thousand companies, was created within ten years of the construction of Britain's first aeroplane.

Foundation of the SBAC

On 23 March 1916, the main constructing firms came together to form an interest group through which to voice their common concerns. This was the Society of British Aircraft Constructors (SBAC), an organisation that continues to be a spokesman for the industry today. The founder members include a significant number of firms that are less than familiar today. The initial list of forty founder members, as published in April 1916, was as follows:

Aircraft Manufacturing Co. Ltd
Airships Ltd
The Austin Motor Co. (1914) Ltd
Wm Beardmore & Co. Ltd
The Blackburn Aeroplane & Motor Co. Ltd
Boulton & Paul Ltd
The Brush Electrical Engineering Co. Ltd
The Coventry Ordnance Works Ltd
The Daimler Co. Ltd
Darracq Motor Engineering Co. Ltd
Wm Denny & Brothers
The Dudbridge Iron Works Ltd
Fred^k Sage & Co. Ltd
G. & J. Weir Ltd
The Grahame-White Aviation Co. Ltd
Handley Page Ltd
Hewlett & Blondeau Ltd
Jouques Aviation Works
Mann, Egerton & Co. Ltd
Mann & Grimmer
Martinsyde Ltd
D. Napier & Son, Ltd
The Norman Thompson Flight Co. Ltd
Parnall & Sons
Phoenix Dynamo Manufacturing Co. Ltd
Robey & Co. Ltd
A.V. Roe & Co. Ltd
Ruston, Proctor & Co. Ltd
S.E. Saunders Ltd
Short Brothers
The Siddeley-Deasy Motor Car Co. Ltd
The Sopwith Aviation Co. Ltd
The Standard Motor Co. Ltd
The Sunbeam Motor Car Co. Ltd
Vickers Ltd
Wells Aviation Co. Ltd
Westland Aircraft Works
J. Samuel White & Co. Ltd
Whitehead Aircraft Co. Ltd
Wolseley Motors Ltd

This group of companies, plus a few others which joined the SBAC shortly thereafter (such as Sir W.G. Armstrong, Whitworth & Co. Ltd) made up the aircraft industry at the end of the First World War. Not one survives today as a wholly British aircraft manufacturer, although Shorts (as a subsidiary of Bombardier) and AgustaWestland are honourable near-survivors.

3
Collapse and Re-birth
Between the Wars (1919-1939)

The inter-war period was marked by the near complete collapse of the military aircraft market, and the closure of many of the companies that had contributed to the First World War production effort. The larger companies were restructured to avoid Excess Profit Duty, and all faced competition from their own products, now being marketed by The Aircraft Disposal Co. Military sales were very limited in number, although Fairey Aviation (with its long-lived Fairey IIIF) and Hawker (with a multiplicity of Hart variants) were cushioned from the worst of these problems. In the 1930s, the light aircraft movement resulted in expansion of civil production, and many new concerns were established, only to be cut off at the start of the Second World War. Re-armament began in 1935, and provided a lifeline for the main manufacturers. These phases of activity are discussed in more detail below.

The Aircraft Disposal Co. (stock available)

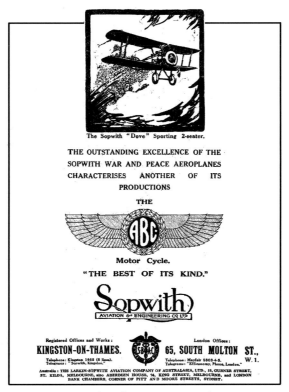

Sopwith (selling ABC motorcycles)

Post-war Collapse

What brought about this position? Quite simply, the need for aircraft evaporated virtually overnight. Once the war stopped, the country had neither the resources nor the need to sustain the aircraft production juggernaut. Many orders were cancelled, and the enormous stock of war surplus aircraft was sold on favourable terms to The Aircraft Disposal Co. at Croydon. In consequence, any firm attempting a new aircraft venture during the immediate post-war period inevitably found itself competing with its own, or its competitors', second-hand products. When this difficulty was combined with the effects of Excess Profits Duty, it is not surprising that wholesale re-organisation took place. Most of the sub-contractors either went into liquidation or returned to their former trades. The prime contractors also re-organised, slimmed down, or went into liquidation; many flirted with the motor trade and other forms of diversification. A number of those that entered voluntary liquidation emerged in new, fitter guises to carry on in the aircraft business. The survivors drew the protective cloak of the SBAC tightly around themselves.

Examples of survival-driven diversification include:

- AIRCO: manufacture of car bodies.
- Grahame-White: car manufacture, furniture.
- Martinsyde: motorcycles.
- Sopwith: ABC motorcycles, coachbuilding, furniture, kitchen utensils.
- Fairey: Daimler car bodies built by Fairey & Charles Ltd, a company set up for this purpose, using the existing aircraft company production capacity.

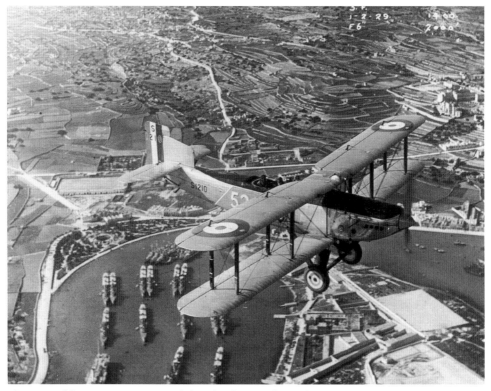

The successful Fairey IIIF series provided, with other mainly naval types, sustained production for Fairey Aviation during the bleak inter-war years. (Ken Ellis Collection)

The scale of the contraction after the Armistice was incredible. On 11 November 1918, 25,000 aircraft were on order. The Air Ministry sought to shut down production of all obsolete types immediately, and to only accept delivery of those contracts from which they positively could not extricate themselves. Those obsolete types that could not be cancelled would be sent directly to store. By cancellation of these orders, the number of aircraft that the Ministry was obliged to accept was reduced to 13,432. Scrapping for the recovery of useful parts proved not to be very economic, and it was recommended that greater savings would be made if the engine were to be removed, and the rest of the machine burned.

RAF manpower dropped from 291,175 at the end of the First World War to 29,730 by 8 March 1920, just fifteen months later. Hilary St George Saunders in *Per Ardua – The Rise of British Air Power* indicates an establishment at the end of the First World War of ninety-five squadrons and seven flights in France, Belgium and the Rhineland, together with thirty-four squadrons and eight flights in other theatres, and a Home establishment of fifty-five operational and no less than 199 training squadrons, for a grand total of 383 squadrons and fifteen flights. Within eighteen months, this was reduced to eighteen squadrons overseas, eight in India and seven in the Middle East, plus only two Home squadrons.

AIRCO, British & Colonial Aeroplane Co. Ltd, Nieuport, Martinsyde, Central Aircraft, Grahame-White and Sopwith had all closed and/or entered receivership and/or re-organised by the end of 1920. By November 1920, the RAF had been reduced to less than one-tenth of its strength at the armistice. By June 1922, only ninety-seven British civil aircraft had Certificates of Airworthiness, down from 240 in 1920. By the mid-1920s, the industry had reduced to sixteen major manufacturers: Sir W.G. Armstrong Whitworth Aircraft Ltd; A.V. Roe & Co. Ltd; The Blackburn Aeroplane & Motor Co. Ltd; Boulton & Paul Ltd; The

Bristol Aeroplane Co. Ltd; The de Havilland Aircraft Co. Ltd; Fairey Aviation Ltd; Gloucestershire Aircraft Co. Ltd; Handley Page Ltd; H.G. Hawker Enginering Co. Ltd; George Parnall & Co. Ltd; S.E. Saunders Ltd; Short Brothers (Rochester & Bedford) Ltd; The Supermarine Aviation Works Ltd; Vickers Ltd; and Westland Aircraft Works (Branch of Petters Ltd). Many of these companies form part of the heritage of British Aerospace (BAe), whose family tree, together with that of GKN Westland Helicopters, is presented in Chapter Nine.

Military Production in the 1920s and 1930s

From this point onwards, military aircraft manufacture was virtually reduced to the modification and development of the existing in-service types, and the development of a smattering of prototypes. The prototype activity was spread across the industry and just about sustained the industrial base. The lack of active operations meant that only small production volumes of largely obsolete aircraft were required to fulfil the needs of the RAF. Shorts, for example, built less than forty aircraft during the whole of the 1920s.

Fairey Aviation was a significant exception to this bleak scene: the Fairey IIIF, Gordon, Seal, Fawn, Flycatcher, Swordfish and Battle ensured continuous production through this difficult period. Another successful military manufacturer was Hawker at Kingston upon Thames, which, after a period of limited production in the early 1920s, found production success and stability with the Hawker Hart, and its subsequent long line of variants, eventually leading to the Fury and the Hurricane. Handley Page at Cricklewood worked initially on civil derivatives of their First World War bombers (leading to the W8), before reverting to familiar ground with bomber versions of the same types (Hyderabad and Hinaidi). The Heyford, Hampden, Harrow and Halifax then saw the company through to mass production for the Second World War.

One measure of the desperation of the industry was that key military requirements, likely to lead to significant production contracts, would lead to a rash of official and private venture prototypes being produced. A good example is provided by requirement N.21/26 for a single-

The Hawker Hart family was similarly a mainstay for Hawker. Production of the Hart family was also extensively contracted out across the industry, but this Hind was built by the parent concern. (Via Author)

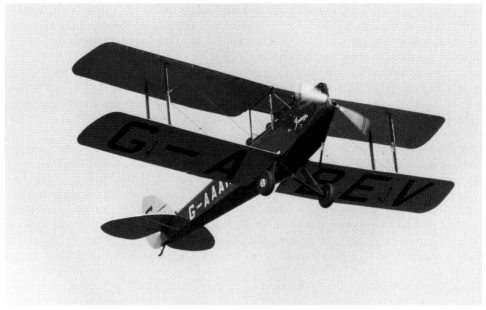

The de Havilland Gipsy Moth was the foundation stone of the light aircraft industry. (Author)

seat fleet fighter to replace the Fairey Flycatcher. Ten designs were produced to compete for this single contract, with competing prototypes as follows:

    Armstrong Whitworth Starling (private venture, A-1)
    Armstrong Whitworth AW XVI (private venture S1591)
    Fairey Firefly III (private venture, F1137 later S1592)
    Fairey Flycatcher II (N216)
    Gloster Gnatsnapper (N227)
    Hawker Hoopoe (N237)
    Hawker N.21/26 (private venture, later officially adopted as the Nimrod, becoming S1577)
    Parnall Pipit (N232, N233)
    Vickers 141 (private venture, ex G-EBNQ)
    Vickers 177 (private venture based on Type 143, no markings)

The military market remained stagnant until, during the late 1930s, tension rose within Europe leading to progressive re-armament from 1935. From this point onward, the military manufacturers saw increasing orders and the start of sub-contract/dispersed production to increase capacity. This is discussed in Chapter Four.

Civil Production and the Light Aeroplane Movement

Immediately after the First World War, there were limited attempts to generate an air transport market, with Blackburn (North Sea Aerial Navigation Co. Ltd), Handley Page (Handley Page Transport Ltd) and AIRCO (Aircraft Transport & Travel Ltd) all starting airline services, mainly using converted military aircraft. These efforts were unsuccessful and, although small numbers of commercial aircraft were sold to independent airlines, there was no real demand for air travel. Even after the formation of Imperial Airways, airliner production in Britain was restricted to modest production runs from Armstrong Whitworth, de Havilland, Handley

Page and Shorts. The appearance of the de Havilland Dragon (1932) and Dragon Rapide (1934) saw production quantities increase. However, it is fair to say that, with the exception of de Havilland, and Empire flying boat production at Shorts, military aircraft production dominated the affairs of most companies.

Whilst the Lympne Light Aircraft Competitions generated much publicity for the potential of privately owned aircraft, the competing aircraft themselves were not a great success. The appearance of the de Havilland Moth, and the availability of subsidies for flying schools, radically changed this picture. New companies emerged and prospered, including the famous names of Airspeed, de Havilland, General Aircraft, Percival, and Miles (then as Phillips & Powis (Aircraft) Ltd). Much of this activity was concentrated in, and near, London, as flying gathered popularity as a fashionable activity. Light aircraft manufacturing in the capital was centred upon de Havilland at Stag Lane (until 1934, and then at Hatfield), Croydon Airport (which re-opened after development in 1928), Heston (officially opened in 1929), and Hanworth Air Park (also opened in 1929). The number of companies formed from the late 1920s onward in an attempt to exploit this market indicates the degree of commercial interest in the light aircraft sector. London-based companies included: Arpin Aircraft Manufacturing Co. Ltd; BAC (1935) Ltd; British Klemm Aeroplane Co. Ltd/British Aircraft Manufacturing Co. Ltd; Chrislea Aircraft Co. Ltd; Comper Aircraft Ltd; Desoutter Aircraft Co. Ltd; Foster Wikner Aircraft Co. Ltd; General Aircraft Ltd; Heston Aircraft Co. Ltd; Hordern-Richmond Aircraft Ltd; Robinson Aircraft Co. Ltd; The Tipsy Aircraft Co. Ltd.

A new phenomenon also arose in the form of the craze for the Flying Flea sparked by the design of the tandem-wing *Pou de Ciel* by Henri Mignet. Although ultimately (and in some cases tragically) unsuccessful, the Flea served to legitimise the eccentric British habit of constructing home-built aircraft. This had originated in the pioneering period by the enthusiasm of the likes of Mr Jezzi at Eastchurch, being continued after the First World War by such characters as F.H. Lowe at Heaton, and the Blake brothers at Winchester. This tradition has been carried on to this day in Britain by individuals such as John Isaacs, John Taylor, Ivan Shaw and many others, now under the very professional administration of the Popular Flying Association.

The Mignet Pou de Ciel, *or Flying Flea, produced a wave of enthusiasm for homebuilt aircraft – a sector which remains significant today.* (Flying Flea Archive)

4
Second World War
Mass Production (1939-1945)

Rearmament and the Shadow Factory Scheme

The expansion of the aircraft production programme against the threat of war built up gradually from 1935. It is inseparable from the Second World War aircraft production effort, and is therefore discussed in this section. Whilst to many eyes the move to re-arm Britain's forces came perilously late, moves began some five years before the Second World War broke out. The first step was the adoption of an expansion plan in July 1934, known as Scheme A, to increase the size of the Air Force. Under this scheme, the Metropolitan Air Force was intended to grow to 1,252 operational aircraft by the spring of 1939.

Hitler had become Chancellor in January 1933, but his repudiation of the Treaty of Versailles, reoccupation of the Rhineland, the Austrian *Anschluss*, the annexation of Czechoslovakia and the Nazi-Soviet Pact were still years ahead. It is clear, therefore, that some early positive decisions were made and, as a result, the armaments industry began to grow. The real difficulty lay in the lack of investment in modern designs and technology, and the drastic reduction in production capacity caused by the lean years of the 1920s and early 1930s. Consequently, when expansion came, it was initially concentrated on types that were to prove of limited value in the struggle to come.

The pace of re-armament in the aircraft industry quickened with Scheme C, which was instituted in May 1935 and which brought about further significant increases in both the size of the RAF and the production of new aircraft types. From October 1936, the need for increased production led to the formation of the 'shadow factory' scheme. New factories were constructed using public funds, owned by the Government, but run by private industry to boost the production of (initially) aero-engine components where the shortfall in production capacity was even more marked than in the airframe industry.

In addition to Bristol (whose engines were to be produced), the five companies initially involved in the shadow factory scheme were The Austin Motor Co. Ltd, The Rover Co. Ltd, The Daimler Co. Ltd, Rootes Securities Ltd (Humber), and The Standard Motor Co. Ltd. In February 1937 the scheme was extended to allow Austin and Rootes to construct airframes as well as engines. Despite this early recognition that engine availability was critical to the acceleration of airframe production, there were periods, as in the First World War, when engineless airframes were in plentiful supply.

The early expansion schemes favoured light day-bombers, such as the Fairey Battle and Vickers Wellesley. Unfortunately, the concept of the light day-bomber proved to be a blind alley, with the Battle, in particular, suffering from high operational losses whilst trying to stem the Blitzkrieg across the Low Countries during 1940. (Fairey Battle losses between 10 May and 14 May 1940 were sixty aircraft out of the 108 deployed operationally during attacks against troop concentrations and the Albert Canal bridges). From 1936 onward, types such as the Blenheim, Wellington, Hurricane and Spitfire began to be ordered in quantity through parent and shadow factories. Later on, the focus switched to heavy bomber production (particularly the Halifax and Lancaster), anticipating the need for a bomber offensive against Germany.

Production Difficulties

Large-scale orders were one thing; production proved to be quite another problem. Production difficulties were encountered with the accelerating demands placed on both airframe and engine manufacturers, particularly as the British industry was only just accommodating retractable undercarriages, variable pitch propellers, and all-metal stressed skin monoplanes. In contemporary reports, one finds reference to:

- Poorly organised initial production by Supermarine at Woolston, with mismatched wing and fuselage production rates.
- Similar problems at Filton with the Blenheim, with thirty-two fuselages produced before any wings appeared.
- Humber's difficulties with establishing Mercury supercharger production which had knock-on effects across the shadow scheme.
- The initial inability of the Morris-run Castle Bromwich shadow factory to get the Spitfire into production.
- Production levels in 1937-1938 running at around one-third of those planned for the Battle and Blenheim, and virtually zero for the Spitfire.
- Miles Master development and production dictated by availability of particular engine types.
- Master, Oxford and Tiger Moth airframes dispersed into storage to await their engines.
- Fairey's problems of excessive dispersal of its factories, including delays to the Albacore due to problems with its Taurus engine. The delay to Albacore production lead to a delay of about a year in establishing Firefly production. A delay of two years to the Barracuda was attributed to priority being given to other types in production by Fairey at Heaton Chapel and Errwood Park. Sir Stafford Cripps intervened to introduce new personnel and re-organise project management at Fairey Aviation.
- Bristol's engineless Beaufighters towed by road from the factory at Filton to Whitchurch to await completion.
- Dozens of Typhoons at Brockworth without engines being ferried to maintenance units using 'slave' engines. The engines were then removed, sent back to the Gloster factory, and refitted to the next aircraft for its delivery.
- Slow production build up for the Halifax by the London Aircraft Production Group at Leavesden.

The setting up of the Shadow Factory scheme was a drain on the resources of the parent firms due to their need to produce additional drawings and tooling, and to provide oversight of the expansion factories. One should not, however, forget the scale of the task, and the depleted production resource initially available for the effort.

Production Quantities and Standardisation

Despite all these difficulties, expansion in the immediate pre-war period was more successful than has been widely acknowledged. In 1935, 893 military aircraft were produced. This figure was more than doubled in 1936, and by 1939 reached 7,940, a nearly nine-fold increase in only five years. In 1941, the figure was more than 20,000, and by 1944 it exceeded 26,000.

The main production effort during the Second World War was split between the following organisations:

- The main design firms of A.V. Roe & Co. Ltd, Sir W.G. Armstrong Whitworth Aircraft Ltd, Blackburn Aircraft Ltd, Bristol Aeroplane Co. Ltd, The de Havilland Aircraft Co. Ltd, The Fairey Aviation Co. Ltd, Handley Page Ltd, Hawker Aircraft

Standardisation limited the number of aircraft and engine types in production during the Second World War. More than 50,000 of these four famous Merlin-powered types were built. (Author)

Ltd, Short Brothers (Rochester & Bedford) Ltd, and Vickers-Armstrongs Ltd. Of these concerns, Fairey (Hayes), Hawker (Kingston upon Thames) and Handley Page (Criklewood) retained production capacity in London. De Havilland operated primarily from nearby Hatfield, and there was also production and/or flight test activity at Brooklands (Hawker and Vickers), Langley (Hawker), Radlett (Handley Page), Leavesden (de Havilland and London Aircraft Production Group), and Rochester (Shorts).

- Shadow and dispersed factories controlled either by aircraft industry parent firms, or by the motor industry (Rootes Securities Ltd, The Austin Motor Co. Ltd, Morris Motors Ltd, Standard Motor Co. Ltd, etc.), mainly in the Midlands and the north-west of England.
- Smaller companies, such as Phillips & Powis (Aircraft) Ltd/Miles Aircraft Ltd, Percival Aircraft Ltd, Airspeed (1934) Ltd, Taylorcraft Aeroplanes (England) Ltd, Cunliffe-Owen Aircraft Ltd, and Heston Aircraft Ltd.
- Civilian Repair Organisations, such as SEBRO at Cambridge, AST Ld at Hamble, and RAF Maintenance Units, such as Henlow and Kemble.

The risk of bomb damage to main factory sites led every firm to set up dispersed operations. As in the First World War, large numbers of firms were involved, and, as early as mid-1939, some 1,200 companies were involved in sub-contract aircraft production. Peak production in the Second World War reached 2,715 aircraft per month (March 1944) with, in addition, more than 500 aircraft per month returned to service after repair.

Unlike the First World War, there was a general policy of limiting the number of types in production. The increased efficiency and production volume that resulted offset the loss of some potentially outstanding designs, such as the Martin-Baker MB5, the production of which was blocked.

The main Second World War production types are summarised thus:

Main Second World War Production Types

Fighter	Bomber	Trainer/Liaison	Other
Defiant	Hampden	Tiger Moth	Swordfish
Hurricane	Battle	Oxford	Sunderland
Spitfire	Blenheim	Master	Firefly
Typhoon	Wellington	Magister	Seafire
Tempest	Stirling	Anson	Walrus
Beaufighter	Halifax	Auster	Lysander
	Lancaster	Proctor	Beaufort
	Mosquito	Dominie	Barracuda

By about 1941, the production of front-line machines, and most of the industry's production capacity, had been grouped on the Stirling, Halifax and Lancaster bombers, the Beaufighter, the Mosquito, the Spitfire, and the Barracuda. The reduced number of types produced reflects the technical maturity of the industry; it was no longer possible for the enemy to produce a new design that would completely change the balance of air power overnight. The Messerschmitt Me262 might have had such an effect, had it been available earlier and in larger numbers, but in general it was found that progressive improvement of existing British designs could keep pace with new enemy designs. Thus, the Spitfire was able to maintain its operational utility, through progressive engine, carburation and airframe developments, in the face of the Focke Wulf Fw190 and its developments.

The Second World War saw the return of the female population to aircraft production, as shown by this excellent photograph of Mosquito fuselage production. (BAE SYSTEMS)

Some idea of the scale of production in the Second World War can be gained from this photograph of Halifax front fuselages at the London Passenger Transport Board factory at Aldenham, near Elstree. (Handley Page Association)

Figures released at the end of the war by the Ministry of Aircraft Production stated that wartime production totalled some 125,000 complete aircraft, the largest numbers being (in sequence) Spitfire, Hurricane, Wellington, Anson, Lancaster, Mosquito, Halifax, Beaufighter, Blenheim and Oxford (all 5,000 aircraft or more). (Note that the published list does not seem to include non-operational types, such as the Tiger Moth, more than 8,800 of which were built).

It is also worth noting, in the light of the post-war domination of the industry by the USA, that, although starting later, the US industrial machine outstripped UK production by a comfortable margin. The US built some 360,000 aircraft in the Second World War, nearly 96,000 of them in 1944 alone.

5
Post-war
(1945-1960)

When peace came, the various car industry-controlled shadow factories were no longer required and were closed, or converted for car and engine manufacture. The aircraft industry set about meeting the challenges that it faced. These were the relatively unfamiliar demands of the commercial market and the race to exploit the new technologies of war as tensions mounted between the West and the Soviet Bloc. The industry's efforts were made more difficult by the weakness of Britain's war-shattered economy.

Commercial Aircraft Developments

A key decision, which has shaped the post-war commercial aircraft industry, was that wartime transport aircraft production was allocated to the USA. As a result, the excellent C-47 Dakota or DC-3 was immediately available for opening up the post-war air routes, with longer range services provided by the DC-4 (C-54 Skymaster), the later DC-6, and the Lockheed Constellation. Not only were these excellent aircraft in their own right, but they also proved capable of development into a line of successful derivative aircraft.

What then of Britain? New aircraft types were needed; Britain's pre-war airliners had, after all, not exactly led the world in their performance or technology. Despite the strain on the economy, an attempt was made, through the Brabazon Committee, to identify and develop a fleet of new aircraft covering a wide range of commercial applications. Unfortunately, these designs could not be created overnight and, in the short-term, stop-gap designs and converted bombers were all that was available to compete for airline markets.

Worse was to follow as, when the new types appeared, they were (with a couple of notable exceptions) not well suited to the prevailing market conditions. One common fault seems to have been the specification of too few passenger seats. Perhaps this reflected the view that few people could afford to fly, and those that could would expect a suitably civilised environment!

To modern eyes, the first post-war commercial offerings from British Industry seem brave but, in many cases, doomed from the outset. Among these were:

- The hurriedly converted bombers – the Halton, Stirling V, and Lancastrian.
- Britain's only true transport of the war – the Avro York – itself a Lancaster development.
- The Sunderland flying boat conversions and developments – the Hythe, Sandringham and Solent.
- Non-starters – Bristol Brabazon, Portsmouth Aerocar, Cunliffe-Owen Concordia, Percival Merganser, Armstrong Whitworth Apollo.
- And finally the honourable exceptions – the new designs which reached production. These were the Avro Tudor, Handley Page Hermes, Handley Page (Reading) Marathon, Vickers Viking, Bristol Freighter, Airspeed Ambassador, de Havilland Dove, de Havilland Comet and Vickers Viscount.

Sadly, the vast majority could not compete with the operational economics of the American designs, nor the economies of scale afforded by the US production machine. Of British commercial aircraft in the immediate post-war period, only the de Havilland Dove and the

The Avro Lancastrian was surprisingly attractive for a converted bomber but, with its limited passenger capacity, it could not compete with the economics of American purpose-built transport aircraft. (BAE SYSTEMS)

Vickers Viscount were unqualified successes. It is indeed tragic that the Comet, which could have achieved a generation of British leadership in the skies, proved to be unexpectedly flawed. Although redesign of the Comet eventually produced a robust and successful aircraft, the moment had been lost as far as potential British domination of the commercial air transport market was concerned.

Bristol's mighty Brabazon looms over the Black Sheds at Farnborough. (BAE SYSTEMS)

BSAA Avro Tudor IV G-AHNN Star Leopard undergoes propeller tests at Hatfield. (BAE SYSTEMS)

Military Aircraft Programmes

On the military side, the defeat of Germany and Japan brought peace but no reduction in tension, because of the development of the 'Cold War' with the Soviet Union. The end of the war had seen the development of long-range surface-to-surface rockets, jet and rocket-propelled aircraft, and the atomic bomb. German technical progress with the development of the thin swept wing was also opening the door to much higher speeds and the prospect of supersonic flight. Britain, and indeed the whole developed world, therefore plunged into a race to develop and exploit these technologies in the military field.

Britain's brilliant lead in jet engine technology saw operational fruit with the Meteor and Vampire, but was rapidly surpassed by the pace of development in both the USA and the USSR. In these nations, the significance of German swept-wing developments was better understood and built upon, resulting in the superlative North American F-86 Sabre and Mikoyan & Guryevich MiG 15/17. Despite 'super-priority' programmes, Britain was unable to bring its own Swift or the Hunter quickly into service, and had to suffer the indignity of the interim operation of the F-86 Sabre in order to preserve a credible operational capability.

In the field of bombers, the superb Canberra was flown in 1949 and continues in RAF service in 2002, more than fifty years later. The Canberra was followed by the challenging V-Bomber programme, which demonstrated that Britain could indeed produce world-class designs. How extraordinary, however, that after all its deprivations in the Second World War, the country could actually afford to carry all three V-Bombers — the Valiant, Victor and Vulcan — into production in the face of the Cold War threat.

The de Havilland DH104 Dove was one of the relatively few outright successes of the immediate post-war period. (Author)

Britain's Aviation Heritage is epitomised by this evocative photograph of the prototype Comet 1 G-ALVG banking over the Bristol Brabazon 1 G-AGPW. (BAE SYSTEMS)

It now seems incredible that Britain should simultaneously produce three completely different types of strategic bomber – the V-bomber force. (Via Author)

Re-structuring of the Industry

As the 1950s came to a close, it was clear that an industry in which every company built every type of aircraft could not be sustained. With anything up to seven manufacturers competing for business to supply a single class of aircraft, the industry was looking at an unsustainable future. The Government recognised that this situation could not be allowed to continue, and applied great pressure on the industry to produce rationalisation. Duncan Sandys' 1957 Defence White Paper of 4 April 1957, 'Outline of Future Policy', has become somewhat notorious for its suggestion that missile technology was now maturing at such a rate that it would supplant the manned aircraft in many roles. It stated that in view of 'the good progress made towards the replacement of the manned aircraft of RAF Fighter Command with a ground to air missile system, the RAF are unlikely to have a requirement for fighter aircraft of types more advanced than the supersonic P1, and work on such projects will stop'. Development of a supersonic manned bomber was not to be started, emphasis being switched to atomic weapons and guided missiles.

Clearly great changes in the aircraft industry were becoming inevitable. The first step was the formation of the British Aircraft Corporation Ltd in January 1960, the Government having indicated that it would only support the TSR.2 programme if it were produced by a single company. This resulted in Vickers, Bristol and English Electric joining forces, with Hunting Aircraft following shortly afterwards.

In parallel, the companies in the Hawker Siddeley Group – Armstrong Whitworth, A.V. Roe & Co. Ltd, Blackburn, Gloster and Hawker – found themselves being progressively joined by new bedfellows. These consisted of Folland (in 1959), de Havilland and its Airspeed Division (in 1960), and Blackburn (also in 1960). In July 1963, this group was further reorganised to generate Hawker Siddeley Aviation Ltd.

Thus was created what *Aviation Week* has called the 'Society of Both Aircraft Companies'. This was something of an exaggeration, as Short Brothers & Harland continued in Belfast, as did Scottish Aviation Ltd at Prestwick, Handley Page Ltd at Radlett and Auster at Rearsby.

In London, a major change took place when Fairey Aviation was absorbed into Westland Helicopters Ltd. This was part of a similar Government-dictated rationalisation, in which Westland acquired the helicopter interests of its competitors: Saunders-Roe Ltd (in 1959); Bristol (in 1960); and Fairey Aviation (also in 1960).

London's Airfields

Another change that took place in this post-war period was a further reduction in the number of airfields within the boundaries of the modern Greater London area. One major influence was the establishment of Heathrow Airport as the main international airport serving London. Conflicting air traffic control requirements resulted in the immediate closure of Heston and Hanworth, together with the nearby Hawker airfield at Langley. Croydon lost its role as an international airport and closed in September 1959. Hendon remained in RAF use until November 1957, later becoming the site of the RAF Museum.

By 1960, there were no manufacturers' airfields in Greater London, although Fairey Aviation/Westland Helicopters, Hawker Aircraft Ltd and Handley Page Ltd retained their manufacturing facilities at Hayes, Kingston upon Thames and Cricklewood, respectively. Just on the outskirts of Greater London, Hatfield and Brooklands remained active, in the hands of Hawker Siddeley Aviation Ltd and the British Aircraft Corporation, respectively.

The TSR.2 programme proved to be a major catalyst for the enforced rationalisation of the aircraft industry. (J.S. Smith)

6
Rationalisation:
The BAC and Hawker Siddeley
Years (1960-1977)

Market Trends – Commercial and General Aviation

BAC and Hawker Siddeley inherited a civil market which was struggling to break out from American domination. It is unfortunate that during the initial post-war period, a unique British ability to market the wrong products (combined with the wartime ceding of the military transport field to the USA) had resulted in the commercial market for piston-engined aircraft being dominated by the USA. It was doubly unfortunate then that, despite the success of the Viscount, the Comet disasters opened the door to the Boeing 707 and DC-8.

If possible, worse was to follow. Myopic specifications from Britain's nationalised airlines (BEA and BOAC) and political indifference to the commercial aircraft industry undermined the potential of the Vanguard and VC-10, BAC One-Eleven and Trident. The technically brilliant Concorde was economically, politically and environmentally flawed, particularly after the oil price shock of the 1970s, and the on-off development of the HS146 (later the BAe 146 and Avro RJ family) appeared to be driven by pure politics.

Despite its undoubted technical excellence, the BAC/Aerospatiale Concorde failed to achieve commercial success. (BAE SYSTEMS)

Britten-Norman's classic utility aircraft, the Islander, is seen here on the gravel airstrip of Out Skerries in the Shetland Isles. (J.S. Smith)

In a significant move for the future, the Hatfield Division of Hawker Siddeley entered into an agreement to develop wings for the new European consortium, Airbus Industrie. This followed inter-governmental agreement to support Airbus project definition, signed in September 1967. From May 1969, the UK government withdrew from further project funding, but Hawker Siddeley took the decision to continue in the project on a purely commercial basis.

In the field of general aviation, the 1960s scene seemed more positive; Beagle (British Executive & General Aviation Ltd) was set up in October 1960, drawing upon the creative abilities of Auster at Rearsby, and F.G. Miles at Shoreham. New designs emerged in the shape of the Beagle Pup, the twin-engine Beagle 206, and the Bulldog military trainer. De Havilland had seen the value of the executive jet market and designed their DH125, initially known as the Jet Dragon, which was taken up and marketed by Hawker Siddeley as the HS125 with great success worldwide.

At Bembridge, Isle of Wight, John Britten and Desmond Norman had, through their operation of agricultural aircraft in some of the more basic areas of the world, identified the need for a simple robust utility aircraft capable of operation from short airstrips in all climates. The design which resulted, the Islander, fulfilled the designers' concept in every respect. On a larger scale, Shorts were also successful in bringing the utilitarian Skyvan into production for both civilian and military users.

In the helicopter arena, Westland Helicopters Ltd built a solid base from its manufacture of Sikorsky products under licence. The Whirlwind and Wessex attracted large-scale orders, and the Saunders-Roe P.531 was developed successfully into the Scout and Wasp. Westland boomed in the 1970s as the Anglo-French helicopter deal came to fruition, with WHL building its own Lynx, and the Aerospatiale-designed Puma and Gazelle. Simultaneously, the company secured large national and export orders for the Sea King helicopter, which it built under licence from Sikorsky in the USA. The ex-Fairey factory at Hayes benefited from manufacture of the Scout, Wasp and Puma, before the eventual closure of the site.

Following rationalisation, Westland Helicopters' success was built upon the Anglo-French helicopter programme with the production of the Gazelle, Lynx and Puma. (Westland)

Commercial Casualties

Handley Page Ltd, having had only modest sales of the Herald, conceived a twin turboprop feeder liner – the Jetstream. The Jetstream was greeted with enormous enthusiasm in the marketplace, with large numbers of sales achieved before the first flight of the prototype. This sales success was in large measure dependent upon the aircraft delivering its declared performance, within its FAA certification limited maximum weight of 12,500lb. In the event, this could not be achieved.

Handley Page Ltd had invested in tools and facilities for large-scale production, and were now faced with a difficult and expensive development programme, whilst bearing the costs of their unfulfilled production expectations. The company proved unable to withstand the financial pressures and entered voluntary liquidation in August 1969, ceasing to trade in June 1970. The subsequent development of the aircraft by British Aerospace shows that this was, regrettably, another case of that British trait, most familiar in the field of sport, of defeat snatched from the jaws of victory.

Similar difficulties were encountered at Beagle. Here, despite the sale of nearly 400 Pup aircraft, financial support to the company was withdrawn by the Government in December 1969. Beagle eventually produced 152 Pup aircraft and eighty-five Beagle 206. Even the hugely popular Islander suffered from the problems brought about by sales success. Although the aircraft survived and remains in limited production, the company suffered a seemingly never-ending series of financial crises, including a number of periods in receivership.

The troubled Handley Page Jetstream was successfully developed by British Aerospace at Prestwick as the Jetstream 31. (BAE SYSTEMS)

Beagle's instant classic, Beagle Pup 150 G-AXJO, shows the clean lines of a thoroughbred. (Author)

Military Developments and Collaborative Ventures

In the military field, an almost mortal blow was struck when BAC, having been drawn together to produce the TSR.2, saw it cancelled by Dennis Healey in April 1965. BAC military efforts were then concentrated on the completion of Lightning production, supplemented by export Canberra refurbishment and the development of the pressurised Jet Provost T. Mk 5, and the BAC167 Strikemaster. BAC then moved on to the collaborative development of the Jaguar.

In the late 1960s, the RAF identified the requirement to reduce its number of front line types, whilst achieving the following aims:

- The progressive replacement, from the late 1970s of the Canberra and the V-bomber fleet.
- To establish the capability to carry out the low level penetration roles that were to have been the province of the TSR.2.
- In the long term, to phase out the Lightning and Phantom from their air defence roles.
- Also in the long term, to replace the Buccaneer in its low level strike, reconnaissance and maritime strike roles.

With all these objectives in mind, a further collaborative project emerged known as the Multi-Role Combat Aircraft (MRCA), later named Tornado. BAC joined with MBB and Aeritalia to form Panavia to produce the Tornado, which first flew in 1974.

Hawker Siddeley faced their own political traumas, with the cancellation of the supersonic V/STOL P.1154 project, the Royal Navy variant being cancelled by Peter Thorneycroft in February 1964. The RAF version followed under the Healey axe of 1965, which also saw the cancellation of the HS.681 V/STOL transport. Despite these difficulties, Hawker Siddeley prospered on the strength of the products that it had inherited from its parent companies. Of particular note were the Harrier from Hawker, the HS.748 from A.V. Roe & Co. Ltd, and the HS125 from de Havilland. Other work included the Buccaneer (ex-Blackburn), the Nimrod maritime patrol aircraft, Hunter refurbishment and production of the Trident.

During this period Hawker Siddeley designed what may prove to be Britain's last purely home-grown military aircraft, the HS.1182 Hawk trainer, which first flew in 1974, and continues to be one of the world's most successful trainer aircraft. The Hawk was built at Kingston, and test-flown from Dunsfold. With the closure of the factories of Fairey Aviation at Hayes and of Handley Page at Cricklewood, the Hawker Siddeley works at Kingston upon Thames was the only aircraft production facility within Greater London when the next major stage in the development of the British aircraft industry took place: the creation of British Aerospace – the 'Single British Aircraft Company' – in 1977.

7
Modern Times

The Nationalisation and Privatisation of British Aerospace

British Aerospace (BAe) was formed as a nationalised corporation in April 1977 as a result of the Aircraft and Shipbuilding Industries Act 1977. In January 1981, BAe converted from a nationalised corporation to a public limited company (plc) in preparation for privatisation. The UK government sold 51.57% of its shares in February 1981, and all but a single £1 'golden share' in May 1985.

When BAe was founded, it employed some 50,000 people on eighteen sites – Bitteswell, Brough, Chadderton, Chester, Christchurch, Dunsfold, Filton, Hamble, Hatfield, Holme-on-Spalding Moor, Hurn, Kingston, Preston, Prestwick, Samlesbury, Warton, Weybridge and Woodford.

Since 1977, BAe has taken on an ever more international flavour. The BAC collaboration on Jaguar was followed by the tri-national Tornado programme. Tornado production for Saudi Arabia has now ended, and BAE SYSTEMS has started for production of Eurofighter, in partnership with Spain, Italy and Germany.

Something of a defining moment for the industry came on 24 December 1998 when new-build Sea Harrier FA.2 NB18 was 'bought off' by the Royal Navy customer. The completion of this aircraft was said by BAe to mark the last delivery of an all-British fighter aircraft to the UK armed services. February 2002 saw the announcement of the plan to withdraw the

The future of BAE SYSTEMS's military aircraft production is focused on Eurofighter and Nimrod MRA.4, together with the F-35 JSF. (Author)

The transatlantic aspects of BAE SYSTEMS' business are summed up by this photograph of the Lockheed Martin X-35B JSF prototype accompanied by a Boeing (ex-McDonnell Douglas) TAV-8B Harrier. (Lockheed Martin)

Sea Harrier FA.2 from service by 2006. One national programme, the Hawk, continues to go from strength to strength. Private venture developments of the Hawk 100 and Hawk 200 have allowed the type to remain effective, and it continues to be selected as the preferred training and light attack aircraft of many armed forces around the world.

By the time of the merger of British Aerospace with Marconi Electronic Systems to form BAE SYSTEMS on 30 November 1999, the number of sites manufacturing aircraft components was down to eight – Brough, Chadderton, Chester, Filton, Prestwick, Samlesbury, Warton and Woodford – less than half the number of sites taken over in 1977. The ex-Sopwith/Hawker/Hawker Siddeley factory at Kingston upon Thames was closed at the end of 1992, bringing aircraft manufacture within the Greater London area to an end.

Further ahead is the JSF programme, with BAE SYSTEMS teamed with Lockheed Martin to produce the supersonic CTOL/ASTOVL F–35 multi-role strike fighter for the USAF, US Navy, US Marine Corps and the RAF. Other transatlantic military co-operations include the T-45 Goshawk for the US Navy, and the AV-8B Harrier II and II Plus with McDonnell Douglas (now Boeing). Development work is underway on an extensively modified Nimrod, the MRA.4 (with new wings and engines), to preserve Britain's maritime patrol capability.

BAe/BAE SYSTEMS Commercial Programmes

In the civil field, the establishment of the Airbus consortium has at last introduced a note of success into Britain's involvement in commercial aviation. Much against many observers' expectations, Airbus has proved to be a worthy rival to Boeing, achieving initial market penetration with the A300 and A310. These types have been followed up by the smaller, and hugely successful, A320 family, and the A330 and A340 long haul transports. Airbus has now launched

Sea Harrier FRS.2 development aircraft ZA195 demonstrates its firepower in this BAE SYSTEMS photograph.
(BAE SYSTEMS)

Commercial aircraft success for BAE SYSTEMS has come through its stake in the Airbus programme, more than 4,500 Airbus aircraft having been sold by July 2002. (Author)

its super-wide body project, the A380, and is also the nominated project management organisation for a joint European military transport project, the Future Large Aircraft A400M.

Elsewhere, the civil market has not proved a happy experience for British Aerospace/BAE SYSTEMS.

Corporate jet activity was continued with production of the BAe125 (previously HS125, previously DH125). The aircraft has been extensively developed throughout its production life, the final BAe production versions being the Hawker 800 and Hawker 1000. BAe sold its corporate jet business to the Raytheon Corporation in June 1993.

BAe's regional turboprop products were the Jetstream and the Advanced Turbo-Prop, or ATP, a stretched and re-engined development of the Avro/HS 748. The ATP was manufactured at Woodford until October 1992, when production was transferred to Prestwick, and the aircraft re-launched under the designation Jetstream 61. At this time the regional turboprop activity was re-styled Jetstream Aircraft Ltd. At Prestwick, meanwhile, a growth version of the Jetstream, the Jetstream 41, was launched. Market conditions proved initially unfavourable due to production over-capacity in this sector. BAe responded by forming an alliance with Aerospatiale and Alenia known as Aero International (Regional), AI(R), with a view to rationalising product lines. An early casualty was the ATP/Jetstream 61 which, together with the original Jetstream 31, were not taken up by the AI(R) consortium. BAe continued with the Jetstream 41, but announced in May 1997 that the production line would close by the end of 1997. The AI(R) consortium was, itself, disbanded in 1998.

In the regional jet market, BAe produced the 146, taken over from Hawker Siddeley. Although produced in significant numbers (219 aircraft), initially at Hatfield and then at Woodford, the 146 was not a financial success for BAe. Production costs were high and many aircraft were leased on terms which ultimately proved unprofitable to BAe. The aircraft was re-launched as a family of types known as the Avro RJ (Regional Jet) series. Unfortunately, the terrorist attack on the New York World Trade Center on 11 September 2001 sounded the death knell for the RJ/RJX programme. On 27 November 2001, BAE SYSTEMS announced that it would be withdrawing from the construction of commercial aircraft at Woodford and would close the RJ and RJX programmes, with a consequential loss of 1,669 jobs. This decision, following the earlier suspension of the Jetstream 41 and 61 programmes at Prestwick, marked the end of BAE SYSTEMS' construction of complete aircraft for the civil market.

The Wider Industry

Outside of BAe/BAE SYSTEMS, Shorts produced the SD330 and 360 developments of their 'ugly-duckling' Skyvan, and went on to supply the RAF with an extensively developed version of the Embraer Tucano for basic training. The last SD360 was built in 1991, and the last Tucano in 1992. Purchased by Bombardier in 1989, the company has become increasingly centred upon aerospace component manufacture and assembly. It is unlikely that the company will ever build another complete aircraft again.

The boom that Westland experienced in the late 1970s could not last. As a result of its ill-starred WG30 civil helicopter venture, Westland found itself in financial difficulties in 1986. A huge political row erupted over whether WHL should accept a possible European rescue package, or one offered by Sikorsky. After much acrimony, including the resignation of Michael Heseltine from the cabinet, the Sikorsky option was taken.

Westland, like BAe, has taken an increasingly international route to secure its future. This has centred on the EH101 helicopter developed with Italy, the RN production variant, the

The Jetstream 41 was produced at Prestwick by British Aerospace, but was an early casualty of an over-capacity marketplace. (BAE SYSTEMS)

The commercial aerospace market has proven troublesome for BAE SYSTEMS. The two RJX prototypes are seen here flying together, shortly before the programme was cancelled in the aftermath of the terrorist attack on New York on 11 September 2001. (BAE SYSTEMS)

Merlin, being managed by Lockheed Martin Government Systems as prime contractor. WHL was purchased by GKN in 1994. During 1998, GKN announced its intention to combine its helicopter operations with those of the Italian company Agusta SpA. This merger has resulted in the formation of a new company, AgustaWestland, which has a mix of civil and military products, and involvement in both the EH101 and NH90 programmes. In the UK, the company has the EH101 and the WAH-64 Apache in production. The long-lived Lynx also remains in production, having gained export success in the form of the Super Lynx 300. This Lynx variant is also under study for a number of UK requirements. The helicopter market-place worldwide still features over-capacity, and AgustaWestland will continue to need good penetration in export markets to secure its long-term future.

In the general aviation sector, the almost immortal Islander continues in limited produc-tion. Private aircraft have, for the most part, remained a bleak area for the British industry. Success has, however, been achieved by three products – the Slingsby T67 Firefly, the CFM Shadow, and the Europa.

Slingsby redesigned the wooden Fournier RF6 (T67A), adopting an all-composite structure and installing increased power to produce a highly successful fully aerobatic trainer, which has found favour at entry level with a number of air forces around the world.

The CFM (Cook Flying Machines) Shadow was designed by David Cook of Leiston, Suffolk: more than 400 of these aircraft have been built in a number of variants, including the high performance Streak Shadow which flies at up to 105 knots on its 64hp. The Shadow and Streak Shadow have been sold in more than thirty-six countries, and have completed many notable flights, including from England to Australia.

Ivan Shaw's all-composite Europa, designed for the home-built and kit construction market, first flew in September 1992. Within seven years, more than 550 kits had been sold in twenty-nine countries, and more than seventy aircraft were flying.

Future Prospects

Where does the future of the British industry lie? Shrinking defence markets have forced rationalisation in the United States of America. To some extent, this was also the engine for the creation of Hawker Siddeley and BAC, and subsequently the formation of British Aerospace and BAE SYSTEMS. With an increasing trend toward collaborative projects, and the large scale of investment required to launch new projects, aerospace is rapidly moving towards being a global business.

Lockheed, Martin Marietta, General Dynamics (Fort Worth Division), IBM, Loral and Vought have already coalesced into a single corporation. Northrop and Grumman have merged, as have Boeing, McDonnell and Douglas. Faced with these giant businesses, European re-structuring has become inevitable. British Aerospace took a 35% share in Saab of Sweden and spent a period in ultimately unsuccessful restructuring discussions with DaimlerChrysler Aerospace of Germany (DASA).

On 19 January 1999, BAe and GEC announced that they had reached an agreement on the merger of BAe with the GEC defence interests (Marconi Electronic Systems). This merger, effective from the end of November 1999, created BAE SYSTEMS, then Europe's largest defence company, ranking at third largest in the world, with a workforce of nearly 100,000 employees.

Developed using the Lynx dynamic system, the WG30 was a brave but unsuccessful attempt by Westland to diversify into the civil market. (Author)

The all-composite Europa has been an outstanding success with more than 550 kits sold in twenty-nine countries, including more than 100 in the USA. (Europa Aircraft Co.)

In response to the creation of BAE SYSTEMS, DaimlerChrysler announced in June 1999 that they were acquiring the Spanish company CASA, thereby strengthening their position for future restructuring discussions. An agreement with Aerospatiale Matra followed, leading to the formation of EADS (European Aeronautic Defence & Space Co.) on 10 July 2000. EADS is the world's third largest defence organisation, behind Boeing and Lockheed Martin, and displacing BAE SYSTEMS from this position.

The strong pressure to unite Airbus as a 'Single Corporate Entity' finally bore fruit with the announcement of the formation of the Airbus Integrated Co. on 23 June 2000, BAE SYSTEMS taking a 20% share. With both BAE SYSTEMS and EADS indicating their interest in transatlantic as well as European partnerships, it seems that the future will continue to be turbulent.

With transatlantic projects such as JSF looking to secure global export markets, overtures from the major players in the USA may not be long delayed. A future global aerospace business may yet be created by one of the major US defence conglomerates acting in partnership with BAE SYSTEMS and/or EADS. In ten years' time, it is hard to believe that the current structure of the industry will not have seen further upheaval – we will have to wait and see. By that time, indeed, it may seem almost quaint to refer to the British Aircraft Industry.

8
The Genealogy of
British Aerospace/BAE SYSTEMS
and GKN Westland Helicopters

The preceding narrative has charted the evolution of the British aircraft industry. Much of the manufacturing capacity of the industry is now in the hands of only two companies: BAE SYSTEMS, previously British Aerospace plc, manufacturing military and commercial fixed wing aircraft; and AgustaWestland (previously GKN Westland Helicopters Ltd) manufacturing military helicopters.

Although the narrative has shown how political and commercial imperatives led to progressive re-structuring of the industry into these companies, the impact of these changes is best appreciated when presented graphically in the form of a family tree. BAE SYSTEMS came into being with the merger between British Aerospace and the defence interests of GEC, Marconi Electronic Systems (MES). As MES did not include any UK aircraft manufacturers in its heritage, the following family trees represent only the British Aerospace heritage that passed into BAE SYSTEMS.

Four diagrams are presented:

1. British Aerospace: The Big Picture
2. BAe: Hawker Siddeley Companies
3. BAe: British Aircraft Corporation and Scottish Aviation
4. British Rotorcraft Industry

Whilst in many respects, these diagrams speak for themselves, a few observations are worth making:

- British Aerospace was formed in 1977 by the merging of three companies: Hawker Siddeley, Aviation Ltd, the British Aircraft Corporation (BAC) and Scottish Aviation Ltd. Short Brothers & Harland were the only major fixed-wing aircraft manufacturer that remained independent of this group.
- Because Scottish Aviation Ltd had acquired the rump of the Beagle Aircraft Ltd and Handley Page Ltd activities, they brought with them into the BAe family tree the heritage of these firms. This encompasses (via Handley Page Ltd) Martinsyde Ltd and Phillips & Powis/Miles Aircraft Ltd, and (via Beagle) Auster Aircraft Ltd and Taylorcraft Aeroplanes (England) Ltd. In Diagram 3, the dotted line from Miles Aircraft Ltd to F.G. Miles Ltd shows the links between the two companies and the new aviation activities of Mr F.G. Miles after the take-over of his original company by Handley Page Ltd.
- Hawker Siddeley Aviation Ltd (HSAL) added Blackburn & General Aircraft Ltd, The de Havilland Aeroplane Co. Ltd and Folland Aircraft Ltd to the group of Hawker Siddeley companies, which had already been merged in 1935, although continuing to trade under their original identities (A.V. Roe & Co. Ltd, Hawker Aircraft Ltd, Gloster Aircraft Co. Ltd, Sir W.G. Armstrong Whitworth Aircraft Ltd).
- The less familiar antecedents of HSAL include H.H. Martyn & Co. (via Gloster),

William Denny & Bros Ltd, General Aircraft Ltd and CWA Ltd (via Blackburn) and Airspeed Ltd, May, Harden & May and Wycombe Aircraft Constructors (via AIRCO/de Havilland).

- Only four companies were grouped into BAC, these being English Electric Aviation Ltd, Bristol Aircraft Ltd (previously the Bristol Aeroplane Co. Ltd), Vickers-Armstrongs (Aircraft Ltd) and Hunting Aircraft Ltd (previously Percival Aircraft Ltd). The Vickers-Armstrongs heritage includes The Supermarine Aviation Works Ltd and Pemberton-Billing Ltd. The aircraft interests of The English Electric Co. Ltd were originally formed by merging the aircraft activities of Coventry Ordnance Works, Phoenix Dynamo Co. Ltd and Dick, Kerr & Co. in December 1918.
- Between 1919 and 1921 many company names were changed, and a number of new companies were founded following the closure of closely linked predecessors. This reflects the impact of taxation imposed after the First World War on companies which were considered to have made excess profits.
- On the helicopter side, only one major cycle of contraction is apparent with the Saunders-Roe Ltd, The Bristol Aircraft Ltd (Helicopter Division) and The Fairey Aviation Co. Ltd helicopter interests merging into Westland Aircraft Ltd in 1959-1960. Saunders-Roe had acquired the helicopter interests of The Cierva Autogiro Co. in 1951. Both The Fairey Aviation Co. Ltd and Saunders-Roe Ltd were, of course, notable manufacturers of fixed-wing aircraft, in addition to their helicopter interests.

BAe – The Big Picture

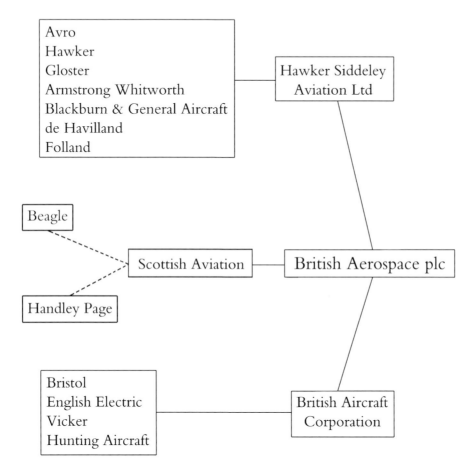

British Aerospace – Hawker Siddeley Companies

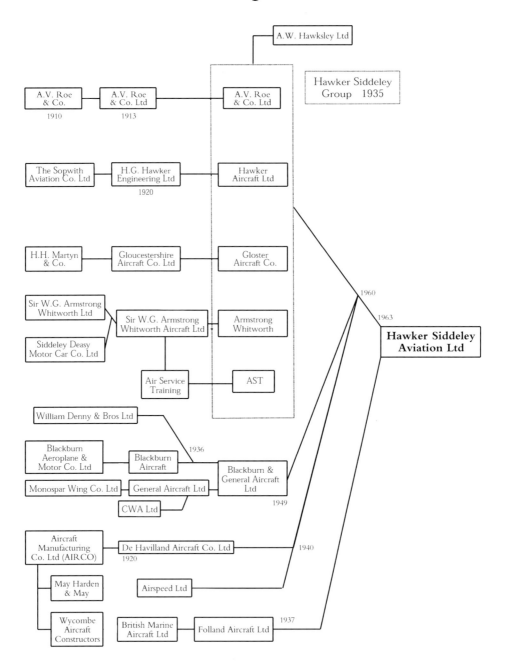

BAe: British Aircraft Corporation & Scottish Aviation

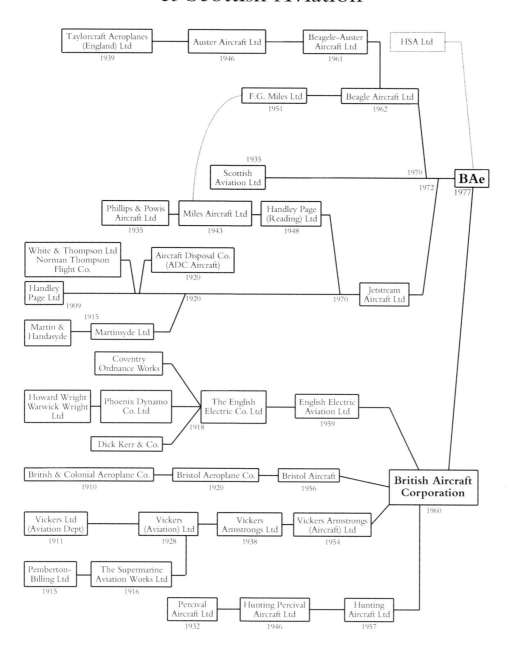

British Rotorcraft Industry

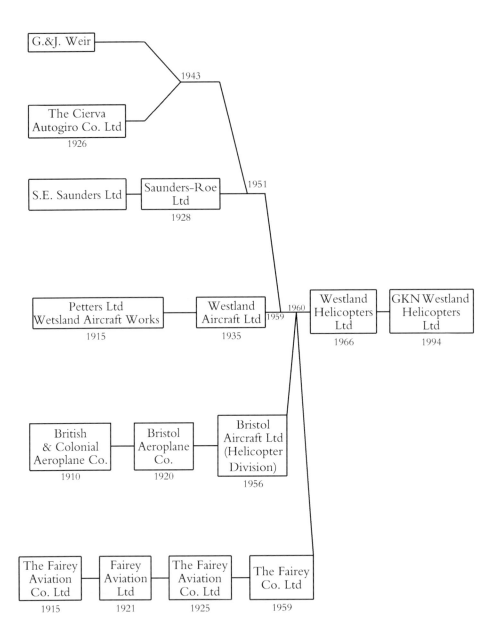

The Aircraft Manufacturers
of Greater London

Abbey Wood

The **Barnes** monoplane, a single-seater powered by a 20hp JAP, flew at least once in October 1909 at Abbey Wood, covering a distance of 1.5 miles. Its constructor, G.A. Barnes was injured at Folkestone, at the end of September 1910, in a fall from his Humber-Blériot monoplane in which he suffered head and wrist injuries. Mr Barnes was a racing motor-cyclist who was a pioneer pilot, gaining Royal Aero Club Aviator's Certificate No.16 in June 1910.

Acton

The Acton Aviation Grounds were located between the A406 and A4000, north-east of the Central Line underground railway and on the south side of the present A40 Western Avenue, with Mason's Green Lane as the western boundary. The main entrance to the aerodrome lay at its southern corner, close to the present West Acton underground station.

Visiting this area today, the general suitability of the site can be appreciated by looking at the flat expanse of the North Acton Recreation Ground, alongside Noel Road, immediately to the south-east of the airfield site.

An early burst of flying activity at the Acton Aviation Grounds was brought to a premature end by a fire to the hangars which destroyed five aircraft in May 1911. Although some testing is reported by Mr Dixon in 1913 (see below), the site seems to have been largely dormant until the arrival of Ruffy, Arnall & Baumann and the Alliance Aeroplane Co. in the later years of the First World War.

The characteristic roof structure of this building marks it out as the remaining portion of The Alliance Aeroplane Co. factory at Acton. (Author)

During the Second World War, de Havilland made use of the First World War Alliance factory at Acton, in this case for the construction of Oxford wings. (BAE SYSTEMS)

The Alliance Aeroplane Co. Ltd was registered on 26 January 1918, with the considerable capital of £451,000. The offices were at 45 East Castle Street, London, W1, the works at Cambridge Road (also given as Cambridge Grove), Hammersmith, and aerodrome at Noel Road, Acton. The company was founded by Samuel Waring of **Waring & Gillow** (partially in the light of concerns over Excess Profit Duty arising from his other concerns, including the White City tent factory). When first set up (as the **Hendon & Alliance Aeroplane Co.**) it operated at the Waring & Gillow works, but soon expanded into new premises, with 'subsidiary works in various parts of England'.

The factory itself was a very impressive brick structure surmounted by steel cross–girders to support large hangar door openings. The girders remain a prominent identification feature on the southern part of the factory which is still standing alongside Alliance Road, on the eastern boundary of Acton Aerodrome. The factory took fifteen months to complete, work not being finished until 1919.

A woodworkers strike in June 1918 originated with the sacking of a foreman at the Alliance Aeroplane works on 26 June. As a result of the intervention of the Minister of Munitions (W.S. Churchill) the factory was put under Government control on 10 July 1918, with the Superintendent of the Royal Aircraft Establishment being called in to manage 'the Alliance Aeroplane Erecting Shop'. Such action was a relatively common occurrence in the aircraft and munitions industries with the Defence of the Realm Act being used to quell unrest in the industry. In December 1917, for example, the London District Aircraft Woodworkers Council refused to accept a change in conditions to 'payment by results' (i.e. piece work).

Production by Alliance during the First World War comprised parts for ten Handley Page V/1500s ordered from Alliance but completed by Handley Page; 200 DH10s ordered but possibly not delivered; and 350 DH9s with serials from H5541-H5890. The DH9 aircraft were constructed at Acton, whereas the V/1500 components are thought to have been manufactured at Hammersmith.

During the summer of 1918, Alliance took over Ruffy, Arnall & Baumann, producing a single modified version of the RAB15 as the Alliance P1 K159/G-EAGK. This was followed by the long-range P2 Seabird, two of which were built, the type being designed by J.A. Peters, previously of Robey & Co. The first non-stop flight between London and Madrid was made on 31 July 1919 by an Alliance P2 Seabird K160/G-EAGL, having taken off from Acton.

ALLIANCE TYPE P1.

The Owner-Driver's Machine.

Extremely simple in details. Robust construction. Fuel cost $3\frac{1}{4}$d. per mile. Speed variation 30 to 77 M.P.H. range with pilot and two passengers, or 300 lbs. of mails, 300 miles. Dual control can be fitted if required.

ALLIANCE TYPE P4.

This machine has been specially designed for passenger-carrying over medium distances.

With four passengers and a pilot in a comfortable saloon, it has a range of 800 miles at a fuel cost of $4\frac{3}{4}$d. per mile.

It has a top speed of 107 M.P.H. and a landing speed of 40 M.P.H., which, combined with a wide tracked oleo undercarriage, renders it capable of being landed almost anywhere. The wings fold for storage purposes, bringing the span down to 15 ft.

For terms and particulars of this and other types, and appointments for demonstrations, apply to :—

The ALLIANCE AEROPLANE Co., Ltd.

Registered Offices:
45 EAST CASTLE STREET, LONDON, W.

Works:
CAMBRIDGE ROAD, HAMMERSMITH.

Works & Aerodrome:
NOEL ROAD, ACTON.

Longest Commercial Flight in the World
LONDON TO MADRID NON-STOP—900 miles in $7\frac{3}{4}$ hours.

ALLIANCE. P.3. (Eleven Seater).

THIS is the type of machine which has been adopted by Messrs. Waring & Gillow for their Intercommunication Services between their various Houses in London, Paris, Brussels, Madrid, Buenos Aires, etc. The first flight between London and Madrid was made on July 31st :—a distance of 900 miles in $7\frac{3}{4}$ hours. It is to be noted that the actual fuel cost on this flight was $7\frac{1}{4}$d. a mile.

On a service of this length these machines are capable of carrying a TON of goods or mails or TEN passengers, in addition to the pilot and fuel, for the non-stop flight. The passengers are very comfortably seated in a totally enclosed cabin, free from noise and draughts and provided with ample window area, affording a clear view of the country below.

For terms and particulars of this and other types, and appointments for demonstrations, apply to :—

The ALLIANCE AEROPLANE CO., Ltd.

Registered Offices :
45 EAST CASTLE STREET, LONDON, W.1.

Works:
CAMBRIDGE ROAD, HAMMERSMITH.

Works & Aerodrome:
NOEL ROAD, ACTON.

Contemporary advertising announced the 'longest commercial flight in the World. London to Madrid non-stop in 7 ¾ hours'. The second aircraft G-EAOX was intended for a flight to Australia which ended in a disastrous crash on 13 November 1919. Soon after this accident the company closed down, the factory building remaining in use by the parent company, Waring & Gillow, with the airfield being developed for the housing that stands on the site today.

During the Second World War, the ex-Alliance factory was requisitioned from Waring & Gillow by the Ministry of Aircraft Production. The factory was put to further aircraft manufacturing use by **The de Havilland Aircraft Co. Ltd** for the manufacture of Mosquito wings and ailerons for assembly on the production line at Leavesden.

The **HS Dixon** Nipper No.1 canard monoplane was tested at Acton with limited success during Autumn 1911. Mr Dixon, of 73 Twyford Avenue, Acton, was reported in late 1912 and early 1913 to be experimenting at Acton Aviation Ground with a canard pusher monoplane (known as the 2-1-P-O tailless monoplane). This machine is reported to have repeatedly 'got-off' in runs of less than 100 yards. It is not clear whether this report in *Flight* of March 1913 actually refers to the previously mentioned Nipper as the date of publication and different designation suggests a new design.

The **International Aircraft Works**, of 12a Emmanuel Avenue, Acton, was registered in January 1918. Nothing else is known.

Long Monoplane – this machine was flying at the 'Acton Aviation Grounds' in 1911. It was designed by J.D.B. Long and was clearly based on the Blériot, but for a different undercarriage arrangement.

D. Napier & Son Ltd: Napier built a new factory for its expanding car production on a four acre site at 211 The Vale, Acton, in 1903, expanding the works in 1904 and 1906. During the First World War, the company produced some 600 aircraft under contract, comprising fifty RE7s, 400 RE8s and 150 Sopwith Snipes. After this airframe construction activity, the company was to become justifiably famous for its aero-engines including the Lion, Dagger, and Sabre.

After 1940, Napier engine testing was conducted from Luton. A factory was also set up in Liverpool for manufacture of the Napier Sabre during the Second World War, but significant problems were experienced in getting this complex engine into production. Partially as a result of this, D. Napier & Son Ltd was taken over by **The English Electric Co.** on 23 December 1942. English Electric maintained an office at 47, The Vale, Acton, that was involved in designing modifications for the Canberra aircraft used in the 1953 air race from

E6938 is a Sopwith 7F1 Snipe, built by D. Napier & Son, and preserved in the Canadian National Aeronautical Collection. (J.S. Smith)

London to Christchurch, New Zealand. This unit also worked on the design of the forward fuselage of the English Electric P.1B and on the Canberra B(I) Mk.8, for which a mock-up was built at the same address.

Nieuport (England) Ltd, later **Nieuport & General Aircraft Co. Ltd**: The Nieuport London triplane bomber was first flown at Acton on 13 April 1920, this being reportedly the last flight from the aerodrome. Two Nieuport Londons were built, H1740 and H1741, from an order for six aircraft. Development ceased when the company was effectively wound up in July 1920. One other Nieuport aircraft known to have been active at Acton was the second Nieuport Nighthawk prototype F2910.

The hydroplane experimenter **Piffard** lived in Acton and, during 1911, was advertising for 'volunteer assistance to help experiment with aero-hydroplane at South Coast', from an address of 18 Addison Road, Bedford Park, W4.

From 1909 onward, Piffard experimented with various designs from a small field behind the present North Ealing Station, to the west of Mason's Green Lane. This field lay immediately to the south-west of the later Acton Aviation Grounds. Piffard's first machine was built in his studio at Bedford Park, assembled in a rented shed in Turnham Green and moved to the field in Acton for testing. Piffard had a long association with flying at Shoreham, West Sussex.

Ruffy Arnall & Baumann Aviation Co. Ltd opened their new aerodrome at Acton on 28 February 1917, there being by this time considerable pressure on the civilian flying schools operating at Hendon. It would be more accurate to say that they restored Acton Aviation Grounds to use as Acton Aerodrome. The company origins were in the **Ruffy School of Flying** at Hendon, which became the **Ruffy-Baumann School of Flying** in February 1915, Ruffy being joined by the two Swiss Baumann cousins, Edouard and Ami. The company was again reformed into the **Ruffy, Arnall & Baumann Aviation Co. Ltd** which was registered in January 1917 and provided instruction at Acton mainly on Caudron G.2 aircraft. Ruffy, Arnall & Baumann built the RAB 15, this type being taken over by the **Alliance Aeroplane Co. Ltd** as the Alliance P1 when Alliance took over the company in 1918. The flying school cannot have been wholly satisfactory as it was told to cease operation in July 1918. The grounds for this order included obsolete equipment (presumably the Caudron fleet) and inadequate instruction.

Ruffy-Baumann had offices and works at Portman Square. In April 1916, auxiliary works were in use at 'The Burroughs, Hendon'. The rather grand BBC Outside Broadcast Unit building, which fronts onto Alliance Road is located on the reported site of the Ruffy, Arnall & Baumann Flying School hangars. See also the entry for Hendon.

The **Twining Aeroplane Co.**, of 29b Grosvenor Road, Hanwell, was established in 1910 by E.W. Twining and produced model aircraft, together with three full-size designs which were tested at Acton. One of the model designs is said to have inspired the design of the Dixon Nipper (see above). The Nipper used a patent Twining's propellor design. The Twining Aeroplane Co. advertised its abilities as 'Builder of flying machines. Models. Experimental Aeronautical Work. Model flying machines for inventors. Strictest secrecy. Consultations'.

The full-size designs comprised a glider and two biplanes, the first of which was exhibited at Olympia in 1910.

Ultra Electric of Western Avenue, Acton, manufactured Short Stirling components during the Second World War, including rudders, bomb bay doors, elevators and instrument panels.

Waring & Gillow Ltd are well known as superlative furniture manufacturers with a long history of supplying the finest houses and the greatest families of the land. Sir Samuel (later Lord) Waring turned his company's capacity over to aircraft manufacture during the First World War. He was also instrumental in investing in a number of new companies, including BAT, British Nieuport/Nieuport & General Aircraft, Wells Aviation Co. Ltd, Chelsea Aviation Co. Ltd and the Alliance Aeroplane Co. Ltd.

Waring & Gillow advertised as 'Contractors to the War Office and The Admiralty. Aviation Department, Cambridge Road, Hammersmith, W6. Head Office Oxford Street, W1'. Contract production during the First World War included 500 DH9 from D5551. During the Second World War, Waring & Gillow were involved in the group manufacture of a large number of General Aircraft Hotspur gliders.

Barking/Fairlop

Handley Page Ltd was formed on 17 June 1909 with its initial workshop and registered offices at 3a William Street. A factory was established on land between Barking, Creekmouth and Dagenham, covering some 10,000sq.ft; one of the first in Britain to be built specifically for aircraft manufacture. In view of the location of the factory, it seems likely that the company's offices were at William Street, Barking, close to Creekmouth, although other sources specify Woolwich on the opposite bank of the River Thames.

Four experimental monoplanes, the Handley Page A, C, D and E, were constructed at Barking. The Type A was tested in May 1910, but proved to be capable of only short hops. The Type B biplane (or HP2) was built for **Planes Ltd** and flown, in modified form, at Freshfield, Merseyside, which see for details.

Subsequent Handley Page monoplanes featured a crescent wing planform with considerable tip wash-out. This configuration showed the influence of José Weiss, with whom Handley Page had collaborated at Fambridge, Essex.

The field by the factory at Barking, which had originally been purchased as a flying ground by the Aeronautical Society, proved to be too rough and too small, and in 1911 Handley Page rented a field at Fairlop to continue testing. The most successful of the designs to be built at Barking was the Handley Page E (or HP5), which was flown at Fairlop late in 1911. In September 1912, Handley Page transferred his offices and works to 110 Cricklewood Lane, moving his flying operations to nearby Hendon. The Handley Page E remained in use at Hendon and elsewhere well into the summer of 1913.

Barnes and Putney

A.V. Roe: The first A.V. Roe biplane was built during 1907 at 47 West Hill, Putney, SW15, in stables behind the surgery of his brother, Dr Stephen Verdon Roe. On completion, the aircraft was moved to Brooklands.

Messrs Boon & Porter Ltd, of 163 Castelnau, SW13, were controlled by **Blackburn Aircraft Ltd** during the Second World War to generate modification kits for Grumman aircraft, Blackburn being nominated as a sister firm to Grumman. The company delivered no fewer than 40,000 modification kits for four types of aircraft.

Handley Page supplied aeronautical components to other pioneers from its Barking factory. This photograph shows propeller manufacture underway in 1910. (Handley Page Association)

The interior of the Handley Page works at Creekmouth, Barking, is seen here in 1909. At the rear is the Weiss-inspired Handley Page glider, which made short hops here. (Handley Page Association)

The Handley Page Type A monoplane, Bluebird, was modified to become the Type C, seen here at Barking. This type achieved only limited success. (Handley Page Association)

The original Handley Page, Yellow Peril, at Barking in 1911. (Handley Page Association)

Palladium Autocars Ltd, of Felsham Road, Putney, SW15, were pre-First World War car manufacturers catering for the 'middle-class' market. After a period of making (and advertising) specialised trailers for the transport of aircraft, the company began aircraft construction. The major contracts were for 146 DH4s, the first being F5699. A further order for 100 Sopwith Salamanders was cancelled. Palladium Autocars also built the cabin DH4A H8263.

Battersea and Clapham Junction

Hardingham Bros, of the Star Aeroplane Works, Church Road, Battersea, SW11 advertised as 'Manufacturers of Aeroplane Parts – Contractors to the British Government'.

Harris & Others Ltd, Old Town, Clapham, SW4: This company was advertising in 1918 as 'Aircraft Constructors'.

Hewlett & Blondeau had premises at 55 St James' Street, SW1; 77 King's Road, SW3; and Omnia Works, Vardens Road, Clapham Junction. The Omnia Works were formerly occupied by Mulliner Coachworks, having previously been a skating rink. In December 1912, Hewlett & Blondeau were constructing three Hanriot monoplanes under contract to Hanriot. The main assembly shop at that time measured 150ft by 60ft. In February 1913, the company was advertising 'Aeroplanes of any description from customers' designs'. The company constructed the Dyott 1913 monoplane, and later the BE2a, BE2c and other types, moving to a new factory at Leagrave near Luton, Bedfordshire, to expand production capacity. The Omnia Works extended to nine acres.

The Dyott was an extremely successful streamlined monoplane, looking rather like a Nieuport monoplane with reduced (29ft) wingspan. The aircraft was built in April 1913, power being provided by a 50hp Gnome, and fuel for three hours was carried. One unique feature was that the machine was fitted with a recording drum which could show the pilot's movement of the controls during flight. Flown initially from Hendon, the Dyott monoplane toured the USA with great success in 1913 and was latterly reported as being based at Shoreham.

In May 1913, the factory built a Caudron for W.H. Ewen under War Office contract, this being delivered with Service Serial No.51. By February 1914, BE2 aircraft built by Hewlett & Blondeau were flying at Eastchurch. In April 1914, the company **Hewlett & Blondeau Ltd** was formed to carry on the business.

Mrs Hilda Hewlett, wife of the novelist Maurice Hewlett, was the first female pilot to obtain a Royal Aero Club Certificate (No.122, in August 1911, flying a Henri Farman), and is said (in *The Aeroplane*, October 1917) to have founded the first flying school at Brooklands. One notable person whose first flight was in the Hewlett & Blondeau Farman at Brooklands was Thomas Sopwith, later much associated with Brooklands himself.

Mrs Hewlett taught her son, Francis E.T. Hewlett, to fly in 1911. He became a pilot in the RNAS and had the misfortune to be the only British seaplane pilot missing after the Cuxhaven raid. After getting lost in cloud, the engine of his Short 135 began to misfire and overheated due to loss of oil. He landed on the sea near a Dutch trawler, the *Maria van Helten*, to ask for oil, his request being refused. Hewlett then holed the floats of his machine and let the aircraft sink. He was able to return to England on 3 January 1915, having been missing over the Christmas period. He was almost certainly the only pilot in the First World War who was taught to fly by his mother!

Ten different types of aircraft were built at Battersea (including Hanriot, Caudron and Dyott types) before the move to Leagrave. The Leagrave site was equipped to build complete aeroplanes, taking in only raw material – all required processes, components and details being completed on site. Aircraft built at Leagrave were flight tested at Hendon.

The **Morley Aviation Co. Ltd**, of 1 Renfrew Road, SW11, was registered in September 1918. Nothing else is known.

H.J. Mulliner Ltd, of Vardens Road, Clapham Junction, constructed a monoplane, which was exhibited at the 1910 Olympia Show, and the 1911 Skinner monoplane. This firm was the very first coachworks to specialise in car bodies. Its Omnia Works were taken over and used for aircraft production by Hewlett & Blondeau (see above). Mulliner also provided financial backing to The Varioplane Co. Ltd.

The **Short Brothers'** initial London works were located at Queen's Circus, Battersea Park, and also at Clapham. These works were used for balloon manufacture from 1906, and are said to have been located under the railway arches next to the gas works to take advantage of the convenient supply. Some thirty balloons were built by the Short Brothers at Battersea.

Windham's Works, Clapham Junction, advertised two new Farman biplanes and parts for three others in October 1912.

Warwick Wright Ltd, Battersea Railway Arches, and 110 Marylebone High Street, NW1. This firm was originally a partnership between Howard Wright and J.T.C. Moore Brabazon which was set up on 28 November 1906 for motor car construction, with a workshop at Battersea, underneath the arches of the London, Brighton & South Coast Railway. In 1907 aircraft construction was started, with the designers being Howard Wright and W.O. Manning.

Horatio Barber's **Aeronautical Syndicate Ltd** occupied one of the neighbouring arches and the prototype Valkyrie was built by Warwick Wright. A number of Blériot-inspired mono-planes were followed by an aircraft commissioned by the Scottish Aeroplane Syndicate which was initially known as the Golden Plover. This was tested at Brooklands early in 1910, and subsequently re-named the Avis. The Avis was Howard Wright's most successful design.

Warwick Wright Ltd was subsequently taken over by **The Coventry Ordnance Works** at the end of 1911, with COW aircraft then being tested at Brooklands. In January 1912, *Flight* reported that the Howard T. Wright company was being absorbed by The Coventry Ordnance Works.

Bexleyheath

Vickers Ltd established an experimental works at Gravel Hill, Bexleyheath, which was notably used for the construction of the first three prototypes of the Vickers Vimy, which first flew 30 November 1917. Small numbers of FB5, FB9 Gunbus, FB11 and FB16 were also built here.

Bickley (near Bromley)

The **Thomas Bros Aeroplane Co.**, of the United States, maintained an office at Bickley during the First World War. The office address was O.W. Thomas, Denbridge Road, Bickley, Kent.

Bow Common, Bromley, Limehouse

The Lusty family (of the furniture manufacturers William Lusty & Sons Ltd) were closely involved in the **Foster, Wikner Aircraft Co. Ltd**, with J.F. Lusty, W.K. Lusty and F.A.M. Lusty all serving on the company board, together with Mr Victor Foster and Mr Geoffrey N. Wikner (both of Ilford). The company was registered on 9 September 1936 as a private company with nominal capital of £100 to manufacture and repair aircraft at its factory, Lusty's Works, Colin Street, Bromley-by-Bow, EC3. The company produced the Foster Wikner Wicko, the prototype flying at Stapleford Tawney, Essex, and production took place at Eastleigh, Hampshire.

Standard Aircraft Manufacturing Co. Ltd, of Effingham House, Arundel Street, London, WC2, and 28 Bow Common Lane, London, E3, advertised 'Aircraft and parts to official spec-ifications', 'Contractors to the War Office'. The types and quantities are unknown, although the company is listed as an aircraft manufacturer in *The Aviation Pocket-Book, 1919-1920*. The company was registered in May 1916, with capital of £100.

Brentford and Isleworth

Brentford Aircraft Ltd, of the Market Place, Brentford, was registered with £10,000 capital in April 1918. Nothing else is known.

During 1919, **The Fairey Aviation Co. Ltd** used the River Thames at Isleworth for the testing of some early production Fairey III seaplanes.

Bromley

Mr P.G.L. Jezzi built two successful biplanes at Bromley, Kent, in 1910 and 1912, which were flown at Eastchurch. The first machine resembled a Wright Baby and flew in mid-1910, and was continuously modified to improve performance. The second machine was a small tractor biplane with wings of unequal span, and with a large gap between the wings in which the fuselage was suspended. Later the lower plane was extended to create a two-bay biplane configuration. This diminutive aircraft was powered by a 35hp JAP engine and had a wing span of 27ft 7in.

First flown in Spring 1912, the second machine was built in a workshop in Mr Jezzi's private house at Bromley. Both Jezzi machines were good flyers; it was reported regularly in *Flight* throughout 1911 and 1912 that 'the Jezzi biplane was out for trials at Eastchurch'. Also, 'the machine displays high speed and extreme steadiness'. Despite the low power, the second machine would readily fly with pilot and passenger.

Camberwell

Cremer Aircraft & Industrial Works Ltd, of Lorn Road, Brixton, was registered in September 1918 as aircraft manufacturers, engineers, etc., acquiring the existing business of the same name with capital of £10,250 (and therefore a company of reasonable substance).

Martin & Handasyde used the Trinity Works, at Camberwell, SE5, for the construction of their series of monoplanes built prior to the First World War. These aircraft were flown at Brooklands, Surrey.

Camden Town

Camden Engineering Co. (address unknown): George Holt Thomas/AIRCO acquired these works in Camden Town for aircraft component manufacture. The main products were items such as fuel tanks because this area of North London provided a ready supply of skilled sheet metal workers.

Canning Town

The Aircraft Construction Co., Harley Aeroplane Works, Beckton Road, E16: This company was formed by Mr R.P. Grimmer (formerly of **Mann & Grimmer**). In November 1917 it was advertising 'ribs, spars, longerons, tanks, wiring, plates and every description of metal fitting' and 'Aeronautical Designers and Engineers. Speciality: Windscreens complete with Non-Flamoid. Every accessory and component part of any aeroplane supplied at the shortest notice'. Mr Grimmer's initial activity was aircraft parts manufacture, with the ultimate intention of complete machines. The company also had premises at Great Alfred Street, Nottingham.

Estler Bros, of South Molton Road, Victoria Docks, is listed as an aircraft manufacturer in *The Aviation Pocket-Book, 1919-1920*. Nothing else is known.

Above: The Aircraft Construction Co. was founded by Mr R.P. Grimmer and manufactured aircraft components and windscreens.

Right: Hooper & Co., who built Sopwith designs under contract, were coach-builders of the finest pedigree.

Chelsea

Hooper & Co. had works at 77 King's Road, Chelsea, and offices at 54 St James Street, London, W1. In December 1916 the company was advertising as 'Aircraft Contractors to the War Office', 'Aeroplane Builders to HM Air Council'.

The heritage of the company was also made clear as follows: 'Royal Warrant coachbuilders', 'Motor body builders and coachbuilders to the King, Queen, Queen Alexandra, King of Spain, King of Norway. Coachbuilders to Queen Victoria and King Edward'.

The company was a significant manufacturer of Sopwith machines, building 250 Sopwith 1½ Strutters (the first being A1511), at least 300 and possibly as many as 375 Camel aircraft, and 216 Sopwith Dolphins from orders for 350 aircraft. Different production figures can also be found, for example 150 1½ Strutters and 238 or 309 Dolphins. Hooper-built machines were delivered to No.2 Aircraft Acceptance Park at Hendon. Hooper & Co. are reported to have had a further factory at Wembley in use during the First World War.

The Rivers Engineering Co. Ltd, of Lots Road, Chelsea, in January 1917 was advertising: 'Tail units, undercarriages, metal parts, tanks, cowls, engine bearers, etc'. The company is listed under aircraft accessories in *The Aviation Pocket-Book, 1919-1920*.

R.F. Wells & Co., 'constructors of the Reo biplane', later became **Wells Aviation Co.**, of 10a Elystan Street, Chelsea, and 30 Whitehead's Grove. Wells Aviation Co. was registered in April 1916, with capital of £10,000. Types manufactured by Wells Aviation during the First World War included the Sopwith 1½ Strutter (between twenty and sixty aircraft from orders for 100), and eighteen Vickers FB12C's. An order for 100 FE2b's was cancelled.

The Vickers FB12 was a single-seat fighter of pusher layout, distinguished by a small nacelle of circular section. The prototype was flown in June 1916, leading to Wells Aviation building a single FB12B in early 1917. A contract for fifty FB12C's followed, eighteen of which were built with a number of different engines. The company were sub-contracted for the manufacture of Vickers FB14 fuselages.

The company was also agent for Benoist Aeroplane Co., Chicago, and was the British agent for Roberts Aero Engines (65hp to 350hp) which were used by the Benoist Flying Boats. The works used to be 'an art pottery', known as Coldrum Pottery.

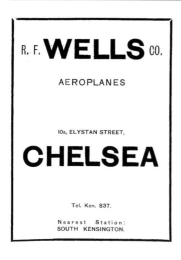

R.F. Wells later became Wells Aviation Co. Ltd, a major manufacturer of Sopwith designs.

In April 1916 the advertising style was '**Wells Aviation Co. Ltd**, Aeroplanes and Seaplanes'. Due to expansion, by September 1916 additional office space had been purchased in Whitehead's Grove, and the works had expanded to a building in Jubilee Place, which had previously been used for the storage of scenery for the Alhambra Theatre. The company was reported to be starting up a new flying field 'down Chichester way' in October 1916. By October 1917, however, the company was in liquidation, and the creditors voted to accept 10 shillings in the pound from Mr S.J. Waring – see **Chelsea Aviation**, below.

Chelsea Aviation Co. Ltd, of 30 Whiteheads Grove, Chelsea, was formed in June 1918 to take over the assets of **Wells Aviation**, 'and to enter into an agreement with S.J. Waring'.

The Chelsea Motor Building Co. Ltd, also of Whiteheads Grove, Chelsea, was, presumably, the last company in the **R.F. Wells & Co. – Wells Aviation Co. Ltd – Chelsea Aviation Co. Ltd** sequence. This company was formed in June 1920.

Whiteheads Grove and Elystan Street bordered grand apartment buildings in this prosperous area, where it is now difficult to imagine that a significant aircraft manufacturing business was once conducted.

The **Worms Aircraft Construction Co.**, of 4 Sackville St., Piccadilly, advertised 'complete metal and wood components for all types of aircraft' with works at Twickenham and Chelsea. In April 1918, the company changed its name to **Worms Aircraft Construction Co. Ltd** with works at Bournemouth.

Chiswick

Chiswick Aviation Works Ltd: this company was registered in November 1917 as manufacturers and dealers in aircraft, motors, etc., with capital of £1,000. Nothing else is known.

Chittenden-Robinson: J.P. Chittenden and L.P. Robinson built two biplanes and one monoplane in 1909-1910. The second biplane was of single-seat tractor configuration and had a very practical air about it. The fact that none of these aircraft were widely reported in the aircraft press suggests that they may not have been successful irrespective of appearances.

EH Industries Ltd, of 500 Chiswick High Road, was formed in June 1980 to undertake development of the EH101 helicopter, managing the activities of Westland Helicopters and Agusta SpA of Italy. The further development of the EH101 to create the RN production version (Merlin) is managed by Lockheed Martin Government Systems. EH Industries later moved to Farnborough.

WELLS AVIATION CO.
LIMITED,

WHITEHEAD'S GROVE.
CHELSEA

CONTRACTORS' TO
H.M. WAR OFFICE

Tel. : KEN. 6163.   Nearest Station : S. KENSINGTON.

City

The following listing consists mainly of registered offices, and is complemented by a considerably longer list under London (Central). The list is not likely to be comprehensive and the information presented is often limited to the street address of the relevant office. **City** is bounded by Blackfriars, Tower Bridge, Aldgate, Liverpool Street, and Holborn Viaduct.

Aerial Navigation Ltd, of 13 Copthall Avenue, EC, was registered in November 1912. Nothing else is known.

Aerogypt High Speed Development Co. Ltd, Caxton Street, SW1, was registered in February 1945 to continue post-war development of the Helmy Aerogypt.

The Aircraft Investment Corporation Ltd, of 148 Leadenhall Street, EC3, was set up in July 1929 to produce the Segrave Meteor, the company being the joint owners Blackburn and Saunders-Roe.

Anderson Aerocars Ltd, 61 Crutched Friars, EC3, was founded on 15 October 1935, becoming the **Deekay Aircraft Corporation Ltd** in October 1936, and built the Deekay Knight at Broxbourne, Herts.

Ashford Aircraft Works Ltd, of Cree House, Gracechurch Lane, EC3, was registered in December 1917 with £10,000 capital. Nothing else is known.

Boulton & Paul Ltd, 1 Pall Mall East, SW1, and 135-7 Queen Victoria Street, London, EC.

BAT (British Aerial Transport Co. Ltd) registered in June 1917 at 90 Cannon Street, EC, with capital of £100, and later at 38 Conduit Street, London, W1. See also Hendon and Willesden.

British Marine Aircraft Ltd had offices at 79 Lombard Street, EC3.

The Cierva Autogiro Co. Ltd, River Plate House, 12-13 South Place, EC2: this office address was in use in 1953. In addition to their London activities at Hanworth, the company operated at Hamble, Henley and Eastleigh.

The Commercial Aeroplane Wing Syndicate Ltd, see the entry for **Varioplane Co. Ltd**, below.

Croydon Aviation & Manufacturing Co. Ltd, of 2 Gresham Buildings, Guildhall, EC, was registered in March 1919, with capital of £20,000, acquiring the business of **Croydon Aviation & Engineering**, Effingham House, Arundel Street, Strand, WC2.

Dunne/Blair Atholl Aeroplane Syndicate, of 1 Queen Victoria Street, advertised the 'Dunne Patent Safety Aeroplanes, single and two-seater, mono or biplane'. Flying activities were carried out at Farnborough, Blair Atholl/Glen Tilt and Eastchurch.

Eldon Aviation Co. Ltd, 46 Eastcheap Buildings, EC3: it is not known if this company, which was registered in late 1917 with capital of £5,250, was successful.

The English Electric Co. Ltd, 3 Abchurch Yard, EC: this was the registered office in December 1918. The company subsequently moved to Kingsway.

General Aviation Contractors Ltd, 25-28 Crosby Buildings, Crosby Sq., Bishopsgate EC2: this company was in liquidation in November 1917.

Handasyde Aircraft Co. Ltd, of 1 Laurence Pountney Hill, London, EC4, was registered in early 1921. The company works were at Woking, Surrey.

Hanriot (England) Ltd, of 412 Moorgate Station Chambers, EC, was registered in May 1912.

Harris & Sheldon Ltd had offices at 70 Wood Street, EC2, and works at Birmingham, West Midlands.

Leconfield Aircraft Works Ltd, with offices at 345 City Road, E1, was registered in April 1918, taking over Leconfield Works, Canonbury, N1, as aircraft manufacturers, sheet metal workers, etc.

The Monospar Wing Co. Ltd, of 4 Broad Street, London, EC2, was founded in November 1928. The Monospar Wing Co. patents were subsequently exploited by **General Aircraft Ltd** at Croydon and Hanworth.

The **Navarro Safety Aircraft Ltd** (see Heston) designed and built the three-engine, three-seat Navarro Chief, which featured a radically unconventional control system. This company had offices at Finsbury House, Blomfield Street, London, EC2. Related Navarro companies are listed under London (Central).

Nieuport (England) Ltd, of 28 Milk Street, EC, was registered in January 1914 and moved almost immediately (in February 1914) to 45 Marlborough Street, South Kensington. The company listed its flying grounds as Hendon and Southampton (waterplanes). Mr G.M. Dyott was retained as pilot. See also Cricklewood.

Piggott Bros & Co., of 220-226 Bishopsgate, London, EC2, was advertising canvas aeroplane sheds in 1911. The company built a biplane in May 1910, and a monoplane in 1911. Both these aircraft are believed to have been unsuccessful. In 1919 the company was claiming that 'Piggott's aeroplane tents are the cheapest and most portable aeroplane shelters in existence'.

Robey & Co. Ltd had offices at 91 Queen Victoria Street, London, EC4, and works at Lincoln.

Sturtevant Engineering Co. Ltd, 147 Queen Victoria Street: although listed in *The Aviation Pocket-Book, 1919-1920* as an aeroplane manufacturer, the company's advertising material suggests that its products were mainly engines and spare parts. The company (then at Southern House, Cannon Street, EC4) was still advertising for Engineers and Draughtsmen in 1958.

Tibbenham's Aviation Co. Ltd, of Dunster House, 12 Mark Lane, EC, is listed in *The Aviation Pocket-Book, 1919-1920* as an aeroplane manufacturer and had works at Ipswich.

The Varioplane Co. Ltd, of 34-36 Gresham Street was registered in October 1913 to exploit Holle patents for the Alula wing. The Varioplane Co. Ltd was backed by H.J. Mulliner Ltd, coach builders. After the involvement of Robert Blackburn, a new company, **The Commercial Aeroplane Wing Syndicate Ltd**, was registered at the same address.

Construction and/or experimental flying was undertaken at Northolt, Sherburn-in-Elmet, and Addlestone.

C.C. Wakefield & Co. Ltd, of Wakefield House, Cheapside, EC2, is listed in *The Aviation Pocket-Book, 1919-1920* as an aeroplane manufacturer.

T.K. Wong Ltd, of 17 Ironmonger Lane, EC2, built the *Wong Tong Mei*, which was flown at Shoreham.

Whitfield Aviation Ltd, of 14 Paternoster Row, EC, and 10 Dane Street, High Holborn, WC (offices): this company was registered in September 1918 and was reported in November of that year to be acquiring Pulvo Engineering Co. Ltd. The address of the company works was given in March 1919 as Friars Lane, Richmond, Surrey.

The Willoughby Delta Co. Ltd had registered offices at 56 Moorgate, London, EC. This company was registered on 8 October 1931 to develop the Willoughby Delta design, which was test flown at Witney (Oxford).

Crayford (near Dartford)

Vickers Ltd (Aviation Department) set up an aircraft design office at Crayford in August 1914, adding production capacity later in the same year. The design office was moved to Weybridge in 1915. One hundred and fifteen FB5 Gunbuses, and forty-five FB9 (an improved Gunbus with a neater undercarriage and rounded wing tips) were built here, together with fourteen Vimys. Other FB5 and FB9 aircraft were built by S.A. Darracq at Suresnes, France. A small number were also built in Denmark. Contract production at Crayford included the following types: BE2c (sixteen); 150 Sopwith 1½ Strutter (first aircraft A1054); and SE5A (515). The ABC Dragonfly engine was also built at Crayford.

Cricklewood

Companies operating at Cricklewood are listed alphabetically below, the chief among these being Handley Page Ltd, who were responsible for establishing the airfield at Cricklewood and retained a factory there after removing their flight operations to Radlett, Hertfordshire.

G.W. Beatty. The Beatty School moved from Hendon to Broadway, Cricklewood, following the War Office move to take complete control of Hendon in February 1917. Flying operations made use of the Handley Page aerodrome at Cricklewood.

The **British Caudron Co. Ltd** had works at 255, The Broadway, Edgware Road, Cricklewood, and built substantial numbers of Caudron aircraft, here and at Alloa. The original flying school was at Hendon, but the offices and works were moved to Broadway in January 1915, occupying the premises previously used by Messrs Morgan & Sharp, car body makers.

The company also set up a Scottish factory at Alloa. The precise split in production between the British Caudron factories is not clear. Production included:
- One Caudron G.2
- Sixty-one Caudron G.3
- At least four of twelve Caudron G.4 ordered
- Fifty AIRCO DH5 (believed to have been at Cricklewood)
- Fifty BE2c/e (believed to have been at Alloa)
- 100 Camel from orders for 350 aircraft
- Fifty Handley Page O/400 (shared with Harris Lebus)

CONTRACTORS TO H.M. ADMIRALTY, WAR
OFFICE, AND FOREIGN GOVERNMENTS.

THE BRITISH CAUDRON CO. Ltd.

—SOLE BUILDING AND SELLING RIGHTS FOR—

Caudron Aeroplanes

——AND——

Hydro-Aeroplanes

— FOR —

THE BRITISH EMPIRE AND DEPENDENCIES.

HEAD OFFICE AND WORKS—BROADWAY, CRICKLEWOOD, N.W.
CABLE AND TELEGRAPHIC ADDRESS—"CAUDROPLAN, CRICKLE, LONDON."   PHONE—5651 HAMPSTEAD

SCOTTISH FACTORY AND AERODROME—ALLOA.
CABLE AND TELEGRAPHIC ADDRESS—"CAUDROPLAN, ALLOA."   PHONE—52.

- Twenty Avro 504B (shared with The Regent Carriage Co., who completed sixteen of the total).

Of these, the fifty BE2c/e and 100 Camel were built at Alloa, and the shared O/400 and Avro 504B orders are most likely to have been built at Cricklewood, the collaborating companies being London firms. The first British-built twin engine Caudron (Service Number 3332) was built in November 1915 and used 100hp Anzani radial engines, rather than the usual rotaries.

The company's November 1917 advertising copy ran: 'Contractors to HM Admiralty, War Office, and Foreign Governments. The British Caudron Co. Ltd. Sole building and selling rights for Caudron Aeroplanes and Hydro-Aeroplanes for The British Empire and Dependencies. Head Office and Works – Broadway, Cricklewood, NW2. Scottish factory and aerodrome – Alloa'.

Edgware Engineering and Aircraft Co. Ltd. This company was registered in December 1917, but may well have been only a speculative enterprise in view of its modest authorised capital of only £100.

Handley Page Ltd. After initial operations at Barking, Handley Page moved to new head-quarters at 110 Cricklewood Lane (a converted riding stables), with works close by in Claremont Road, Cricklewood. The works were to be used by the company for the rest of its existence. The removal of the Handley Page Ltd works from Barking to 'their new and larger works at Cricklewood' was announced in September 1912.

Although Handley Page initially produced a series of monoplanes, these had begun to fall out of favour by November 1913, and Handley Page reacted by producing a biplane derived directly from his monoplane designs. The resultant 100hp Handley Page G was outstandingly stable (it was demonstrated flying with no fixed tailplane to prove the point) and possessed a wide speed range. Advertising in 1914 stated: 'the special design of the Handley Page Planes gives the aeroplane that inherent stability which makes this machine so easy to learn upon, so simple to fly.'

The pace of production built up rapidly during the First World War; by late 1915, Handley Page was using a local Rolls-Royce repair depot, Cricklewood Broadway skating rink, and the local maternity home (as a drawing office), in addition to the riding school at Cricklewood Lane. By April 1916, the advertising styling was 'Aeroplane Manufacturers, Contractors to HM Admiralty and War Office'.

Famous for their bombers, Handley Page developed the O/100 and O/400 after Commodore Sueter, Director of the Admiralty, famously requested that Handley Page

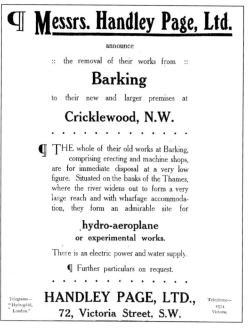

develop a 'bloody paralyser' of an aeroplane. Forty O/100 were built, all by Handley Page, in two specially built sheds at Claremont Road, Cricklewood, which was later to become the site of Cricklewood Airfield.

Initially, the large Handley Page prototypes were moved by road to Hendon for testing (e.g. O/100, on 9 December 1917), until Cricklewood Airfield could be opened. The party responsible for the O/100 moved the aircraft at night using ropes pulled by a team of sixty men. Trees and inconvenient lampposts had to be removed en route.

Eight hundred and forty Handley Page O/400 bombers were ordered, more than 400 of these being built before the Armistice brought production to a halt. O/400 contractors included: the Birmingham & Midland Carriage Co.; Clayton & Shuttleworth; Harland & Wolff Ltd; Metropolitan Carriage, Wagon & Finance Co.; National Aircraft Factory No.1; and the Royal Aircraft Factory. The lifting capacity of these machines was illustrated by the freelance test pilot Clifford B. Prodger flying the second O/100 to 10,000ft with ten passengers on 23 April 1916, and to 3,000ft with sixteen passengers on 7 May 1916. The same pilot followed this up later by flying a Handley Page (O/400) to 7,180ft carrying twenty-one passengers (reported in *Flying* magazine of October 1917).

The O/400 was one of the types that had the distinction of being selected for production in the United States of America. The first such aircraft was built by The Standard Aircraft Corporation, and flew at Mineola on Long Island on 6 July 1918. Civilian conversions of the O/400 made an important contribution to British commercial aviation. The type pioneered a number of air routes in the service of Handley Page Air Transport. New O/400 aircraft were delivered to store at Castle Donnington, and a number of these were converted for Handley Page Air Transport. Subsequent variants included the O/7 which first flew in July 1919, and the O/10 and O/11 with various engine installations and cabin arrangements. These latter aircraft were selected from the surplus holdings of The Aircraft Disposal Co. Ltd, itself managed by Handley Page.

The V/1500 was an even bigger bomber, with a 126ft wingspan and the unprecedented bomb load of 7,500lb. The V/1500 was built with a view to being able to bomb Berlin, but, of the 255 ordered, relatively few were delivered – thirty-eight complete aircraft and a further

This aerial photograph dating from around 1918 shows that, even then, urban housing was established close to the airfield boundary. (Handley Page Association)

By the 1960s, the Handley Page Ltd factory buildings were surrounded by housing, with the airfield site nowhere to be seen. (Handley Page Association)

The Type G biplane was essentially a biplane derivative of the earlier monoplane series. Built at Cricklewood, the Type G was flown at Hendon. (Handley Page Association)

This Handley Page O/400 is being flown quite vigorously for an aircraft of more than 100ft wingspan. (Via J.S. Smith)

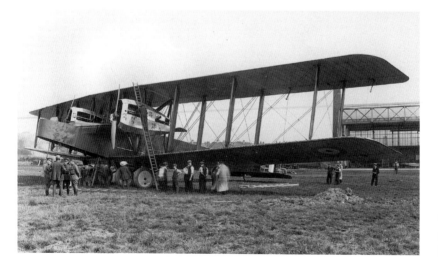

The prototype V/1500 at Cricklewood. (Handley Page Association)

Final assembly of the Handley Page W8 G-EAPJ. (Handley Page Association)

twenty-two as unassembled spares. The first prototype B9463 was flown at Cricklewood on 22 May 1918.

Handley Page Transport ran a London to Paris transport service from Cricklewood, which suffered from the reliability problems of the day. More than 100 forced landings were suffered during this service. Handley Page Transport operated a total of thirty-four O/400 conversions, from the (then) fields of Cricklewood, from May 1919 until May 1921 when transport operations were transferred to Croydon.

The Handley Page W8, a new design for civil transport, first flew here on 2 December 1919, to be followed by the W8b in April 1922. In January 1920, the brand-new W8 was advertised thus: 'Handley Page W8 – The World's most luxurious commercial aeroplane.' The W8 G-EAPJ won the 1920 Air Ministry Civil Aircraft Competition in the Large Aircraft section. G.T.R. Hill (later of Pterodactyl fame) was a test pilot for Handley Page Ltd and flew the Handley Page W8 to an altitude of 13,999ft with a 1,500kg payload on 4 May 1920.

By 1919, the Cricklewood works extended to fifteen acres, adjoining the 160 acre airfield. Cricklewood was not the most ideal of sites; the longest run was only 800 yards, and the site became progressively surrounded by the housing of the expanding London suburbs. The relatively basic production conditions of 1923 are illustrated by the fact that the dope shop and wind tunnel were partitioned off from the rest of the erecting shop by surplus O/400 wings propped up on their leading edges.

Handley Page Ltd manufactured forty-five Hyderabad twin-engine bombers based upon the W8 design, the prototype J6994 being flown in October 1923. The Hyderabad itself led to a further derivative, the Hinaidi, the prototype of which was a modification of Hyderabad J7745. This aircraft was first flown at Martlesham Heath on 26 March 1927; including prototypes, forty-nine Hinaidi were built. A limited number of a transport derivative, the Handley Page Clive, were also built, one of these (G-ABYX) being used by Sir Alan Cobham for in-flight refuelling trials.

Like many other companies, Handley Page Ltd rebuilt a number of DH9A aircraft in the 1920s, the aircraft being allocated new serial numbers. Important experimental work was

Handley Page Ltd was one of a number of manufacturers to run its own airline services (as Handley Page Transport Ltd) after the First World War.

The Handley Page Clive was a transport derivative of the Hyderabad and Hinaidi bomber family, this example being J9949. (Ken Ellis Collection)

Handley Page pioneered development of the automatic slat to reduce landing speeds. The first slatted aircraft to fly (with fixed slats) was the HP17 J6906 on 22 April 1920. This aircraft was a modification of a surplus AIRCO DH9, H9140. (Handley Page Association)

This dramatic photograph of Hamlet G-EBNS taking off shows both its use of leading edge slats, and the creeping proximity of housing to Cricklewood Airfield. (Handley Page Association)

The Handley Page Gugnunc G-AACN was one of the last aircraft to be built and flown at Cricklewood before Handley Page flight operations moved to Radlett. (Author)

Cricklewood remained in use as a manufacturing site after the Handley Page final assembly and flying operations were transferred to Radlett. This photograph shows the manufacture of Canberra fuselages in the 1950s. (Handley Page Association)

This Sopwith Snipe is painted as E6837; the original aircraft bearing this serial was one of a batch of at least forty built in Cricklewood by Nieuport & General Aircraft Ltd. (Author)

carried out at Cricklewood leading to the development of the Handley Page automatic slat, which was patented in October 1919. A number of trial installations were carried out, on such types as the HP17 J6906 of 1920 (a DH9 with full-span slats on upper and lower wings), and the HP20 (DH9A fuselage plus monoplane wing with full-span slat), eventually giving rise to the widespread adoption of this ingenious device. The Handley Page HP32 Hamlet G-EBNS was one of the first Handley Page designs to exploit this invention. The HP39 Gugnunc G-AACN was designed to compete in the 1929 Guggenheim Safe Aircraft Competition (in which it was placed second), and is preserved today by the Science Museum at Wroughton.

Radlett was purchased in June 1929, and Cricklewood closed for flying in February 1930. The airfield was then sold for £100,000 to the Golders Green Development Association, although the factory was retained, and the site was 'soon covered with roads and houses of an estate arranged in concentric ovals around a grassy central park'.

Handley Page Sayers monoplanes: three aircraft (all of similar appearance) were designed by Captain Sayers (designer of the Grain Kitten) and built by Handley Page at Cricklewood for the 1923 Lympne Light Aeroplane Trials. Unfortunately the first (No.23) resolutely refused to fly. The second (No.25) was flown at Lympne in October 1923. The third (No.26/J7265) was delivered to the Royal Air Force at Martlesham Heath; it was never assembled, and was eventually burned. Not a very auspicious type record!

Nieuport (England) Ltd, **Nieuport & General Aircraft Co. Ltd**, of Langton Road Cricklewood, London, NW11, were situated between Temple Road and the railway line at Cricklewood. Nieuport & General Aircraft Co. Ltd was registered in November 1916, the firm having been founded by Sir Samuel Waring. Like many contemporary companies, its advertising featured the slogan 'Contractors to HM Admiralty and War Office'.

At first the company acted as a contractor, producing Sopwith fighter aircraft in the form of 358 Sopwith Camel from orders for 400 and at least forty Snipe from orders for 100. The British Nieuport BN1 C3484 was flown in February 1918. This aircraft was followed in April 1919 by the Dragonfly-powered Nieuport Nighthawk (prototype F2909), which entered production. Nieuport & General Aircraft built at least sixty-four Nighthawk from total orders for 286 of the type. The Nighthawk was designed by Henry Folland who had joined the company in 1917, with several of his colleagues from the Royal Aircraft Factory. In view of the unhappy service record of the Dragonfly engine, it is perhaps not surprising that a number of Nighthawk aircraft were used to support the development of the Jaguar and Jupiter engines.

A significant number of airframes were completed without engines or armament, these later playing a significant part in the affairs of the Gloucestershire Aircraft Co. Ltd, who were also contracted to build the type at Cheltenham.

The Nieuport Nighthawk gave rise to a series of spectacular racing derivatives. These comprised Nighthawk K-151, Nieuhawk G-EAJY, and Nieuport Goshawk G-EASK. The latter, with 320hp and only 21ft 6in span, set a Class C4b speed record of 166.5mph. Harry Hawker was tragically killed whilst testing this aircraft.

The company adopted the advertising style of '**British Nieuport & General Aircraft Co. Ltd**', this name also being used by *Flight* in referring to the Nighthawk (e.g. 27 November 1919). This apparent use of two names for one company has been a source of some confusion. Lord Waring was later reported (*The Aeroplane*) to have combined **British Aerial Transport (BAT) Co.**, **Alliance Aeroplane Co.**, and **British Nieuport Co.** into a single combine – presumably this could have been **British Nieuport & General Aircraft Co. Ltd**, although some sources report that the BAT works were taken over after December 1919 by **General Aeronautical Contracts Ltd**.

The Nieuport London was an ABC Dragonfly-powered triplane bomber which was first flown at Acton on 13 April 1920. Two aircraft were constructed, H1740 and H1741; only the first being flown.

Folland left Nieuport on 1 August 1921, moving to the Gloucestershire Aircraft Co. Further development of the Nighthawk continued under Folland at Cheltenham. The Nieuport & General Aircraft works were later occupied by Smiths Instruments.

One of the trade addresses given for **Parnall & Sons** was North Circular Road, Neasden, although the company activities at this site are not described. The registered office was 8 South Street, London W1, and the company's main activities were at Bristol and Yate.

In October 1911, the **Compton Paterson** biplane was tested 'in a field near the Welsh Harp', where it took off in a 20-yard run. This machine, unlike Compton Paterson's Liverpool-based designs (flown at Freshfield), was constructed by **Messrs. Lawton** in their motor body works at Cricklewood.

The **Stanley Aviation Co. Ltd** had works at Stanley Works, Langton Road, Cricklewood, and other facilities at 67 Kingsland Road, E2, and Chatham Place, Morning Lane, Hackney, E9. This company was registered in April 1916 (with a capital of £1,000 to manufacture flying machines and components parts), and advertised as 'Government Contractors' in July 1917. Other advertisements running through to August 1918 refer to the company as 'Manufacturer of Stanley Propellers' and supplying 'propellers, fuselages, planes, rudders, fins, skids, etc'.

Croydon

In December 1915 an RFC airfield, known as Beddington Aerodrome, was established at Croydon, based on an area of land at New Barn Farm, with its buildings on either side of Plough Lane. This airfield was also sometimes known as Wallington Aerodrome.

From 1918, the Waddon National Aircraft Factory No.1 (which was managed by Cubitt Ltd) was established, occupying the north-east corner of the site, in the junction of Stafford Road and Coldharbour Lane. The area between Coldharbour Lane, Stafford Road and Plough Lane was flattened and used for flight testing, becoming known as Waddon Aerodrome.

During the early 1920s, the airfield was known as London Terminal Aerodrome, having been adopted as the Customs airport for London (in succession to Hounslow) on 29 March 1920. The Beddington Aerodrome buildings remained in use until 1927. This was made possible by the construction of a level crossing on Plough Lane, allowing aircraft to move from the Beddington hangars to the aerodrome surface. During this period the RFC hangars were used by companies such as Instone Air Line Ltd, Air Transport & Travel Ltd and Handley Page Transport Ltd.

In the late 1920s, the airport was extensively redeveloped to become the London terminus for Imperial Airways, the remaining Plough Lane buildings being demolished and new hangars, hotel accommodation and administrative buildings being constructed. The new buildings were located on the eastern boundary of the site adjoining Purley Way, and to the south of the National Aircraft Factory buildings.

Demolition of the central (Plough Lane) buildings allowed a much larger operating area, with Plough Lane being closed off to allow the entire surface to be used. This improved safety by allowing a significantly longer run to be used, particularly when the wind was blowing from the south-west. Although operations from Croydon Airport were underway in 1927, the formal opening of the new airport buildings did not take place until 2 May 1928.

Croydon Airport was officially closed on 30 September 1959, the last scheduled service from the airport being flown by Morton Air Services using de Havilland Heron G-AOXL. A Heron aircraft bearing these markings is displayed in front of the main airport building. After the closure, much of the western part of the site was redeveloped as Roundshaw Housing Estate. The northern industrial area continues to make use of some of the buildings originally used by the National Aircraft Factory. Within this area, the street name Cubitt Street recalls the origins of the site.

The first two British-registered **Aeronca** (C2) aircraft, G-ABHE and G-ABKX, were assembled in the ADC works during 1931.

The **Aircraft Disposal Co. Ltd** (ADC) (managed by Handley Page Ltd) was established at Croydon on 15 March 1920 to refurbish war surplus aircraft and engines for civil and military use. The company purchased the entire government surplus stock of aircraft and engines that had previously been handled by the Aircraft Salvage Depot system. Statements made in setting up the organisation are reproduced below:

All surplus aeroplanes, seaplanes, engines, accessories and spares in England have been sold to the Imperial and Foreign Corporation Ltd for £1,000,000. The purchasers must hand over 50% of the profit on resale, and take over responsibility for storage and insurance. The syndicate formed is known as The Aircraft Disposal Co. Ltd, offices: Regent House, Kingsway. Whereas previously the machines were sold by the Disposal Board as they stood, ADC will carry out detailed inspection and provide certificates of airworthiness for all machines sold.

The existence of ADC will stabilise the industry by issuing a price list, fixed for all purchasers. A rebate will be given to all British aircraft manufacturers and merchant firms dealing in aircraft. A further fixed rebate will be given to those firms who desire to purchase back machines of their own design originally supplied by them to the government. The presence of these stocks means that industry has to face a period when little manufacturing will be required.

The quantity of equipment was staggering, including:

10,000 aircraft including Vimy, DH10, DH9, DH9A, DH6, Sopwith Pup, Camel, Dolphin and Snipe, Avro 504K, Bristol Fighter, Martinsyde, SE5, FE2b, BE2e, a few Handley Page O/400, and large and small flying boats of the F, H and NT types. 35,000 engines include Rolls-Royce Eagle and Falcon, Napier Lion, Siddeley Puma, Wolseley Viper and Adder, 200hp and 300hp Hispano Suiza, Curtiss, Renault, RAF, Anzani, ABC, Le Rhone, Clerget, BR2, Monosoupape, etc. as well as an immense quantity of engine and aeroplane spares, hangars, etc.

The greater part of this stock is absolutely new and has never been used.

Flight reported that the ADC facility at Waddon consisted of 'numerous sheds in which were stacked packed and piled literally acres of aeroplanes, engines, airscrews, landing gear, instruments, magnetos, carburettors, nuts, bolts, split pins. The depot is one of six which were equally full.' Supplies include 500-1,000 tons of ball bearings, 100,000 magnetos and 350,000 spark plugs.

In 1920, The Aircraft Disposal Co. were advertising:

£100 million worth of aircraft, motors and accessories. Types included virtually every RAF type – Armstrong Whitworth, BE2e, FE2b, SE5A, Martinsyde, Bristol Fighter, Avro 504, Pup, Snipe, Camel, Dolphin, Vimy, O/400, DH6/9/9A/10, and a wide range of flying boats (F.3 and NT.2b). (Aircraft for immediate delivery with military equipment) [...] No machine leaves Waddon Works until it has been tested.

Not, perhaps, surprisingly a huge amount of space was required, with many aircraft being stood on their noses inside the hangars to minimise their storage space. ADC purchased the hangars of the National Aircraft Factory for use as storage space.

In April 1923 The Aircraft Disposal Co. took over **Martinsyde Aircraft Co.**, including a number of unconverted Martinsyde F4 airframes. The company was later renamed **ADC Aircraft Ltd** after its parent company ceased trading in 1930. Significant numbers of ADC Martinsyde F4 airframes were sold abroad, including aircraft supplied to the Polish Government. In May 1923, ADC were flying a modified F4 with 300hp Hispano Suiza engine, cooled by Lamblin 'lobster pot' radiators. In 1924, the design was updated by John Kenworthy (previously of the Royal Aircraft Factory and designer of the Austin Whippet and later of the Robinson Redwing).

The Martinsyde ADC1 G-EBKL was first flown on 11 October 1924, it being a Martinsyde F.4 with a Jaguar radial engine. Eight ADC1 were exported to Latvia. ADC set up its own engine production organisation under Major Frank Halford, producing the Cirrus, Hermes and Nimbus engines. Two Nimbus-powered Martinsyde aircraft (G-EBOJ, G-EBOL) were flown in 1926. The final Martinsyde derivative was the AV1 G-ABKH, which was flown in 1931.

Many other war surplus aircraft were subject to radical modifications to produce civilian machines. The Aircraft Disposal Co. modified significant numbers of DH9/9A aircraft for civil use, together with more than twenty SE5As for private use. By 1923 civil aircraft dealing was also undertaken, this being reflected in contemporary advertising: 'ADC commercial types for delivery – DH18, Westland Limousine, Vickers Viking, Vickers Vulcan.' G-EBAN was a DH9B modified from a DH9A at Waddon with a Rolls-Royce Eagle engine and Lamblin radiators between the undercarriage legs. This aircraft was equipped to carry five machine guns and bombs. ADC also converted and sold ten Renault-powered Avro 548 aircraft, and created four examples of the Avro 504K powered by the Bristol Lucifer radial (in effect Avro 504N) which were exported to Argentina.

In 1930, the company still had plenty of equipment for sale, reflected in the following advertisements from May and November of that year:

ADC Aircraft Ltd: Largest suppliers of aircraft equipment in the world. Stocks include Avro 504K type, De Havilland 9, Martinsyde machines; Puma, Nimbus, Eagle VIII, Falcon III, Hispano Suiza, Liberty, Viper engines.

ADC Aircraft Ltd, Suppliers of Aircraft and Aero Engines for all purposes. 504K, DH9, Martinsyde F4 plus new and unused Le Rhone, Sunbeam Dyak, Clerget, Wolseley Viper, Siddeley Puma, Hispano Suiza, Fiat and Rolls-Royce Eagle.

The Koolhoven-designed Desoutter monoplane was built at Croydon. Here G-AANE approaches to land at its birthplace. (Via Author)

In retrospect, perhaps ADC's greatest contribution to the industry was to employ Major Frank Halford to find practical ways of using the mountain of surplus engines and parts available. It was this step which led directly to the development of the Cirrus series of engines, with which it became possible to design practical light aeroplanes such as the Moth.

Brant Aircraft Ltd built the prototype Abbott-Baynes Scud glider here in 1930, it first flying in January 1931. Later the type was produced at the Farnham factory of E.D. Abbott Ltd.

Brian Allen Aviation Ltd was a distributor for the Tipsy S – 'The small machine with the Large Performance'. Brian Allen was later a director of **The Tipsy Aircraft Co. Ltd** at Hanworth.

The **Cooper-Travers** Hawk Monoplane was a Rolls-Royce Hawk-powered, cantilever monoplane with a wing of thick section and low aspect ratio. The aircraft was built at Brentwood and flown at Croydon, after assembly in The Aircraft Disposal Co.'s premises. Such was the depth of the wing section that accommodation was provided in each wing root for a passenger seated alongside the pilot. A number of short hops and straight flights were successfully made in late 1923 and early 1924, before the aircraft was destroyed in a fatal accident on 14 February 1924.

Croydon Aviation & Engineering Co., of 57A Southend, Croydon, is listed as an aircraft manufacturer in *The Aviation Pocket-Book, 1919-1920*. Nothing else is known.

Cubitt Ltd managed the **National Aircraft Factory No.1**, generally known as Cubitts. Work on construction was authorised on 16 September 1917 and was completed in eight months, including the erection of fifty-eight buildings covering some 650,000sq.ft. Aircraft manufacture began in January 1918, in parallel to the completion of factory construction. The first aircraft to be built, a DH9, was completed only fifty-eight days later on 14 March 1918. The total workforce was more than 3,200, half of whom were women.

In addition to manufacture of the DH9 and O/400, the factory also produced some 3,000 sets of aircraft machine gun interrupter gear. Cubitt Ltd are credited with the manufacture of at least 276 DH9 from an order for 500 aircraft, the first having the serial D451. In the guise of the National Aircraft Factory No.1, a further 142 DH9 were completed from an order for 300. A single Handley Page O/400 F5349 was erected at Ford Junction from components manufactured by the National Aircraft Factory No.1. A final order for 400 Sopwith Salamander was cancelled.

At the start of 1919 aircraft production was stopped, the National Aircraft Factory becoming National Salvage Depot No.3 (or Waddon Salvage Depot). The National Aircraft Factory site was purchased in April 1920 by Handley Page Ltd, for the use of The Aircraft Disposal Co. (later ADC); see the above entry for ADC. Car manufacture by Cubitt Ltd failed after the First World War.

The **Desoutter Aircraft Co. Ltd** was formed by Marcel Desoutter in December 1928 to manufacture in Britain the designs of the Dutch Koolhoven company and, specifically, the FK41. G.H. Handasyde was appointed to act as works manager and engineer. British-built aircraft differed from the Dutch FK41, having a low-set tailplane and revised cowlings and cockpit glazing. A total of twenty-eight Desoutter I were built, nineteen of which were delivered to National Flying Services. The Desoutter II, thirteen of which were built, adopted the inverted Gipsy III engine, and further refinement of the cockpit glazing and empennage. The aircraft were built in the ex-ADC factory at Croydon. The designer, Koolhoven, had served with companies including Deperdussin, Armstrong Whitworth and BAT.

Film Aviation Services Ltd produced three Tiger Moth-based replicas for the film *Lawrence of Arabia*, these flying as a Fokker D.VII (based on T7438), and two Rumpler C.V. built up from G-AHHF and G-ANNC.

General Aircraft Ltd was formed at Croydon on 27 February 1931 to take over the operation of **The Monospar Wing Co. Ltd** and exploit its patents, following the encouraging success of the ST3. General Aircraft used the rear part of the west hangar, formerly used by The Aircraft Disposal Co. The first production design was the ST4 Monospar whose prototype, G-ABUZ, flew in May 1932. Seven ST4 Mk I and 22 ST4 Mk II were built. The ST4 was followed by the ST6 with a five-seat cabin, three being built. In October 1934, General Aircraft Ltd was restructured and moved to Hanworth.

Martinsyde – see ADC. The main activities of the company were conducted at Woking and Brooklands in Surrey.

Morrisons Engineering Ltd were advertising in 1945 using an artist's impression of a Hawker Hurricane, and the slogan 'Morrisons Croydon and elsewhere. Construction, Maintenance and Repair'. By 1946, the text was more specific in location: 'Morrisons – Croydon and Peterborough, Aircraft Construction, Maintenance and Repair. To the private owner we offer the same aircraft maintenance and repair service that we rendered to the fighting services. Morrisons Engineering Ltd. Morrisons Aircraft Services. Offices 11 Upper Grosvenor Street, London W1.' During the Second World War, the company managed a repair organisation at Horsey Toll, Peterborough, that specialised in work on the Hawker Hurricane.

The **Robinson Aircraft Co. Ltd** was incorporated on 12 August 1929 with offices in Stafford Road, Wallington, Surrey. The company was established to build the Robinson Redwing and changed its name to **Redwing Aircraft Co. Ltd** from 16 March 1931. The company initially had offices in Stafford Road, but began to occupy its Croydon premises from 19 October 1929. The Redwing biplane G-AAUO first flew on 6 June 1930 at Croydon and was designed by John Kenworthy.

Kenworthy was a notable designer, whose career took him from being Chief Designer of the Royal Aircraft Factory (responsible for the FE8 and FE9), to Austin Motors, where he designed the Austin Whippet. Subsequently, he worked as Chief Designer for ADC, and was employed by a number of other firms in the industry. At the time of the construction of the first Redwing, Kenworthy was acting as a consultant to the firm, whilst retaining his post in

G-APTZ is a Rollason-built Turbulent seen here, as so often, display flying with the Tiger Club. (Author)

A Puss Moth comes in to land over the Redwing Aircraft Co. Ltd hangars at Croydon. (Via Author)

The last surviving Redwing, G-ABNX, was one of the three built during the company's spell at Colchester. (Ken Ellis Collection)

*G-ASRC displays
the factory colour
scheme of a
Rollason-built
D62C Condor.*
(Author)

the AID (Aeronautical Inspection Directorate of the Air Ministry). Kenworthy took up a full-time position with Robinson Aircraft Ltd on 1 July 1932.

The first Redwing was christened by Air Vice Marshal Sir Sefton Brancker, Director of Civil Aviation, on 19 June 1930. The aircraft was particularly noted for its slow landing speed (30mph), short take-off run (60yds) and good climb performance. The standard equipment included two suitcases to fit the luggage locker, grease gun, floor mat, engine tool kit, picketing rings and a standard red and cream colour scheme. Other features included a rearward extension to the luggage locker for the carriage of long items such as golf clubs. The aircraft was advertised as 'Britain's cheapest side-by-side light aeroplane' at £575.

Like a number of other Croydon-based firms, initial production took place in one of the former ADC hangars, themselves part of the former Waddon National Aircraft Factory. Nine aircraft were built at Croydon, and a further three at Blue Barns Airfield, Colchester. The company began to transfer its activities to Colchester at the end of 1931, with production being fully transferred to Colchester by March 1932.

Redwing Aircraft also operated a flying school at Gatwick, owning the aerodrome there for some eighteen months. In early 1934, Redwing Aircraft Co. Ltd moved back to Croydon from Colchester, the move being completed on 26 February. During the years leading up to the Second World War, the company expanded its operations and, by the end of the war, used facilities at Croydon, Thornton Heath, Wolverhampton and Watford.

The main Redwing wartime sites in the Croydon area included:

- No.20 Factory, Progress Way (used for fuel tank repairs).
- Tithe Barn (manufacture of Defiant ailerons and Mosquito fuel tanks).
- Derwent Works (next to the aerodrome and used to construct Wellington and Battle parts and Lancaster engine mounts).
- The main works at Benham Lane, Thornton Heath, which constructed a wide range of Wellington parts.

At Balham, Redwing controlled a Civilian Repair Organisation, which specialised in repairs to Blenheim and Beaufighter wings. Typhoon components and details were manufactured at Willett Road, Croydon, and at Major Motors, Purley Way. Other buildings in the area were used for administrative and storage purposes, and to provide accommodation.

At the end of August 1944, the company name was changed to **Redwing Ltd**. March 1946 advertising copy read: Redwing Ltd 'Designers and makers of components for Aircraft' Redwing House, Stafford Road, Croydon. Works at Croydon and Wolverhampton.

This view of the Surrey Flying Services AL1 in flight shows its comparatively generous wing area. (Ken Ellis Collection)

Capt. W.A. Rollason founded a number of Croydon-based companies, including **W.A. Rollason Ltd**, **Rollason Aircraft Services Ltd** and **Rollason Aircraft & Engines Ltd**. Prior to the Second World War, Rollason designed and implemented the modifications to introduce a third crew position into the Wellesley, for service in the Middle East. Eleven Wellington aircraft were converted to magnetic mine exploding variants by **W.A. Rollason Ltd.** Rollason carried out the civil conversion of large numbers of surplus RAF Tiger Moth aircraft at Croydon. As Rollason Aircraft & Engines Ltd, the company manufactured the French Druine Turbulent and Druine Condor designs and acted as UK agents for the Jodel. They also provided spares support for the de Havilland Tiger Moth and the Stampe SV4, had a long association with The Tiger Club, and built the Rollason Luton Beta racing aircraft. Production comprised thirty Turbulent, forty-eight Condor (two D62A, forty-two D62B and four D62C) and four Beta. The components for these aircraft were manufactured at Croydon, final assembly and test flying being carried out at Redhill Aerodrome. The first Rollason-built Turbulent G-APBZ flew on 1 January 1958.

W.A. Rollason was active at a number of other airfields, including Hanworth, Eastleigh and Shoreham, to which the company moved its offices in 1973.

The **Sanders** Type 1 biplane of 1909 was designed by Capt. Sanders of the **London Aeroplane & Aerial Navigation Co.**, 23 Blenheim Road, Croydon, a company which was formed to publicise the design. The aircraft was erected at Benacre Down, Suffolk, and was first flown there in October 1909. This activity led to the formation of the **Sanders Aeroplane Co.** at Beccles.

The Selsdon Aero & Engineering Co. Ltd, Sanderstead, Croydon, 'Contractors to the Air Board – Pumps for Aero Engines'. The company was founded from a garage at 1 Brighton Road, Croydon, before moving to Sanderstead Road and also had offices at 1 Albemarle Street, W1. In addition to the aforementioned pumps, the company manufactured interrupter gear and the ABC Dragonfly engine. A further indication of their product range is provided by advertising in February 1917: 'Metal components, engine parts, welding, etc'; in October 1917 for 'Parts for DH4, DH6, DH9, SE5, Bristol and Avro'; and finally in August 1918, 'Engine components & parts, gun synchronizing gear, air, oil, water and petrol pumps'. The company was reported in July 1919 to have commenced operation at Somerton Works, Cowes, Isle of Wight, but was closed by October 1919.

Surrey Flying Services. This company constructed a single example of the Surrey Flying Services AL1. This was a two-seat side-by-side wooden biplane powered by a Salmson AC7 radial of 95hp. The AL1 G-AALP was designed by Mr John Bewsher and first flew in

September 1929. The aircraft had an aerobatic Certificate of Airworthiness but failed to enter production, G-AALP being the sole example built.

Surrey Flying Services was originally set up in 1920, and acquired three Avro 504 aircraft from the A.V. Roe & Co. Ltd store at Alexandra Park. The company fitted these aircraft with Clerget rotary engines in 1925 as G-EAKJ, G-EAKM, G-EAKP. These were followed by four more from the same source – G-EBOF, G-EBOY, G-EBRB and G-EBTF – in 1926-1927.

The company changed its name to Surrey Flying Services Ltd on 5 September 1931. The company was also the United Kingdom agents for the Cessna C34 Airmaster, advertising the type in April 1936 as 'Tomorrow's Aircraft Today'. In 1953, the company was still in existence and was manufacturing aircraft components.

Elephant & Castle

Alford & Alder of 53 Newington Butts, London, SE11, is listed in *The Aviation Pocket-Book, 1919-1920* as an aeroplane manufacturer. The company was certainly a Hemel Hempstead-based car industry supplier, being purchased by Standard Triumph in 1960.

The **Morley Aviation Co. Ltd**, of 1 Renfrew Road, London, SE11, was registered in September 1918, its activities being listed as 'Aeroplane, aircraft parts, & piano manufacturers, woodworkers, etc.'

Erith

The **Thiersch Monoplane** of 1910 is reported to have flown successfully at Erith in May 1910. Its wings were constructed by Handley Page.

Vickers Ltd had offices and works at Erith prior to the First World War. The Vickers No.1 monoplane was built at Erith in early 1911 and was based upon the REP design for which Vickers held a licence. The Vickers design had a modified nose section and, like subsequent experimental prototypes, was first flown (in July 1911) at Joyce Green, Kent. Seven other monoplanes in this series were built, together with other pre-First World War production. Aircraft built at Erith during the First World War included contract production of the following types: BE2/2a (thirty-one), BE2c (twelve), BE8/8a (thirty-one).

Fulham

A. Darracq & Co. (1905) Ltd, **Darracq Motor Engineering Co. Ltd** (formed May 1916), **Hendon & Darracq Motor Engineering**, Darracq Works, Townmead Road, Fulham – 'Prices of complete aeroplanes, propellors, [...] on application.' This company was linked to S.A. Darracq of Suresnes, which manufactured ninety-nine Vickers FB5 and FB9 aircraft in France, and are believed to have supplied least sixty-eight FB5 and twenty-four FB9 for British use. The Darracq Motor Engineering Co. Ltd was formed in October 1916 and built ten FB5 at Fulham, these being serial 7510-7519.

The next type delivered was the Royal Aircraft Factory FE8, a pusher biplane designed by John Kenworthy. Darracq Motor Engineering built 220 FE8 from contracts for 245, and was the main contractor for the type. Next came the DH5, of which 200 were constructed, one example being A9435 (which was captured by the Germans and described in *The Aeroplane* of August 1918). The final type built by Darracq was the Sopwith Dolphin, Bruce Robertson indicates a production total of at least 300 (possibly 331) from orders for 400 (other sources give a total of 365). A contract for eleven Vickers FB7 twin-engine fighters was cancelled. Darracq later became part of the Sunbeam Talbot Darracq combine before splitting off in 1935 to continue independent car production.

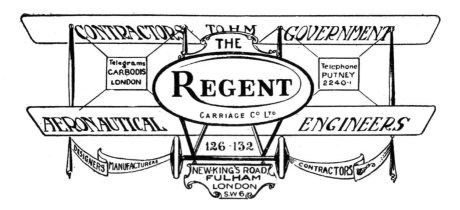

Geoffrey de Havilland. The first de Havilland aircraft was built in a workshop off Bothwell Street, Fulham, in 1909. Unfortunately, this aircraft crashed on its first flight in December of that year. The second, more conventional machine was also built in Fulham and flown successfully at Beacon Hill south of Newbury.

The Mayrow Steel Construction Co. of Lily Road, Fulham, was reported to be very busy on BE parts in March 1915.

Morris & Co., of 79 Lots Road, SW10, is listed in *The Aviation Pocket-Book, 1919-1920* as an aeroplane manufacturer with propeller branch. Nothing else is known.

The Regent Carriage Co. Ltd of 126-132 New Kings Road, Fulham, SW6, built twenty Avro 504B (production being shared with The British Caudron Co.). The company advertised as 'Contractors to HM Government, Aeronautical Engineers, Designers, Manufacturers & Contractors'. It would be interesting to understand what was meant when, in 1918, *The Aeroplane* stated, 'its works are so ingeniously camouflaged through natural circumstance that location by the enemy would be impossible. I had trouble finding them myself, though my exploration was conducted on foot.' The telegraphic address, 'Carbodis, London', clearly indicates the firm's origins.

The **Whitehead Aircraft Co.** had works at the Old Drill Hall, Townshend Road, Richmond, and Lily Road, Fulham – 'Contractors to HM Government'. In fact, Whitehead was a major contractor for the Sopwith Pup, DH9 and DH9A. For further details of this company's activities, please refer to the entries for Richmond and Hanworth.

Hackney and Homerton

A.V. Roe tested his No.1 Triplane, *The Bullseye Avroplane*, at Lea Marshes, Hackney. This aircraft was built at 47 West Hill, Putney, in his brother's stables and tested in 1909, using two rented Great Eastern Railway arches to house the machine. A plaque on the railway arches, unveiled in 1984, records A.V. Roe's temporary use of them. At this time, Roe was assisted by R.L. Howard Flanders and Mr E.V.B. Fisher.

On 13 July 1909, Roe succeeded in making a 100ft hop in this machine, but the very next day the council asked him to quit the site. By 23 July, the maximum distance flown had been improved to 900ft, which was the best to be achieved here. After departure from Lea Marshes, Roe tried the Old Deer Park at Richmond as a flying site, but found it unsuitable. In November 1909, Roe resumed flying operations, being now based at Wembley Park, see which for further details.

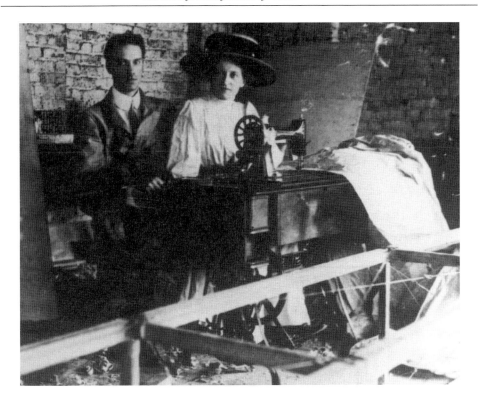

Captain and Mrs de Havilland building the first de Havilland machine at Fulham. (BAE SYSTEMS)

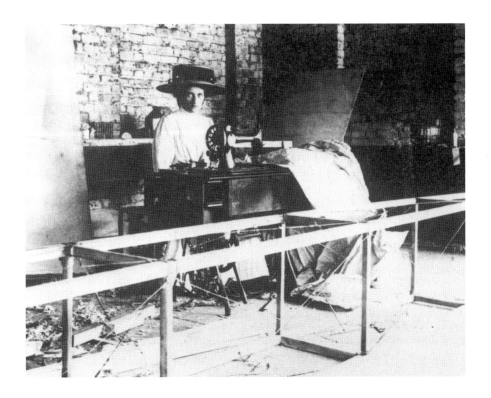

The Roe Triplane I was flying successfully at Lea Marshes by July 1909. (BAE SYSTEMS)

Although bearing the markings of A.V. Roe & Co. Ltd, H5199 was built by The London Aircraft Co. at Clapham. (Author)

Herman & Phillips of Acton Street, Kingsland Road, NE, is listed in *The Aviation Pocket-Book, 1919-1920* as an aeroplane manufacturer with propeller branch. Nothing else is known.

The **Homerton Aircraft Co. Ltd** of Sherry's Wharf, Homerton Bridge, E9, was registered in November 1917. Nothing else is known.

The **Jackson Aircraft Co. Ltd** of 215 Mare Street, Hackney, was also registered in November 1917. It is not known whether this company was successful, see **London Aviation Co. Ltd**, below.

London Aircraft Co. Ltd, 5 Urswick Road, Lower Clapton, NE, advertised quite actively. Examples from 1917 include: 'Aero and seaplane manufacturers. Specialists in automatic wood machinery work. Delivery from stock for all leading types'; 'aeroplanes to official specifications'; and 'Complete machines and spares, experimental and delivery flights by own pilot'.
     Although the company mainly seems to have concentrated upon wood machinery work for aeroplanes, it is also listed as delivering 100 Avro 504 with serials from H5140 (other sources quote the number of aircraft completed from this order as sixty-six). It seems very likely that

the company did undertake complete aircraft manufacture in the light of the last of the advertising slogans quoted above.

The London Aviation Co. Ltd, had its head office and works at 24 and 27-30 Charlotte Road, Great Eastern Street, EC2, a dope shop at 96 Old Street, EC, and other works at New Inn Yard, Shoreditch and 126 Gossett Street, Bethnal Green, EC2. (For further details, see Shoreditch). The business of **The London Aviation Co. Ltd**, of 215 Mare Street, Hackney, E8, was acquired by the **Jackson Aircraft Co. Ltd** in November 1917.

Note: The fact that the first of these companies has its head office and works in Shoreditch, whilst the second only refers to an address in Hackney, may mean that they are not the same company.

Stanley Aviation Co., Chatham Place, Morning Lane, Hackney, E9, and 27/28 Charlotte Street, and 67 Kingsland Road, E2 (both Shoreditch) – 'Government Contractors – propellers, fuselages, planes, rudders, fins, skids, etc.' See also Cricklewood.

The Super Aviation Co. Ltd of 154 Dalston Lane, London, E8, was registered at the end of October 1917. Its comprehensive capabilities were advertised as 'Aeronautical Designers, Constructors and General Engineers. Manufacturers of complete machines and spares. Seaplane and aeroplane manufacturers' at Dollis Hill Works, Duddenhill Lane, Willesden, NW10.

The company changed its name in June 1918 to **Sceptre Aviation Co. Ltd**, to 'avoid confusion with a similarly named firm', presumably The Supermarine Aviation Works Ltd.

The **Thames Aviation Works (Burtons Ltd)** of 141 Curtain Road, EC2 (Shoreditch) was registered in April 1917. This was clearly a significant enterprise involving three sawmills and six other works. In October 1917 the firm was advertising employment vacancies. The text of one of its contemporary advertisements ran: 'Three years experience, Constructors of complete aircraft'.

The company address changed to London Fields Station (Great Eastern Railway), Hackney, E8, and it appears literally to have occupied the station buildings. This can be inferred by the announcement of a further change of address in April 1919, the company moving to 30A Highgate Road, NW5 'as a result of London Fields station being re-opened'.

The company is listed in *The Aviation Pocket-Book, 1919-1920* as an aeroplane manufacturer.

Hammersmith

Wm Cole & Sons Ltd: Works at 235 Hammersmith Road, W6, and offices at 92 High Street, Kensington, London W. (This company also advertised as **Cole Aircraft**.) Although there is no record of the firm delivering complete aircraft, a comprehensive capability is

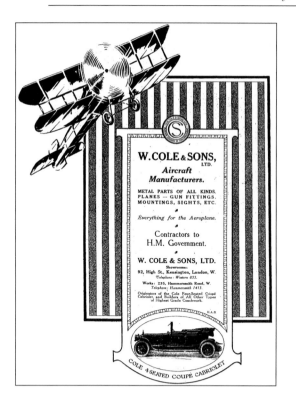

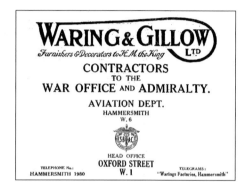

indicated by their advertising copy: 'Aircraft manufacturers, contractors to HM Government'; 'Metal parts of all kinds of planes'; 'Makers of aeroplane parts. Everything for the aeroplane except the powerplant'. These advertisements are from the mid–war period; at the end of the First World War, the company was still advertising as 'Aircraft manufacturers. Contractors to the Royal Air Force' The company origins appear to have been as coachbuilders.

The Davidson Aviation Co. Ltd: Aviation works and offices at 229-231 Hammersmith Road, W6 – 'Designers and Manufacturers of Aircraft. Contractors to HM Government'; 'Contractors to the Air Board'. This company was reported in October 1917 as making wings in large numbers. Having initially obtained minor contracts, rapid expansion led to the company investing in wood production to the extent that it cut down its own trees, and cut and dried the wood to supply its aircraft works. The company also made metal parts for aircraft and built other vehicles. Further advertising offered their capabilities as 'Designers and inventors of aircraft, waterplanes and flying boats'.

At peak production several factories were in use including engineering works at Gt Church Lane, Hammersmith and Airscrew Works at Ravenscourt Avenue, W6.

Gwynnes Ltd of Chiswick/Hammersmith was the British licensee of Clerget Motors. Gwynnes were originally known for pump manufacture, and later were involved in some vehicle manufacture. In addition to the Clerget rotary, Gwynnes received orders for the Bentley BR1. Although not a familiar name today, Gwynnes are said to have been the largest British engine producer during the First World War.

Hendon & Alliance Aeroplane Co., Cambridge Road, Hammersmith – for details of this company and its production, see Acton. The company was founded by Sir Samuel Waring (of Waring & Gillow Ltd) and initially used that company's works.

Waring & Gillow Ltd. This famous and long-established furniture manufacturer expanded into aircraft manufacture during the First World War at the instigation of Sir Samuel Waring. The company were keen to state their origins in its advertising, a typical example being: 'Furnishers and Decorators to HM the King. Contractors to the War Office and Admiralty. Aviation Department, Cambridge Road, Hammersmith, and 164-180 Oxford St'. The street address of the aviation department was never given in detail – presumably the name Waring & Gillow was enough to find them,

Production types are believed to have included the DH4 (some sources indicate forty-six aircraft starting with H5894, although Bruce Robertson attributes these to Palladium Autocars), and the DH9 (no less than 500 aircraft). The company was also responsible for a small number of DH4A cabin conversions.

Hanworth (Feltham)

The **No.7 Aircraft Acceptance Park** operated here during the First World War, the airfield being sited on the private estate of Mr J.A. Whitehead.

After the First World War, the airfield had a resurgence of activity and popularity when Hanworth Air Park (also known as The London Air Park) was officially opened on 3 August 1929. Wooded gardens and lawns surrounded the clubhouse/hotel, and the whole estate covered some 230 acres, including two separate landing areas. The ground to the north of the hotel was used for commercial flying, and that to the south for private operations. Houses and trees surrounded the airfield, and the longest run available was around 1,000 yards. The airfield was owned by Blackburn and was the home of their Bluebird/B2-equipped flying school, Flying Training Ltd, later styled National Flying Services (NFS). The British Pacific Trust who backed General Aircraft Ltd purchased the airfield lock, stock and barrel in 1934 from NFS, after NFS went into receivership in June 1933.

British production of the American **Aeronca** light aircraft followed its initial distribution by **Light Aircraft Ltd** of Hanworth (registered on 26 August 1935) which had obtained a licence to produce the Aeronca C-3 in Britain. Sixteen American-built aircraft were assembled at Hanworth. On 15 April 1936, the formation of the **Aeronautical**

This DH9, which is preserved in France, was constructed by the British manufacturers of fine furniture, Waring & Gillow Ltd. (Author)

*G-AEFT is an
American-built
Aeronca C-3,
distributed from
Hanworth by Light
Aircraft Ltd. (Author)*

Corporation of Great Britain Ltd was announced, with a registered capital of no less than £300,000. The company directors included Mr H.V. Roe (the brother of A.V. Roe), Mr J.V. Prestwich (the son of J.A. Prestwich, the later manufacturer of the Aeronca-JAP two-cylinder air-cooled engine), and Mr W.G. Gibson (previously the Works Manager at the Westland Aircraft Works), with S.D. Davis as Chief Engineer (previously of Hawker and Vickers). The company took over the interests of **Light Aircraft Ltd** and the **Lang Propeller Co. Ltd**. The Aeronautical Corporation of Great Britain also entered into an agreement with **Fred^k Sage & Co. Ltd**, which led to the company works being established in the First World War Sage works at Walton, Peterborough, where twenty-four Aeronca 100 were built.

L.G. & L.J. Anderson converted the Cierva C.8V Autogiro back to conventional biplane form as the Avro 552A G-ABGO in 1930. The aircraft was then used to tow advertising banners. The Anderson brothers also converted at least six Avro 504N for joy-riding and aerial advertising.

The **Angus Aquila** was a Salmson-powered single-seat low-wing monoplane with a snub-nosed appearance. The sole example, G-ABIK crashed here on 21 March 1931 after only one month of flying, its designer Mr A.L. Angus being fatally injured. The Aquila was built at Sutton Benger, Wiltshire.

M.B. Arpin & Co. Ltd of Longford, West Drayton, built the Arpin A-1 G-AFGB, a monoplane of pusher configuration with tricycle undercarriage and twin tailbooms. Power was provided by a 75hp Salmson AD-9R radial driving a four-blade propeller, and the type also featured a castoring undercarriage. Cooling of the Salmson was unsatisfactory, and it was subsequently replaced by a 90hp Cirrus Minor, the type then being known as the Arpin Mk II.

The Arpin A-1 was built at West Drayton and flown at Hanworth on 7 May 1938. The company was styled the **Arpin Aircraft Manufacturing Co. Ltd** from 26 May 1939, but plans for the type to enter production were frustrated by the outbreak of the Second World War.

The design of the Newbury Eon four-seat light aircraft was carried out by **Aviation & Engineering Projects Ltd** of Feltham. The Eon was the only powered aircraft to be built by the glider manufacturer **Elliotts of Newbury**.

British Aircraft Co./Kronfeld produced the Drone powered glider, of which thirty-three were built. The origin of the Drone was the **Lowe-Wylde** Planette. The Planette was a development of CH Lowe-Wylde's series of BAC gliders, built at Maidstone, Kent, and was (under)powered by a 600cc Douglas engine mounted as a pusher on a pylon above its wing centre section. Refinement of the engine-mounting pylon resulted in a change of name to the Drone.

After Lowe-Wylde's death in May 1933, Robert Kronfeld continued Drone production at a new factory at Victoria Road, Feltham. Robert Kronfeld was well known as a sailplane pilot and enthusiast, and flew the enormous (100ft span) sailplane *Austria* from Hanworth. **BAC (1935) Ltd** was formed in March 1935 to take over production and development of the Drone. In February 1936, we find the company advertising: 'BAC "Super Drone" £275 fully equipped. 2/- per hour for petrol and oil at a speed of 60mph. BAC (1935) Ltd, London Air Park, Feltham'.

The type is reported to have been very underpowered and to have had heavy flying controls. As is the case of many pusher designs, it had a distinctive note (so characteristic of some present-day autogyros and microlights), and this is perhaps why the name Drone was so appropriate. Such was the performance of this machine (and its noise a nuisance?) that it was banned from flying beyond the confines of Hanworth aerodrome, and could only fly between sunrise and noon on weekdays. One notable flight was that made by the Master of Sempill in G-ADUA on a non-stop flight from Croydon to Berlin at a stately 54.5mph in eleven hours. This flight set a Class 4 record for distance in a straight line (570 miles) for aircraft with a take-off weight below 200kg.

The company was re-named **Kronfeld Ltd** (also known as **Robert Kronfeld Ltd**) from 21 May 1936. Various engine changes led to the Super Drone and the Drone de Luxe. In September 1936, the company was advertising 'Super Drone – Folding wings, lands at 22mph, insurance covers field landings, all round visibility. Simplest aeroplane to fly and cheapest to run. De Luxe Drone – Carden Ford twin ignition. Folding wings, split sprung undercarriage, increased performance, trimming device. Safest light engine in the safest airframe. KRONFELD LTD, Hanworth Aerodrome'.

The company also produced a single example of the Kronfeld Monoplane, in essence, a two-seat Drone. The sole example, G-AESG, was a two-seat parasol monoplane with pusher layout. The type was similar to the Shackleton Murray SM1 in configuration, but with a more angular appearance to its fuselage and tail surfaces, very like the modern Woody Pusher. This design followed on from the Drone series, and it flew for the first time on 7 May 1937, construction having been undertaken by General Aircraft Ltd.

By now the Drone was an anachronism, and the Kronfeld Monoplane failed to generate new business. As a result, the company entered receivership on 24 September 1937, component stock and goodwill being purchased by Luton Aircraft Ltd of Gerrards Cross.

The Arpin A-1 featured an unusual configuration, and was the first British aircraft to be designed to use a tricycle undercarriage. (Military Aircraft Photographs)

A long-winged BA Swallow G-AFGE has pride of place on the apron at Shoreham.
(Author)

British Klemm Aeroplane Co. Ltd, **British Aircraft Manufacturing Co. Ltd** Victoria Road, Hanworth. From 1929, Major E.F. Stephen, of S.T. Lea Ltd, imported some twenty-seven Klemm L.25 aircraft, the successful sales of these aircraft leading to the decision that the aircraft should be built in England. As a result, **The British Klemm Aeroplane Co. Ltd** was formed at Hanworth in February 1933.

British Klemm was notable for the pioneering pedigree of its design staff: George Handasyde and Harold Boultbee. Handasyde was a pioneer in his own right, and a partner in Martinsyde, from where he moved to Desoutter, until their collapse in 1930. He then became works manager at British Klemm, finally designing the BA Eagle. Boultbee worked for Bristol, Handley Page Ltd, and his own Civilian Aircraft Co. before becoming the Chief Designer of British Klemm.

The first British-built Klemm Swallow G-ACMK was flown at Hanworth in November 1933. In 1934 the 'All British' Klemm Swallow was advertised as: 'The safest aeroplane in the World. Will not spin, will not stall, flies hands off'. Twenty-eight British Klemm Swallow 1 were built, followed by 105 of the improved Swallow 2 of 1935. The introduction of the Swallow 2 was marked by a change in company name on 4 April 1935 to **British Aircraft Manufacturing Co. Ltd**. The company continued its theme of promoting the safety of the Swallow with a series of advertisements in 1935 and 1936. In September 1935, one of the most fulsome examples trumpeted:

The BA Swallow – The Safest Aeroplane in the World. The BA Swallow is a full cantilever, open two seater, low-wing monoplane, built to meet the demands of Private owners, Clubs and Schools. Safety, quality and economy are the features demanded and the details of the Swallow, as outlined, form a complete and unique answer. An outstanding feature of the Swallow is its low landing speed which enables the pilot to land almost anywhere.

SAFETY – is obtained by a combination of slow landing speed, under 30mph, ample control at low speeds, quick take off and exceptional visibility for pilot and pupil. The presence of all these safety qualities in one aeroplane is absolutely unique and undoubtedly accounts for the fact that the BA Swallow is universally accepted as the safest aeroplane in the world.

QUALITY & ECONOMY – Running costs of petrol and oil are under 1d. per mile, and owing to the highest standard of real workmanship and quality of material used, maintenance is reduced to a minimum.

This beautiful BA Eagle is now the last survivor of the type. This photograph was taken at Wroughton, just after the aircraft had been subject to a comprehensive restoration. (Author)

Other claims made included:

> *IN FULL CONTROL at speeds below the stall. ... Landing at 25mph, taking off in 40 yards and cruising at ninety-eight are true safety features. ... YOU CAN'T SPIN A SWALLOW.*

> *With the Pobjoy Cataract II, Dunlop Brakes, and 'one man' folding wings, the price of the Swallow is £725 complete. No extras needed.*

The second main product of the company was the Eagle three-seat touring aircraft with a retractable undercarriage. The prototype G-ACRG was first flown in early 1934, and a total of forty-three aircraft were built. A typical advertisement for the company's products featured the Eagle as follows: 'BA Monoplanes – Quality, Performance, Safety. Superlative quality, easy handling, economy machines. The Eagle cruises with three passengers at a comfortable 130mph. The top speed is 150mph. The running cost is less than 1½d per mile and the price with Gipsy Major is £1,250'. The company's other products were unsuccessful, these being the sole BA Cupid (G-ADLR), and the twin-engine Double Eagle (three aircraft, the prototype being first flown on 3 July 1936 as Y-1, later registered as G-ADVV). The Double Eagle was a six-passenger twin-engine aircraft with a shoulder-mounted wing and retractable undercarriage.

British Aircraft also constructed a number of Cierva C.40 autogiros in 1938, with Oddie, Bradbury & Cull Ltd supplying assemblies for these machines. The first C.40 G-AFDP was first flown at Hanworth on 21 June 1938. **General Aircraft Ltd** brought out the British Aircraft Manufacturing Co. in January 1938. In 1940 a number of BA Swallow aircraft were converted at Hanworth to glider configuration for trials by the Royal Aircraft Establishment.

The **Broughton Blayney** Brawny was a development of the Perman Parasol and indirectly, therefore, of the *Pou de Ciel*. The Brawny was built by T.H. Gill & Son, of 75 Kilburn Lane, London, W10, of which company Mr Blayney was a director. The **Broughton Blayney Aircraft Co.** was registered at Hanworth on 3 September 1936. The aircraft was first flown at Hanworth on 17 September 1936, but unfortunately two out of the three built were destroyed in fatal accidents. The aircraft is said to have had a tendency to spin off turns, and this was certainly a factor in both fatal accidents. The three aircraft built were registered G-AENM, G-AERF and G-AERG. The company works were later taken over by The Tipsy Aircraft Co. Ltd.

The Cierva Autogiro Co. Ltd. The first Cierva C.30 prototype G-ACFI was assembled at Hanworth in 1933 in the workshops of **National Flying Services Ltd**: the fuselage was modified from a C.19 by **Airwork Ltd** at Heston, the rotor head provided by **Mollart Engineering Co. Ltd** of Thames Ditton, and the blades by **Oddie, Bradbury & Cull** at Eastleigh. Ultimately, eighty-two C.30 were constructed in the United Kingdom, the majority being the 140hp Genet Major 1A-powered C.30A, built by A.V. Roe & Co. Ltd in Manchester and distributed by Cierva at Hanworth. **The Cierva Autogiro Co. Ltd** moved its headquarters to Hanworth on 26 April 1937. An unusual military use of the Autogiro during the Second World War was to provide a slow-flying platform to assist in radar calibration experiments.

Typical Autogiro advertisements of 1935 and 1936 seemed to be unable to decide whether safety or practical enjoyment was the better aspect on which to sell the aircraft. Thus, from July 1935:

> *Across country in confidence. Acknowledged as the safest aircraft in the world, Autogiros offer greater comfort in bumpy weather, combined with the finest view facilities. Real flying enjoyment will be yours, no matter what country you are passing over, safety is assured. Landings can be made without the necessity of using prepared aerodromes – it is more practical to fly by Autogiro to your destination. IDEAL FOR PHOTOGRAPHIC PURPOSES.*

By February 1936, safety was even more prominent:

INDISPUTABLY THE SAFEST AIRCRAFT OF TODAY
- *BECAUSE it cannot stall or spin*
- *BECAUSE it maintains height and is under full control at 20mph (vital in conditions of bad visibility)*
- *BECAUSE it can descend vertically and land without forward run. (No fear of hitting ground obstacles at high speed).*
- *BECAUSE it has a steep angle of climb*
- *BECAUSE of its unrivalled safety characteristics it is the finest aircraft for FLYING INSTRUCTION. Full ab initio course for A licence, by Autogiro experts, at £35 inclusive.*

AVOID ACCIDENTS..............FLY BY AUTOGIRO.

The initial test flying of the unsuccessful **Westland**-built CL.20 Autogiro G-ACYI was carried out at Hanworth from 5 February 1935, the pilot being H.A. Marsh. More than sixty test flights were required to amass a total flight time of 8½ hours before the project was

The Broughton Blayney Brawny was developed from the Perman Parasol. Three were built in a factory that was later to be used by The Tipsy Aircraft Co. Ltd. (Military Aircraft Photographs)

Developed in Scotland, the Weir W-2 and W-3 autogyros were tested at Hanworth, alongside the designs of Cierva and Hafner. (Ken Ellis Collection)

abandoned. Alan Marsh also tested both the **Weir** W.2 and W.3 autogyros at Hanworth. Dr J.A.J. Bennett, who contributed to the technical development of the British-built Cierva machines, later became head of the Fairey Aviation helicopter activity. Another well-known figure in British rotorcraft circles was Reggie Brie, who was sales manager for Cierva at Hanworth, a founder member of the Helicopter Association of Great Britain, and subsequently ran BEA Helicopters. The company also operated at Hamble, Eastleigh and Henley.

General Aircraft Ltd (GAL) was restructured in October 1934, and moved to Hanworth from Croydon, taking up occupation of part of the Whitehead factory site. The pioneer pilot E.C. Gordon England was managing director. The company continued the development of the twin-engine Monospar series with the following types:

- ST10 – an ST4 with improved forward view (two built)
- ST11 – a retractable undercarriage version of the ST10 (two built)
- ST12 – A Gipsy Major powered ST10 (ten built)
- ST18 Croydon – a large ten-passenger transport aircraft with a 60ft wingspan (one only, G-AEDB)
- ST25 Jubilee – the most successful Monospar variant

The ST25 'Jubilee' was so named in celebration of the silver jubilee of King George V. The type replaced the ST10 in production and offered accommodation for pilot and four passengers. Power was provided by two Pobjoy Niagara III engines. A total of fifty-nine ST25 were built in two versions – the ST25 and the ST25 Universal of 1936 with a twin-fin empennage. Ambulance and freighter derivatives of the ST25 were available with a large loading hatch (for freight or stretcher) on the starboard side. The Monospar thus became one of the world's first Air Ambulance types, with examples including G-AEYF (with 6ft 6in side door), and G-AEWN, G-AEGX and G-AEVN. Contemporary articles indicate that ambulance versions were used in the United Kingdom, Romania (YR-SAN), France and Spain. Other export customers for the ST25/ST25U included Aden, Australia, Canada, Denmark, Holland, India, New Zealand and Sweden.

General Aircraft Ltd advertised the Monospar as 'not a flying machine, but a luxury automobile of the air'. This slogan was associated with a 1936 sales campaign which, unusually for the time, was specifically aimed at the female pilot or private owner. Another, perhaps more masculine slogan was: 'Bolt into the Blue – fly by Monospar'. A later slogan was: 'Wings are the wheels of tomorrow'.

G-ADIV is a General Aircraft ST25 Monospar with Pobjoy Niagara engines. This was the most successful Monospar variant. (Ken Ellis Collection)

General Aircraft Cygnet G-AGBN is seen here at Biggin Hill in the 1960s. (J.S. Smith)

The Owlet trainer was flown at Hanworth in wartime 1940 as G-AGBK. (Ken Ellis Collection)

The last of this series was the single, Cirrus Minor-powered GAL26, which carried the test marking T6 when first flown. After 1936, General Aircraft used the prefix GAL in its aircraft designations, reflecting the departure of the designer H.L. Steiger from the company.

General Aircraft built a single example of the GAL33 Cagnet. The Cagnet was a two-seat side-by-side trainer with a tricycle undercarriage, a 50hp Aero Engines Pixie engine in a pusher installation, and twin tailbooms with twin fins. The aircraft, which had a span of 33ft and 23ft length, was first flown marked as T46, subsequently becoming W7646.

General Aircraft built the first aircraft in Britain to have a pressurised cabin, the aircraft being based on the ST25 Monospar Universal. This aircraft, the GAL41, carried the test markings T45 (later T-0222) and was flown on 11 May 1939. Cabin pressurisation was provided by a separate Aero Engines (Douglas) Sprite engine. GAL was influential in the development of high-altitude flight in the United Kingdom through its advocacy of the pressure cabin. This work ultimately led to the pressurised Spitfire and Wellington derivatives. A further experimental development was T42/N1531, an ST25 with a tricycle undercarriage, which was later used by the RAF as N1531.

General Aircraft took over **CW Aircraft Ltd** during the Spring of 1938, developing the CW Cygnet prototype G-AEMA into the GAL42 Cygnet, adopting twin fins and a tricycle undercarriage in the process. The stressed skin GAL42 Cygnet was an advanced machine for its day and was put into production; ten were built, three of which did not acquire civil registrations and may not have flown. The closely related GAL45 Owlet tandem-seat open cockpit trainer G-AGBK flew for the first time at Hanworth on 5 September 1940. The Owlet was advertised under the slogan: 'The 3 wheel trainer for 3 wheel bombers'.

In 1936 the company received an order for eighty-nine Hawker Fury II, serial numbers K8218 to K8306, the first of these being completed in July of that year. In 1938 General Aircraft Ltd converted around 125 Hind aircraft to trainer configuration and converted a number of Blackburn Shark aircraft to Shark III configuration. Wartime activity included construction of the Fleet Shadower, Hotspur, Hamilcar, and Fairey Firefly, General Aircraft building 132 Firefly F.1 from an order for 200. The company also manufactured Skua fuselages, Roc rear fuselages, Albemarle noses, Firefly front fuselages, Whitley wings, bomb racks and structural components, wings and tail surfaces for Spitfires from November 1936, and various fittings for other types. The Albemarle production effort was disrupted as a result of enemy bombing on 3 October 1940. General Aircraft also acted as a repair organisation for Spitfires and converted large numbers of Hurricane aircraft to Sea Hurricane configuration.

The Spitfire repair section used a hangar facing The Jolly Sailor pub. Wartime expansion saw GAL take over all of the Whitehead factory buildings and (with the exception of the Field Aircraft Services hangar) most of the other buildings on the site, including those previously used by Rollason, Cierva and Aircraft Exchange & Mart.

The General Aircraft S.23/37 Fleet Shadower P1758 was an extraordinary and grotesque design (almost identical to its Airspeed AS39 competitor) featuring a high-wing layout, four Pobjoy Niagara engines, a fixed tricycle undercarriage, wing folding and a most un-aerodynamic fuselage. The Fleet Shadower prototype first flew on 13 May 1940. Similarly ungainly in appearance was the GAL47 Air Observation Post (T-47/T-0224/G-AGBL). Other oddities included the half-scale Hamilcar, GAL50 T-0227/DP226 and the twin Hotspur GAL48B MP486.

General Aircraft became an important wartime glider manufacturer. Nearly 1,000 GAL48 Hotspur gliders were built, these being mainly used for training. Twenty-two Hotspur were built by GAL, the remainder being 'group-built' under the leadership of Harris Lebus. The larger GAL49 Hamilcar first flew (as DP206) on 27 March 1942 and could carry a seven-ton tank, or sixty troops. More than 400 were built, twenty-two by GAL and some 390 by group firms. Many sub-contract organisations were involved in glider manufacture – notably that managed by Harris Lebus, which included AC Motors, Birmingham Railway Carriage & Wagon Co., and the Co-operative Wholesale Society. Twenty-two Hamilcar were later converted to powered aircraft with two Bristol Mercury engines as the Hamilcar X, the first of these LA704 flying (from Lasham) in February 1945. Two examples of the boxy GAL55 training glider were built against specification TX.3/43.

In 1943, General Aircraft acted in support of Sikorsky to build the R-3 and R-4 helicopters, before Sikorsky's association with Westland. The company also designed a target-towing modification for the Brewster Bermuda, of which only a prototype conversion was completed.

General Aircraft Ltd had two subsidiary companies: Airtraining (Oxford) Ltd and Airtraining (Fairoaks) Ltd. During the Second World War, these companies, which operated pre-war flying schools, were responsible for the overhaul and reconditioning of over 1,200 RAF aircraft and the training of more than 6,000 RAF pilots. The main types handled were the Hurricane, Blenheim, Mustang and Beaufighter. Numerous garages and similar establishments were used to provide dispersed capacity for GAL in both the Hanworth and Fairoaks areas.

Three GAL36 experimental tailless gliders were built. The first, TS507, was flown on 13 November 1944 (reportedly at Farnborough), and tested in 1945 at Dunholm Lodge. A subsequent series of tests were carried out in 1947 and 1948 at GAL's test facility at Lasham, Hampshire.

General Aircraft Ltd carried out target tug conversions of the Mosquito, demonstrating TT39 PF606 at the 1948 SBAC show. Thirty-one conversions were carried out from Mosquito B Mk 16 aircraft, the prototype being PF489. The TT39 featured a remarkable greenhouse-like glazed nose.

Like many other aircraft companies, GAL entered a period of enforced diversification at the end of the Second World War, constructing pre-fabricated housing, prams and Hillman car bodies. The last of the General Aircraft designs was the GAL60 Universal, which ultimately became the Blackburn Beverley. In its civil guise, the Universal was designed (based on advertising material published in 1952) for the carriage of six motor cars, plus five motorcycles and up to forty-two passengers. General Aircraft Ltd was absorbed into Blackburn & General Aircraft Ltd from 1 January 1949. Work already in hand at Feltham was completed after this merger, and activities thereafter, including development of the Universal and Beverley, were then concentrated on Brough, East Yorkshire.

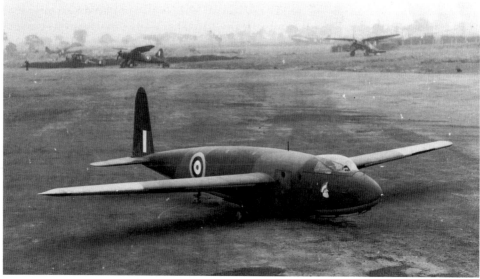

General Aircraft designed both the Hotspur and Hamilcar gliders, which were built in large numbers, mainly 'group built' by dispersed sub-contractors. This Hotspur is seen at Boscombe Down. (Ken Ellis Collection)

The innovative Hafner A.R. III G-ADMV at Hanworth. (Ken Ellis Collection)

The **Hafner** A.R. III G-ADMV was designed by **ARIII Construction (Hafner Gyroplane) Ltd** of 59 High Street, Feltham at Hanworth, built at the Martin-Baker works, Denham, and flown at Heston and Hanworth. The first flight of the Hafner A.R. III G-ADMV is given by both A.J. Jackson (in *British Civil Aircraft Since 1919*) and Bruce Robertson (in *British Military Aircraft Serials 1878-1987*) as 6 February 1937 at Hanworth. This seems to be contradicted by the aircraft being registered in July 1935. In fact, *The Aeroplane* of 18 September 1935 reports the first flight of the type, and includes a photograph of the airborne machine (albeit at low altitude) displaying its registration G-ADMV.

The confusion over dates is explained by remarks made by Hafner in a lecture to the Royal Aeronautical Society in 1937, in which he explained that his:

> *gyroplane [...] was designed in 1934 and made its first flight at Heston in September 1935, piloted by Mr V.H. Baker. Further development work was carried out during the following year and in its final form the machine, to which we give the type number A.R. III, had its first public demonstration when Flying Officer A.E. Clouston, flew it at the Society's garden party on May 9th of this year.*

The type is technically notable for implementing the first use of a full collective and cyclic pitch mechanism on an autogyro. It therefore laid the foundation for successful helicopter rotor-control system applications. The new control system was a great success and contemporary reports all praise the great manoeuvrability of the type.

Pickering Pearson KP2. It is not known if this aircraft, which was built in 1933, actually flew, although it was registered G-ACMR, and was not scrapped until 1935. The most outstanding feature of the KP2 was the complete absence of a tail fin and rudder. Pearson was the designer of the Glenny Henderson Gadfly, and like the Gadfly, the KP2 made use of Pearson rotary ailerons.

The Tipsy B is one of the classic pre-war ultralights, offering two seats, economy and delightful handling on the modest power of a 60hp Walter Mikron II. (Author)

Rollason Aircraft Services Ltd were operating at Hanworth in 1935 and formed, with Taylorcraft at Rearsby, a significant part of the Hurricane Repair Organisation during the Second World War. The Rollason hangars were situated at the entry to the approach road to the hotel that dominated the centre of the airfield.

The **Servotec** Rotorcraft Grasshopper Srs.1, G-ARVN, was built at Feltham Trading Estate and was first flown on 11 March 1962. Development continued under the aegis of **Cierva Rotorcraft Ltd**, who built and flew the Rotorcraft Grasshopper Srs III at Redhill, Surrey.

Tipsy Aircraft Co. Ltd: designed by E.O. Tips of Avions Fairey (the Belgian Division of Fairey Aviation), the Tipsy S2 and Tipsy B were clean, attractive, successful and influential low-powered ultra-light monoplanes. The Tipsy B was produced in the United Kingdom by Tipsy Aircraft Co. Ltd of Slough and Hanworth. The company offices were at 20 Elmwood Avenue, Feltham, with the factory being sited at the junction of Elmwood Avenue and Forest Road. The aircraft was brought up to United Kingdom Airworthiness standards with a number of modifications designed by Fairey Aviation at Hayes, the type being advertised as 'under licence from **Fairey Aviation Co. Ltd**, Hayes'.

The company was registered on 5 June 1937, and announced:

> *Mr Leslie Irvin, Major J.E.D. Shaw, Mr G. Miller, Mr Brian S. Allen and Mr G. Birkett form the board of the new Tipsy Aircraft Co. Ltd which is to build single-seat and two-seat Tipsy designs under licence from Avions Fairey, Belgium. The former premises of the Broughton-Blayney Aircraft Co. at Hanworth have been taken over. Production will start in a few weeks. The intention is to give most attention to the two-seater.*

The initial authorised capital was £20,000. Mr Brian Allen and Mr Birkett were directors of Brian Allen Aviation Ltd of Croydon Airport, this company having been the importers, to the UK, of the Tipsy S single-seater. Nine licence-built Tipsy S aircraft were constructed at Whitchurch by Aero Engines Ltd of Bristol.

The Tipsy B was unusual in offering side-by-side seats in an open cockpit aircraft; the two seats being slightly staggered to provide adequate shoulder clearance in the relatively narrow fuselage. 1939 advertising included the slogan: 'Good looks plus high performance', with an ex-works price of £550.

The first British-built aircraft, G-AFGF, was flying by the spring of 1938. When tested at Martlesham, the aircraft was criticised for lack of rudder authority. The author concurs – I always found the seven-second take-off roll of Tipsy B G-AFSC rather hectic when I owned it, to say nothing of the roll-out in a crosswind. These aircraft were, after all, intended to be operated into wind on a grass airfield. Once in the air, the handling was a sheer delight.

The British-built aircraft differed considerably from their Belgian equivalents, adopting an enlarged, mass-balanced rudder, one-piece elevator, wash-out of the wing tips and, from the sixth aircraft, letterbox slots in the leading edge ahead of the ailerons. The slots were of a most un-aerodynamic design, having a parallel-sided internal geometry and being too far back from the leading edge to be effective in correcting wing drop at the stall, to which the aircraft was prone.

A total of eighteen aircraft were built, three of these (G-AISA, G-AISB, G-AISC) being assembled after the end of the Second World War. Three enclosed Tipsy BC (Belfair) aircraft were also assembled post-war (from Belgian manufactured components) at Sherburn-in-Elmet.

The British-built Tipsy B is widely reported as having been renamed the Tipsy Trainer from the sixth aircraft (with letterbox slots) and, from the ninth aircraft (with an increased all-up weight) the Tipsy Trainer 1. I have not found any contemporary material that makes these distinctions. Most advertising material refers to the British-built aircraft simply as 'the "Tipsy" two seater monoplane'. My own aircraft carried a manufacturer's plate setting out its serial number and flying limitations which was clearly marked Tipsy B M/C No. (machine number) 11. The post-war G-AISA was similarly marked Tipsy B M/C No.17. This strongly suggests that the widespread usage of 'Tipsy Trainer' and 'Tipsy Trainer 1' is at best an informal terminology, probably adopted post-war, to reflect the different build standards which arose during British production of the Tipsy B.

Aircraft constructed by **Whitehead Aircraft Ltd** were test flown at Hanworth Park, which was the private estate and aerodrome of J.A. Whitehead. The Whitehead factory buildings were at the western boundary of the aerodrome. In June 1917, *Flight* published a photograph showing a line of eleven Whitehead-built Sopwith Pup aircraft awaiting delivery at Hanworth. In early 1918, **Whitehead Aircraft (1917) Ltd** was seeking leave to increase its capital. A delay in granting this permission resulted in a question being asked in Parliament on the subject. At this stage the factory extended to 325,000sq.ft. In 1928, the Whitehead factory was used by Union Construction Co. to build trams for London United Transport, and underground trains. After the re-opening of the aerodrome, the Whitehead buildings were used by General Aircraft Ltd and British Aircraft Manufacturing Ltd, with BAC/Kronfeld also occupying part of the site. Additional information can be found under the entry for Richmond.

Harmondsworth (Heathrow)

The Fairey Aviation Co. Ltd. The Great West Aerodrome at Harmondsworth was purchased in 1928 and operated by Fairey Aviation from the summer of 1930 to provide the company with its own flight test facilities, replacing the intermittent use of RAF Northolt. Originally an area of market gardens, the 150-acre Harmondsworth site remained in use by Fairey Aviation until Heathrow was requisitioned in 1944. Initially intended as a base for planned B29 operations, Heathrow was subsequently developed into the new international airport for London, absorbing Fairey's Harmondsworth site in the process.

The Fairey Hendon twin-engine monoplane bomber K1695 was the first design to have its first flight at Fairey's Great West Aerodrome on 25 November 1930. The Hendon was the RAF's first cantilever monoplane bomber. Fourteen production aircraft (Hendon II) were built at Heaton Chapel and served with 38 Squadron for a brief two-year service life. Other types that underwent prototype or production testing at Harmondsworth are listed in the table below:

Fairey-built Swordfishes, including K8872. Of the 2,393 aircraft built, 1,700 were constructed by Blackburn at Sherburn-in-Elmet. (Fairey Aviation Via Ken Ellis)

Type	**Comments**
Fox	J7941 first flown at Hendon on 3 January 1925. Fox IIM J9834, later G-ABFG, first flown Northolt, 25 October 1929. Twenty-eight Fox I/IA were built for the RAF. Twelve Fox IIM were built at Hayes for sale to Belgium, these being tested at Harmondsworth. The type was built in quantity (and in considerable variety) in Belgium. Production quantities are generally somewhat confused. The Putnam *Fairey Aircraft since 1915* indicates Belgian production of up to 189 Fox aircraft, the first Belgian-built example flying on 21 April 1933. The most important version was the Hispano Suiza 12Ydrs-powered Fox VI, of which some eighty-five were built. Fairey Aviation built a demonstration aircraft, known as the Fox III (later Fox Mk IV, G-ABYY), which was flown at Harmondsworth on 22 June 1933.
Firefly	The Firefly biplane was first flown on 9 November 1925. The Firefly II (first flown at Northolt 5 February 1929) was publicised as the fastest interceptor in the world. Eighty-eight Firefly IIM were built for Belgian use, sixty-three of these in Belgium, by the Fairey subsidiary Société Anonyme Belge Avions Fairey, which was registered on 12 September 1931. The first five Belgian aircraft were tested at Harmondsworth during July 1931.
Seal	S1325 first flown as Fairey IIIF Mk VI on 11 September 1930, ninety-one production aircraft were built for the FAA with thirteen aircraft exported to Peru, Argentina, Latvia and Chile.
Gordon	K1697 (Gordon I) first flown at Harmondsworth on 3 March 1931. The Gordon II prototype K3577 was a modification of a Fairey Seal, and was first flown on 23 May 1934. Total Gordon production comprised two prototypes and 186 production aircraft plus seventy-nine aircraft converted from Fairey IIIF. Twenty Gordon were exported to Brazil, and a single example to China.

Type	Comments
Swordfish	TSR II prototype K4190 to S.15/33, first flown on 17 April 1934. There were 2,393 Swordfish built, including the prototype, of which 1,700 were built by Blackburn at Sherburn-in-Elmet. The type served with distinction throughout the Second World War, equipping at its peak some twenty-six squadrons. The famous 'Stringbag' was in continuous production from 1935 until mid-1944.
Fantôme	First flown on 6 June 1935 as P6, later registered G-ADIF. The Fantôme was an extraordinarily beautiful biplane, of which one was built in Britain and three assembled in Belgium from parts manufactured at Hayes.
Battle	P.27/32 monoplane K4303 first flown on 10 March 1936. Production split between Fairey Aviation – at Hayes (the prototype and one production aircraft K7558) and Heaton Chapel – and Austin Motors at Longbridge. See below for production details.
Albacore	L7404 first flown on 12 December 1938, all 800 built at Hayes. The Albacore was an intended replacement for the Swordfish.
Barracuda	Prototype P1767 was first flown on 7 December 1940. The Barracuda torpedo/dive bomber was built by Fairey (1,190, plus two prototypes), Westland (eighteen), Blackburn (700) and Boulton Paul (692). Total production was 2,600 aircraft, plus two prototypes.
Firefly	Naval fighter first flown (Z1826) on 22 December 1941. General Aircraft Ltd built 132 Firefly F.1 at Hanworth. The remaining aircraft were mainly built at Hayes for a grand total of 1,702, plus four prototypes. The Fairey production total is made up of: 740 Mk 1; 591 Mk 4/5/6; fifty-four aircraft for the RNNAS; and 185 Mk 7/8. Later marks were tested at Heston and White Waltham, with the trainer versions built at Heaton Chapel and flown at Ringway. A number of the later aircraft were subsequently converted to pilotless U8 and U9 drones.

The second Fairey Long Range Monoplane K1991, which flew non-stop for 5,309.24 miles between Cranwell and Walvis Bay in February 1933. (Ken Ellis Collection)

The Fairey Long Range Monoplane J9479 carried out its constructor's trials at Harmondsworth and the second machine, K1991, eventually made a non-stop flight from Cranwell to Walvis Bay (5,309.24 miles) lasting fifty-seven hours and twenty-four minutes, starting on 6 February 1933.

Fairey Battle production was made up of the prototype and 2,184 Battle I, 1,029 of which were built by Austin Motors. Included in this total are the 266 aircraft built as Battle Trainers – 200 at Stockport and sixty-six at Longbridge, and the 200 examples built as target tugs by Austin Motors. An additional sixteen aircraft sets of components were built by Fairey at Stockport for assembly in Belgium. Other production figures can also be found.

Fairey was not compensated for the loss of use of Heathrow until 1964 (after the company had been absorbed by Westland).

The **Airspeed** Horsa prototype DG597 made its first flight at Harmondsworth on 12 September 1941, towed behind a Whitley.

Harold Wood

Premier Aircraft Constructions Ltd of Harold Wood was registered on 2 November 1936 and built three Gordon Dove light aircraft, which bore a close resemblance to the Tipsy S.2. The company was placed into receivership at the beginning of September 1939. See also Maylands.

Hayes

The Fairey Aviation Co. Ltd. The Fairey company's initial factory was opened in July 1915, making use of space at the Army Motor Lorries Co., Clayton Road, to the north of the railway line. The company moved to North Hyde Road from 1918, which remained its company headquarters throughout its subsequent existence. The North Hyde Road works were situated alongside the company's original flying field, large new assembly buildings being constructed on this field to expand production facilities in the spring of 1918.

C.R. Fairey was active with the Short brothers during their pioneering days, and set up **The Fairey Aviation Co. Ltd** on 15 July 1915, with authorised capital of £35,000. The first production contract was for twelve Short 827, to be followed by an order for 100 Sopwith 1½ Strutter, built from October 1916, the first aircraft being A954. The first of Fairey's own designs to achieve production success was the Campania seaplane, fifty being built by Fairey and twelve by Barclay, Curle & Co. Fairey also modified the Sopwith Baby, fitting camber changing flaps (a Fairey hallmark) to create the Hamble Baby. The prototype was a modification of Sopwith Baby, serial 8134, and the type was produced by both Fairey (fifty), and by Parnall & Sons (at least 115 aircraft from orders for 130). Two minor activities were the rebuild of Curtiss JN-3 Jenny 3393, and the manufacture of a single AD Tractor No.3374.

The company entered voluntary liquidation in 1921, being restructured as **Fairey Aviation Ltd**, this company being registered on 9 March 1921.

> *Designers and manufacturers of all classes of seaplanes, flying boats, aeroplanes, amphibian aircraft [...] Designers by request of the largest flying boat built for the British Government. Designers and manufacturers of the Fairey Type III. All machines have folding wings and are fitted with Patent variable camber gear giving high performance and lifting power combined with low landing speed.*
> (Tri-lingual advertisement, February 1921. Reproduced on opposite page.)

The large flying boat referred to was the Fairey N.4 (Atalanta and Titania). The N.4 had a wingspan of 139ft and was powered by four 650hp Rolls-Royce Condor engines, mounted

The Fairey Aviation Company,

LIMITED.

CONTRACTORS to BRITISH ADMIRALTY, WAR OFFICE and AIR MINISTRY.

Fournisseurs des Ministères de la Guerre, de la Marine et de l'Air.
Proveedores del Almirantazgo, Departamento de Guerra y Ministerio de Aviación Británicos.

Head Office · · · ·   **HAYES, MIDDLESEX.**
Siège Social—Oficina Principal.

Works · · · ·   **HAYES, MIDDLESEX, and HAMBLE,**
Usines—Talleres.   **near SOUTHAMPTON.**

Sole Patentees of the Fairey Patent Variable Camber Gear for Aeroplanes, Seaplanes and Flying Boats.

Seuls détenteurs du brevet Fairey pour dispositif de cambrure variable pour aéroplanes, hydravions et bateaux volants.
Unicos poseedores de la patente Fairey de dispositivos de combeo variable para aeroplanos, hidroaviones y barcos aéros.

Designers and Manufacturers of all classes of Seaplanes, Flying Boats, Aeroplanes, Amphibian Aircraft, Aircraft specially fitted for Survey and Photographic purposes, Floating Hangars, and complete equipment for same.
Designers by special request of the largest Flying Boat built for the British Government.
Contractors for the laying out and complete equipment of Passenger, Mail and Express Goods Services by Aircraft.
Designers and Manufacturers of the Fairey Type III. Series of Machines as supplied in quantity to the British Government during the War and since its termination. In this series of Machines the Fuselage, Centre Plane, Tail Unit, etc., are standard and are adapted to take different types of wings, chassis and engines of other Machines of the series to suit the particular purpose for which the machine is required. All Machines of this type have folding wings and are fitted with our Patent variable Camber Gear giving high performance and lifting power combined with low landing speed.

Constructeurs de toutes espèces d'hydravions, bateaux volants, aéroplanes, appareils amphibies, avions spécialement-aménagés pour levées topographiques et photographiques, hangars flottants et équipement complet pour ces derniers.
Constructeurs, sur commande spéciale du Gouvernement Britannique, du plus grand bateau volante construit jusqu'à ce jour.
Etude et entreprise de la fourniture du matériel complet pour services de transport aérien rapide de passagers, courrier et marchandises. Constructeurs des Fairey Type III. Série de machines fournies en grandes quantités au Gouvernement Britannique pendant la guerre et depuis la cessation des hostilités. Dans cette série de machines, le fuselage, le plan central et la queue, etc., sont standardisés, et sont construits de manière à pouvoir recevoir des ailes des types différents, ainsi que des châssis et moteurs d'autres machines de la série, de manière à être appropriés à l'usage auquel la machine est destinée dans chaque cas particulier. Toutes les machines de cette série ont des ailes démontables et repliables, et sont munies de notre dispositif breveté de cambrure variable, qui permet les plus grandes performances et qui combine une grande puissance de soulèvement avec une faible vitesse d'atterrissage.

Diseñadores y constructores de hidroaviones, barcos aéreos, aeroplanos, aparatos anfibios, de todas clases, tambien de aparatos especialmente adecuados para el levantamiento de cartas topográficas y fotografias, hangares flotantes y completo equipo para estos mismos.
Diseñadores, á pedido especial del Gobierno Británico del barco aéreo mas grande que se ha construido para este gobierno.
Proveedores de todo lo necesario para servicios de transporte aéreo de pasajeros, correos y mercancías.
Diseñadores y constructores del tipo Fairey III. Serie de aparatos suministrados en cantidad al Gobierno Británico, durante la guerra y después de su terminación. En esta serie de aparatos, el fuselage, el plano central y la unidad de la cola, son standard y fabricados para adaptarse á diferentes tipos de alas, chassis y motores de otros aparatos de series que sean adecuadas para ejecutar los fines particulares para los cuales se requiera el empleo del aparato. Todas las máquinas de este tipo, tienen alas plegadizas y están provistas del dispositivo patentado de combeo variable Fairey que da una alta performance y potencia de ascensión combinada con una velocidad baja de aterrisaje.

in tandem pairs. The superstructure of the N.4 Titania was manufactured at Hayes, being taken to Hamble to be united with its hull, which had been manufactured on the Clyde.

Fairey were sustained through the 1920s by the progressive development of the Fairey III series. The Fairey III family had its origins in the Fairey F.128 seaplane N10 which was first flown (at the Isle of Grain) on 14 September 1917. Modification to the float configuration led to re-designation as the Fairey III and a further change to landplane configuration generated the first production version, the Fairey IIIA.

Fifty Fairey IIIA were built, although a number of these were delivered directly to storage. The landplane Fairey IIIA was followed into production by the seaplane IIIB, which was first flown at Hamble on 8 August 1918. About twenty-eight Fairey IIIB were completed from orders for sixty, some of these emerging as Fairey IIIC with a more powerful Rolls-Royce Eagle replacing the Sunbeam Maori of the earlier aircraft. The IIIC was also first flown at Hamble during July 1918.

The most important and long-serving variants were to be the Fairey IIID and IIIF (which also led to the closely related Gordon and Seal). The IIID three-seat general-purpose landplane/seaplane was powered by either the Rolls-Royce Eagle or the more powerful Napier Lion. The seaplane prototype N9450 was flown at Hamble in August 1920. The Fairey IIID was used for a number of long-distance flights, including Lisbon to Rio de Janeiro in 1922; a flight of 8,568 miles around the coast of Australia by the RAAF; and an RAF flight of 11,000 miles from Cairo to Cape Town and back to the United Kingdom in 1926. Production comprised 207 aircraft for the Fleet Air Arm and a further seventeen for export to Australia and Portugal.

The most numerous version was the IIIF, 622 of which were built, including prototypes and export aircraft; 243 were Fairey IIIF Mk IV (the RAF variant), and the remainder (Mks I-III) being configured as naval aircraft. This places the Fairey IIIF as second only to the Hawker Hart and its derivatives in terms of inter-war production numbers (prior to the expansion years from 1936 onward). The prototype IIIF N198 was flown for the first time at Northolt on 19 March 1926. More than 900 Fairey III aircraft of all variants were built, and the Fairey IIIF was exported to the Irish Army Air Corps, Russia, Argentina, Chile, Greece and New Zealand.

In addition to its service career, the Fairey IIIF was extensively used for engine testing, examples including:

The main entrance building of The Fairey Aviation Co. Ltd still stands imposingly on North Hyde Road in Hayes. (Author)

The Fairey III series (represented here by IIID N9571) was Fairey's most important product during the lean inter-war years. (Ken Ellis Collection)

- Napier Culverin diesel – K1726 tested at Farnborough
- Rolls-Royce Kestrel II – J9173, J9174, N225
- Armstrong Siddeley Jaguar VI – J9154
- Armstrong Siddeley Panther IIA – S1325
- Bristol Jupiter VIII – J9150

The Fairey Gordon and Seal were closely related to the Fairey IIIF. The Gordon was essentially a IIIF, powered by an Armstrong Siddeley Panther IIA. Two hundred and seven Gordon were built, together with more than seventy aircraft converted in service, mainly at Henlow and Aboukir. (As with the Fairey IIIF, other production numbers are also quoted). Ninety-one Seal were delivered to the FAA, with a further thirteen exported – for further details see Harmondsworth.

Intermingled with production of the III series, the Gordon, and the Seal, were the Flycatcher naval fighter and Fawn light day bomber. One hundred and ninety-six Flycatcher were built; the first of four prototypes, N163, being flown on 28 November 1922 at Hamble. The first production example, N9678, was flown on amphibian floats at Northolt on 19 February 1924. The sole Flycatcher II N216 was flown on 4 October 1926 and competed against specification N.21/26.

Seventy-three Fawn were built (plus five aircraft completed as spares), the prototype J6907 being flown for the first time at Northolt on 8 March 1923. The first production Fawn J7182 was also flown at Northolt on 29 January 1924. The Fawn was a landplane derivative of the Fairey Pintail seaplane, of which six were built, three of these being exported to Japan.

A notable development was the Fairey Fox day bomber (first flown unregistered at Hendon on 3 January 1925, later J9515), which combined a streamlined fuselage with imported American technology in the form of the Curtiss-Reed metal propeller, and the Curtiss D12 Felix liquid-cooled engine. At 50mph faster than the fighters of the day, the Fox caused deep embarrassment to the RAF establishment. Only twenty-eight Fox were purchased, but the design effectively forced the modernisation of Air Ministry thinking and indirectly led to both the Rolls-Royce Kestrel engine, and the Hawker Hart family of aircraft. The poor response to the Fox in Britain was not matched by Belgium, who purchased the aircraft in quantity, many being built by Avions Fairey at Gosselies. This collaboration was later to give rise to the beautiful Firefly and Fantôme biplanes.

In May 1925, the firm was re-registered as **The Fairey Aviation Co. Ltd**, becoming a public company under this name on 5 March 1929. In May 1930 the company was advertising with the simple slogan, 'High Performance Service Aircraft'.

The RAF version of the Fairey III was designated the IIIF Mk IV. This is a Mk IVM, the 'M' indicating all metal construction. (Via Author)

The Firefly biplane (see also Harmondsworth and Northolt) was built at Hayes prior to the setting up of the Avions Fairey production line at Gosselies, twenty-five machines being built here. The Firefly was an elegant design, almost matching the Hawker Fury in appearance, with its sleek cowling, under fuselage radiator and rounded wing tips and tail surfaces.

Second World War manufacture included the Swordfish (2,393 in total, with 1,700 by Blackburn at Sherburn-in-Elmet); Battle (for production details, see Harmondsworth); Albacore (800, all built at Hayes); Fulmar (two prototypes and 600 aircraft); Barracuda (two prototypes); and Firefly (see below), with sub-contract production of other types including the Halifax and Beaufighter.

The Battle, in addition to its primary service role was much used as an engine test bed, examples including:

- Exe – K9222
- Dagger VIII – K9240
- Merlin X – K9257, Merlin XII – N2234
- Taurus II – K9331
- P24 Prince – K9370, first flown on 30 June 1939
- Peregrine – K9477
- Hercules II – N2042, Hercules XI – N2184
- Sabre – K9278 (first flown Luton 31 May 1939), L5286

The Fulmar was developed from the P.4/34, the second prototype K7555 being modified in 1938 to become the prototype Fulmar. This aircraft originally flew (as P.4/34) on 19 April 1937, flying as the Fulmar in March 1938. The first true Fulmar prototype (N1854, later G-AIBE) flew at Ringway on 4 January 1940.

The prototype Barracuda dive bomber and torpedo bomber was constructed at Hayes and first flew on 7 December 1940. Two thousand, six hundred Barracuda (in addition to the two prototypes) were built, production being contracted to Blackburn, Boulton Paul and Westland. Fairey built 1,190 of the 2,600 production aircraft; all the Fairey-built aircraft were built at Heaton Chapel with final assembly and flight test at Ringway.

Fairey Aviation built the Firefly fighter in all marks at Hayes. 1,702 Firefly were built, including, in addition to the Hayes production, 132 Firefly F.I by General Aircraft Ltd at Hanworth, and production at Heaton Chapel of some AS.7 (forty-one from the production total of 151 aircraft), together with T.1, T.2, T.3, U.8 and U.9 conversions.

RA356, the first prototype of the unsuccessful Spearfish, was also built at Hayes and first flown on 5 July 1945. Spearfish flight-testing was conducted at Heston. Six prototypes were built, three at Hayes and three at Stockport, although only one of the Stockport-built aircraft (RN241) was flown.

As will be seen from the above, Fairey became something of a specialist manufacturer of naval aeroplanes. This was reflected in the company's own advertising in 1946, thus: '8 out of 9 British Naval Aircraft were Fairey Types.' It has, however, to be said that the highly dispersed nature of Fairey's production operations during the Second World War caused significant production difficulties.

Post-war production at Hayes was concentrated on the Gannet, alongside the development of the unsuccessful but very advanced Rotodyne. The Gannet, with its unusual Double Mamba powerplant, was the first turboprop aircraft to land on an aircraft carrier (HMS *Illustrious*) in June 1950. Each of the Mamba engines drove one of the two contra-rotating propellers, this arrangement allowing one engine to be shut down, and its associated propeller feathered, to reduce fuel consumption and increase endurance during extended patrol missions.

Fairey highlighted these features in their advertising: 'The Fairey 17 Anti-Submarine Aircraft. The first aircraft to fly powered by twin turbines with co-axial propellers (19 September 1949). The first propeller-turbine aircraft to land on the deck of an aircraft carrier (19 June 1950)'. Three prototypes and 349 production Gannet aircraft were built with production split between Hayes and Stockport (where eighty-eight were built – sixty-four AS Mk 1, twenty-four AS Mk 4). Like the Avro Shackleton, the Gannet had a longer than expected service life as a result of its ability to provide a long endurance platform in the airborne early warning role.

One important experimental design was the Fairey Delta 2, the first jet aircraft to fly faster than 1,000mph. Although not itself developed into a production type, it was an important contributor to the knowledge base that maintained Britain's high-speed flight capability. The speed record set by FD2 WG774 on 10 March 1956 of 1,131.76mph exceeded the previous record (held by the F-100 Super Sabre) by more than 30%. Two FD2 were built, WG774 and WG777, the former being subsequently converted to become the BAC221 and used in support of the Concorde programme.

On 31 March 1959 the company was re-styled **Fairey Aviation Ltd**, a subsidiary of **The Fairey Co. Ltd**, shortly before its merger with Westland on 2 May 1960.

Fairey started its helicopter activity in 1945, this work being headed by Dr J.A.J. Bennett, previously of The Cierva Autogiro Co. Ltd. Helicopter flight testing was carried out at White Waltham, which – after a relatively short period of Fairey flight testing at Heston – replaced Fairey's Great West Aerodrome at Harmondsworth, use of which had been lost as a result of the development of Heathrow.

The aviation interests of Fairey Aviation were taken over by **Westland Aircraft Ltd** on 8 February 1960, and Scout and Wasp helicopter production transferred to Hayes from **Saunders-Roe Ltd**, which had already been absorbed into the Westland Group.

The Royal Navy Historic Flight Firefly looks immaculate at the PFA Rally at Cranfield. (Author)

The Gannet was the last Fairey design to enter production for the Royal Navy, providing valuable carrier-borne service in a number of roles. (Author)

The Westland Scout was developed from the Saunders-Roe P531 and manufactured at Hayes after the merger of the helicopter industry. This photograph shows the Hayes production line in full swing. (Westland)

The Westland Scout. (Author)

Seventeen Westland Wasp were exported to South Africa; this example is preserved at the SAAF Museum. (Author)

The third production Puma is seen here at Hayes. Forty-eight were built for the RAF. (Westland)

The Scout prototypes were the two P.531-2 aircraft G-APVL and G-APVM. The Westland-built, Nimbus-powered G-APVL (later XP166) was flown on 9 August 1959, followed by Gnome-powered G-APVM (later XR493) on 3 May 1960. The first pre-production Westland Scout AH.1 XP165 was flown at White Waltham on 4 August 1960. Eight development aircraft (one being the ex-G-APVL) and 141 production machines were built at Hayes for UK service, with limited additional aircraft exported. The first production aircraft, XP846, was flown in 1961.

The first Westland Wasp HAS.1 XS463 was flown at White Waltham on 28 October 1962. Two pre-production aircraft (XS463 and XS476) were followed by ninety-eight production machines built for the Royal Navy at Hayes, with aircraft exported to Brazil (three), The Netherlands (twelve), New Zealand (three), South Africa (seventeen) and Indonesia.

The forty-eight Puma helicopters built for the RAF under the Anglo-French helicopter agreement were also constructed at Hayes. The North Hyde Road site has been redeveloped under the name Westland Development, and is used as a storage facility by two major supermarkets.

Kennedy Aeroplanes Ltd. The Kennedy Giant, RFC serial 2337, was built by Fairey Aviation and The Gramophone Co. Ltd, both of Clayton Road, Hayes. See Northolt for further details.

Hendon

Hendon Aerodrome was established by Claude Grahame-White at Colindale where Mr E.J. Everett had tested his **Everett-Edgcumbe** monoplane. In February 1910 Mr Grahame-White took an option to purchase the land that was to become Hendon Aerodrome, and eight hangars were constructed in ten days to form 'the London Aerodrome'. Three of the eight were leased to the Aeronautical Syndicate Ltd. The official opening took place on 1 October 1910. In mid-1911, the airfield was being advertised as having 'a good rolling surface over the whole area of 250 acres, circuit 2½ miles, easy access from London by train, tube and tram. Only 6 miles from Marble Arch, restaurant on Ground, good sanitary arrangements'. Hendon quickly became a focus for sporting, flying and flight training, Grahame-White doing much to popularise the new sport by organising regular weekly flying meetings at Hendon.

Although control of the aerodrome passed to the RNAS at the outbreak of the First World War, civil flying training continued at Hendon, with a number of schools in operation.

VALKYRIE
MONOPLANES.

THREE TYPES.   40—80 MILES AN HOUR.   FROM £280,

ALL BRANCHES OF AERONAUTICAL ENGINEERING.
DESIGNING AND CONSTRUCTION.

ALL STANDARD TYPES OF AEROPLANES.   · PROPELLERS A SPECIALITY.

TUITION FREE TO PURCHASERS.   *PARTICULARS ON REQUEST.*

THE AERONAUTICAL SYNDICATE, LTD.,
ESTABLISHED MARCH, 1909,

COLLINDALE AVENUE :: WEST HENDON, LONDON, N.W.

Telegrams—"AEROVALKY, LONDON."   Telephone—KINGSBURY 24.

Aircraft manufactured locally were flight tested at Hendon, and a number of other aircraft were brought here for testing. These included the **Perry-Beadle** biplane and the **Pemberton-Billing** '7 day bus', both of which were here in January 1915. Later, the **Mann & Grimmer** biplane was erected and tested here. The RNAS also operated an aircraft acceptance and test activity at Hendon.

The civilian training schools were not taken into official control until August 1916, when they became the RFC Civilian School of Instruction, at which point all private tuition ceased. In February 1917 *Flight* reported that full control of Hendon airfield had been taken over by the Government under the Defence of the Realm Act. In mid-1917, the No.2 Aircraft Acceptance Park was established, taking over the activities of the earlier RNAS acceptance centre. By spring 1918, the Acceptance Park extended to some forty acres of the site.

The No.2 Aircraft Acceptance Park was re-designated as the No.1 Aircraft Salvage Depot in mid-1919, prior to the sale of all government surplus aircraft and engines to **The Aircraft Disposal Co. Ltd** (see Croydon/Waddon).

Famous throughout the 1920s and 1930s for the annual RAF Aerial Pageants, Hendon was used for communications operations during the Second World War. The aerodrome was officially closed to flying on 2 November 1957, although some gliding activity continued until 31 March 1968. Hendon is now the site of the RAF Museum, which was opened by the Queen on 15 November 1974. The RAF Station at Hendon finally closed on 1 April 1987. The last fixed-wing aircraft to land at Hendon was Blackburn Beverley XH124 on 19 June 1968, remaining outside the RAF Museum until it was scrapped in January 1990 under somewhat controversial circumstances.

Aeronautical Syndicate Ltd. Horatio Barber's Aeronautical Syndicate Ltd (ASL) moved to Hendon from Salisbury Plain in September 1910. ASL built three variants of the Valkyrie – the types A, B, and C. The types B and C were three-seaters, and these were used successfully at Hendon for training, although Dallas Brett comments that 'the Valkyrie, a strange pusher monoplane, flew with some success, albeit dangerously'. After the Valkyrie, came the Viking 1. This had a nose-mounted engine providing drive to two laterally disposed tractor propellers and was said to have flown very successfully; its first flight being made on 18 January 1912.

The entire stock of the Aeronautical Syndicate was put up for sale by auction on 24 April 1912. This consisted, among other items, of one practically new Viking, and three Valkyrie (one each of single-seat, two-seat and three-seat configuration). In the event, the company and entire stock was purchased by Handley Page, and subsequently sold to Grahame-White. The reason for the sale was simply that Mr Horatio Barber decided, on cost grounds, to give up his interests in aviation.

The number of aircraft built by ASL is subject to some debate. Whereas a figure of twenty-nine aircraft is sometimes quoted, Peter Lewis in *British Aircraft 1809-1914* merely states that 'several examples of the Type B were built'. Certainly, photographs exist of one example marked Valkyrie Type B No.5. The evidence provided by the sale of assets suggests that a relatively low figure for the total production by ASL may be justified.

The Aircraft Company, **AIRCO**, and **The Aircraft Manufacturing Co. Ltd**, The Hyde, Hendon, NW9. The Aircraft Company was formed by George Holt Thomas in 1911. After initial use of a skating rink at Merton, the company occupied a disused bus/tram depot (previously used by the Metropolitan Electric Tramway & Omnibus Co.) at The Hyde, Hendon, half a mile south of Hendon.

The Aircraft Company held the sole rights in the United Kingdom for the building of Henri & Maurice Farman aeroplanes, which were obtained by Mr Holt Thomas in early 1912. (The Farman Brothers works were at 167 Rue de Silly, Billancourt, France.)

In April 1912, the first advertisement for The Aircraft Company appeared announcing that it held 'Sole rights to Henri & Maurice Farman designs, and Gnome Motors. Will shortly be constructed in England. Flying ground Hendon, and St Stephen's House, Westminster'. In May 1912, the company name was changed to The Aircraft Manufacturing Co. Ltd (often known as AIRCO, this style being subsequently adopted by the company itself). AIRCO made use of a number of factories on either side of the Edgware Road, including a large factory which was subsequently taken over by Henlys. Some aircraft were flown from fields alongside the factory for the short flight to the nearby Hendon Aircraft Acceptance Park. The AIRCO name remained visible for many years on the side of the factory next to Edgware Road.

Geoffrey de Havilland was recruited from the Royal Aircraft Factory as Chief Designer from 2 June 1914 (an agreement engaging him as a designer and pilot of aeroplanes being signed on 23 May). Farman Longhorn aircraft were manufactured by AIRCO in England up to the start of the First World War; thereafter, they were produced by a number of contractors to drawings supplied by AIRCO Contractors involved in Longhorn production included Brush Electrical Co. Ltd (at Loughborough), Phoenix Dynamo Manufacturing Co. Ltd (Bradford), and Robey & Co. Ltd (Lincoln). A survey of RFC and RNAS serial allocations shows that AIRCO constructed at least 825 aircraft of Farman design, the most important types being the Maurice Farman S.7 Longhorn (more than 120), and the S.11 Shorthorn (about 650).

By mid-1915, the DH1 and DH2 were flying actively at Hendon, the DH1 having first flown in January 1915, and the DH2 in July 1915. AIRCO constructed some seventy-three DH1/1A, and 250 DH2. A typical advertising slogan from the First World War read: 'The Largest Aircraft Enterprise in the World'.

The DH4 (No 3696) first flew at Hendon in August 1916. 1,449 DH4 were built in the UK, some 915 by AIRCO, with a further 4,846 in the USA by Dayton-Wright, Fisher Body and Standard. The type was subject to one of the largest single orders of the First World War, this being for 690 aircraft in a block from A7401. Sub-contract orders were placed with F.W. Berwick & Co. Ltd; Glendower Aircraft Co. Ltd; Palladium Autocars Ltd; Vulcan Motor & Engineering Co. (1906) Ltd; and Westland Aircraft Works (Branch of Petters Ltd).

The DH5 fighter, which was first flown in November 1916, was powered by a 110hp Le Rhone rotary and was distinguished by its reverse-wing stagger; about 550 were built, construction being split between AIRCO (who built 200, prototype A5172); Darracq Motor Engineering Co. Ltd; March, Jones & Cribb (at least thirty-eight from an order for 100); and British Caudron Co. Ltd.

The DH6 was described as follows in the 1919 edition of *Jane's All the World's Aircraft*: 'it has rather the appearance of having been built by the mile and cut off to order'. Over 2,250 DH6 were ordered, including those sub-contracted to the following companies: The Gloucestershire Aircraft Co. Ltd; The Grahame-White Aviation Co. Ltd; Harland & Wolff; Kingsbury Aviation Co. Ltd; Morgan & Co. Ltd; Ransomes, Sims & Jeffries Ltd; and Savages Ltd. The DH6 was

More than five hundred AIRCO DH4 were built by sub-contractors; this example was built by the Westland Aircraft Works of Petters Ltd at Yeovil. (Westland)

first flown in late 1916 and a substantial proportion of the total built were produced at Hendon by AIRCO and The Grahame-White Aviation Co. Ltd.

The DH9 A7559 (a modified DH4) first flew in June 1917 and the type was also very extensively sub-contracted. More than 1,300 were ordered from AIRCO, with additional orders placed with Alliance Aeroplane Co. Ltd; F.W. Berwick & Co. Ltd; Cubitt Ltd; Mann, Egerton & Co. Ltd; National Aircraft Factory No.1; National Aircraft Factory No.2; Short Brothers; Waring & Gillow Ltd; G. & J. Weir Ltd; Westland Aircraft Works; and Whitehead Aircraft Co. Ltd. A production total of 3,204 has been quoted.

The twin-engine DH10 C8658 flew on 4 March 1918, and was also the subject of large sub-contract orders. The companies involved included the Alliance Aeroplane Co. Ltd; Birmingham & Midland Carriage Co.; The Daimler Co. Ltd; The Siddeley-Deasy Motor Car Co. Ltd; Mann, Egerton & Co. Ltd; and National Aircraft Factory No.2. A total of nearly 1,300 aircraft were ordered, although it is believed that significantly less than 300 were actually built.

The Eagle-powered DH9A C6350 flew at Hendon in mid-February 1918. The American-designed Liberty engine was selected for production aircraft, the main production line being set up at Westland Aircraft Works, Yeovil. AIRCO themselves received contracts for 600 DH9A. Other companies in receipt of DH9A orders, or involved in their refurbishment included F.W. Berwick & Co. Ltd; George Parnall & Co. Ltd; The Gloucestershire Aircraft Co. Ltd; Handley Page Ltd; H.G. Hawker Engineering Co. Ltd; Mann, Egerton & Co. Ltd; Saunders-Roe Ltd; Vulcan Motor & Engineering Co. (1906) Ltd; and Whitehead Aircraft Co. Ltd.

In 1918, no less than 3,877 de Havilland-designed machines were taken on charge of the RAF when it was formed, the majority being DH9/9A, DH6 and DH4. Some 5,500 aircraft were built by AIRCO during the First World War, this representing 10% of all British production. By January 1919, the company was generally styling itself AIRCO.

The AIRCO Group included **May, Harden & May**, and **Wycombe Aircraft Constructors** and was expanded by the acquisition of the English business of Vanden Plas coachbuilders to provide additional production capacity. AIRCO also bought **Camden Engineering Co.** to make fittings, and **Peter Hooker Ltd** to produce the Gnome

This dramatic heap of AIRCO DH6 aircraft is presumably being scrapped at the end of the First World War. The aircraft at the top of the pile, B2744, was constructed by The Aircraft Manufacturing Co. Ltd, many others being sub-contracted. (Via J.S. Smith)

The main production contractor for the DH9A was the Westland Aircraft Works, whose assembly line is seen here. (Westland)

monosoupape engine. The connection between AIRCO and May, Harden & May is reflected in the production of a batch of eighty Felixstowe F.2A/F.5 flying boats in a batch running from N4480. The hulls of these aircraft were built by May, Harden & May, with the aircraft being assembled by The Aircraft Manufacturing Co. (AIRCO).

Further Holt Thomas companies included the propeller manufacturer **The Integral Propeller Co. Ltd**, which held production rights to the Chauviere propeller, and shared the same business address as AIRCO, and **Airships Ltd** of Merton, Clapham and Wandsworth. Example advertising included the following from November 1917: 'Chauviere's Integral Propellers are used more extensively than any other Propeller in the World. Hold all records and are indisputably the best. Maximum Efficiency. Best Workmanship. The Integral Propeller Co. Ltd, The Hyde, Hendon, NW9.' **Airships Ltd** manufactured balloon fabric for anti-submarine airships, and were one of the founding members of the SBAC.

In 1920 AIRCO formed an alliance with BSA. The complete amalgamation of The Aircraft Manufacturing Co. Ltd with BSA Co. Ltd was announced in March 1920, the identity of AIRCO being 'wholly maintained'. At the end of March, Mr Holt Thomas resigned from the Chairmanship of The Aircraft Manufacturing Co. Ltd. His statement indicated:

> *BSA have obtained control of the AIRCO companies. Their interest lies in the large factories which can be adapted for motor body and other work. They wish to foster this and cut down on production and expense. I could not advise my co-directors to maintain an expensive technical department devoted to the design of aircraft in the light of the present apathetic attitude of the Government. I could also not regard the disintegration of a staff which has proved itself second to none in the world without misgivings. I have therefore decided to resign, leaving this decision to the co-directors without any views expressed for or against. Fundamentally, the utter failure of the authorities to view in the proper proportion the importance of the air [...] is at the root of the matter.*

"A BEATTY BANKER"

The BEATTY School of Flying Ltd

"Beatty" Pupils are dependable.

◻ ◻ ◻

¶. They are trained by pilots with years of experience.
¶. Our aim is to make them a credit to us, and our success in this is shown by the number of "Beatty" Pupils now in both services who are making good.

FOR FULL PARTICULARS
APPLY TO THE SECRETARY.

THE
Beatty School of Flying,
LTD.,
LONDON AERODROME, HENDON, N.W.

- ERNEST B H LANDER 1915 -

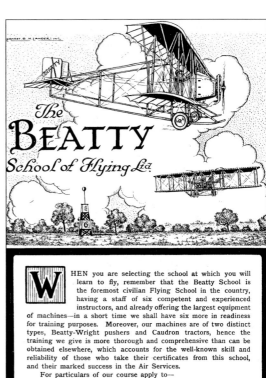

The BEATTY School of Flying Ltd

WHEN you are selecting the school at which you will learn to fly, remember that the Beatty School is the foremost civilian Flying School in the country, having a staff of six competent and experienced instructors, and already offering the largest equipment of machines—in a short time we shall have six more in readiness for training purposes. Moreover, our machines are of two distinct types, Beatty-Wright pushers and Caudron tractors, hence the training we give is more thorough and comprehensive than can be obtained elsewhere, which accounts for the well-known skill and reliability of those who take their certificates from this school, and their marked success in the Air Services.

For particulars of our course apply to—

THE SECRETARY,
THE BEATTY SCHOOL OF FLYING, LTD.,
LONDON AERODROME, HENDON, N.W.
Telephone: Kingsbury 138.

A selection of advertisements for the Beatty School of Flying Ltd.

The BEATTY School of Flying Ltd.

We are the only school at Hendon giving instruction on both pusher and tractor biplanes; you should consider this point when making up your mind as to which school to join.

If you wish to become a really practical pilot, one able to handle successfully any type of machine in use, join up with us at once.

If you wish to enter the R.N.A.S. or R.F.C., a course of tuition at our school is an almost certain means of entry.

Most of our pupils, in fact nearly all, are taken over by either the one or the other of the flying services. The reasons for this are not far to seek: our special means of tuition, fine range of school machines, etc., are the means to the end.

Tuition on Caudron Tractor Biplanes and Beatty-Wright Pusher Biplanes.

Fuller particulars to be had from

THE SECRETARY,
THE BEATTY SCHOOL OF FLYING, LTD.,
LONDON AERODROME, HENDON, N.W.

Telephone : KINGSBURY 138.

ERNEST · B·H·LANDER .

"Just-Off"

The BEATTY School of Flying Ltd.

JUST off on a trial lesson, affording to doubting Thomases, free of any charge, a chance to prove all that we say about our School in our advertisement.

¶ Remember that a school may be loudly advertised and boomed and yet be a bad one for the pupil who wants to get on.

¶ Remember that we are the only School of Flying having sufficient courage and faith in the methods of instruction employed to offer to prospective pupils, before signing on, the chance, quite free of any charge to them, to come and prove by a trial lesson that all that we claim in our advertisements we can prove in facts and actions.

For fuller particulars apply to the Secretary,

THE BEATTY SCHOOL OF FLYING, LTD.,
LONDON AERODROME, HENDON, N.W.

The Beatty School at Hendon used a number of Wright Baby machines for training. By 1916 a mix of Wright and Caudron machines were in use. (Handley Page Association)

AIRCO/BSA subsequently decided to discontinue aircraft production, following which, Geoffrey de Havilland, Charles Walker and Holt Thomas succeeded in obtaining the relevant AIRCO assets and financial backing to create **The de Havilland Aircraft Co. Ltd** on 25 September 1920, with authorised share capital of £50,000, moving almost immediately to Stag Lane. The AIRCO shareholders agreed to the voluntary winding up of the company in December 1920. (The name **AIRCO** was briefly revived as a group of de Havilland, Fairey and Hunting intended to act as a consortium to produce the Trident.)

G.W. Beatty. The Beatty School was formed in February 1914 with Wright and Handley Page machines, taking over the Handley Page School and its pupils at the same time. In April 1915 it was reported that there was a new Beatty machine flying at Hendon. By January 1916, the fleet consisted of four Wright and six Caudron machines. The Wright Baby aircraft favoured by the Beatty School were obsolescent by 1916. When one was modified in April 1916 to have a central nacelle to protect the occupants, *Flight* rudely commented that 'her appearance is a never failing source of merriment'. The company also built a number of engines of their own design.

The Beatty School passed to military control in 1916, and in 1917 the school was forced to move from Hendon, continuing its business at nearby Cricklewood. Mr Beatty is reported to have invented the idea of using a piece of string tied within the pilot's view to indicate sideslip.

Blackburn Flying School. Robert Blackburn ran a flying school at Hendon for about eighteen months in 1912-1913.

The **Blériot School of Flying** was one of the earliest tenants of Hendon (from late 1910), and trained a number of well-known pilots.

The **British Aerial Transport Co. (BAT)** was formed in June 1917 by Sir Samuel (later Lord) Waring. The company is best known for its Bantam, a single-engine single-seat fighter/sporting aircraft designed by Frederick Koolhoven and built in a number of variants (the FK22, FK23 and FK27). A feature of the type was its plywood monocoque fuselage.

It was fast and manoeuvrable, but is reputed to have had 'disastrous' spinning characteristics. The American pilot, Clifford Prodger, flew the Bantam (K-123) in a number of races at Hendon during 1919. At least three FK22, nine FK23 and a single FK27 (K-143/G-EAFA) were built.

The BAT FK24 Baboon was a two-seat training aircraft, which featured the use of many interchangeable parts, including all control surfaces – a concept later to be adoted by the Simmonds Spartan. The Baboon was a small two-bay biplane, with a noticeably broad under-carriage track. The sole FK24 to be built, D9731, later became K-124/G-EACO. The BAT FK26 first flew at Hendon in April 1919, and resembled a large Fox Moth with an enclosed four-seat cabin behind the enormous Rolls-Royce Eagle engine. The pilot was sat well to the rear in an open cockpit, from which a minimal forward view must have been available. The company's advertising ran: 'BAT: We are the first people out with a purely commercial model (not a modified war type), the BAT FK26.' Four FK26 were built, and its influence can (arguably) be seen in the DH18 of 1920, and the 1927 DH50 Giant Moth, which featured a very similar layout.

The FK28 Crow of 1919 could have been a prototype for the modern Whittaker MW6 microlight, were it not for its use of twin tail booms, and a span of only 15ft. Although it was severely underpowered, the Crow is nevertheless reported to have handled well.

BAT was wound up after a BAT Bantam accident in March 1920, the remaining assets being sold in 1921 to Ogilvie & Partners of Willesden.

The British Caudron Co. Ltd – see W.H. Ewen Aviation Co. Ltd.

British Deperdussin Co. Ltd. This company went into liquidation on 23 August 1913, this event being possibly related to M. Deperdussin's arrest for embezzlement, together with failure of the British Deperdussin Seagull design. M. Deperdussin was subsequently convicted of fraud associated with diverting money from other business interests to support both him and his aircraft business, receiving a five-year suspended sentence. In addition to aircraft design and manufacture, the company operated a school of flying.

The Managing Director was Lt J.C. Porte, who later was so instrumental in the development of the flying boat for anti-submarine operations. The designer F. Koolhoven also worked

The BAT FK23 Bantam K-123 was used by Clifford Prodger for air racing at Hendon in 1919. (Military Aircraft Photographs)

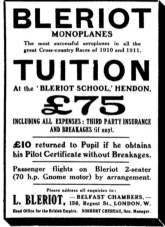

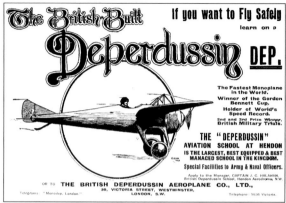

for British Deperdussin, moving on in June 1913 to Sir W.G. Armstrong, Whitworth, and, in 1917, to British Aerial Transport Co. at Willesden.

In May 1916, a photograph was published of a **'Burgess'** machine flying at Hendon. Of generally 'Gunbus' configuration, this was a product of the American company of that name. In fact, twenty-five such aircraft (with serial numbers running from 3657) were erected at Hendon for testing, but subsequently delivered to store. A number of other American-built aircraft, including the Curtiss R-2 (several aircraft including serial 3448) and the Sloane-Day H1 biplane (serial 3701) were erected and tested at Hendon.

The **Chanter** 1911 Monoplane, was a successful, single-seat, Nieuport-inspired machine, which was used at Hendon and subsequently at Shoreham when the Chanter Flying School moved there. This machine was reported as nearing completion at Hendon in October 1911 although, with the move to Shoreham imminent, it was expected to fly first there. In mid-1911 the Chanter school also had a Blériot XI monoplane.

The de Havilland Aircraft Co. Ltd – see The Aircraft Manufacturing Co. Ltd above, together with Stag Lane. The company's other main operating sites include Chester, Christchurch, Hatfield, Hurn Leavesden and Witney.

J.W. Dunne: One example of the Dunne D10 was constructed at Hendon in 1913.

The elegant and efficient **Dyott** monoplane was flying here in October 1913. George M. Dyott learned to fly at the Blériot School, Hendon, and then owned a Deperdussin with which he toured extensively in the USA and Mexico, following which, he also toured extensively with this monoplane of his own design. The aircraft was built by Hewlett & Blondeau at Clapham, and embodied many original features, including provision for the easy replacement of many components. The Dyott monoplane was advertised for sale in December 1913.

The large Dyott Bomber (serial 3687) underwent trials at Hendon from August 1916. The Bomber was a multiple-bay biplane powered by two 120hp Beardmore engines (later replaced by 230hp BHP engines). The armament was intended to be a Vickers two-pounder gun and the type also featured a tricycle undercarriage. Two examples were built, these being constructed, like the 1913 Dyott monoplane, by Hewlett & Blondeau.

The **Everett-Edgcumbe** monoplane was designed by E.J. Everett and was built by Everett-Edgcumbe & Co. Ltd at their Colindale Works, Colindeep Lane. Testing was carried out in a field that later became part of the Hendon aerodrome; evidently the trials were not very successful as witnessed by the type's nickname 'The Grasshopper'. The aircraft had the general appearance of a Blériot or a Deperdussin, but with marked dihedral, squared-off wing tips, a covered fuselage and a triangular fin.

Mr C.R. Fairey assisted in the construction of the aircraft, which was built behind the Messrs. Everett, Edgcumbe & Co. instrument factory. The Everett-Edgcumbe shed was used by Grahame-White to house his Blériot monoplane in January 1910. The same shed was used in April 1910 for the erection of Louis Paulhan's Farman machine, which Paulhan used successfully in his London to Manchester race with Claude Grahame-White.

The **W.H. Ewen Aviation Co. Ltd** was a supplier of 'British Built Caudron Aeroplanes'. W.H. Ewen learned to fly with the Blériot School at Hendon and established a flying school at Lanark, which moved to Hendon in December 1911, obtaining the English agency for Caudron in April 1912. In May 1913, the Hewlett & Blondeau factory built a Caudron for W.H. Ewen under War Office contract, this being delivered with service serial 51.

W.H. Ewen Aviation Co. Ltd was renamed **The British Caudron Co. Ltd** in April 1914 and was soon building aircraft for both the RFC and the RNAS. The company subsequently set up a Scottish factory at Alloa. The precise split in production between the British Caudron factories is not clear. Production included:

- One Caudron G.2.
- Sixty-one Caudron G.3.
- At least four of twelve Caudron G.4 ordered.
- Fifty AIRCO DH5 (believed to have been at Cricklewood).
- Fifty BE2c/e (believed to have been at Alloa).
- 100 Camel from orders for 350 aircraft.
- Fifty Handley Page O/400 (shared with Harris Lebus).
- Twenty Avro 504B (shared with The Regent Carriage Co., who built sixteen of the total).

Of these, the fifty BE2c/e and 100 Camel were built at Alloa, and the shared O/400 and Avro 504B orders are most likely to have been built at Cricklewood, the collaborating companies being London firms.

The company's November 1917 advertising copy ran thus: 'Contractors to HM Admiralty, War Office, and Foreign Governments. The British Caudron Co. Ltd. Sole building and selling rights for Caudron Aeroplanes and Hydro-Aeroplanes for The British Empire and Dependencies. Head Office and Works – Broadway, Cricklewood, NW2. Scottish factory and aerodrome – Alloa.'

Above: *D8350 was built by British Caudron in conjunction with Harris Lebus and was converted by Handley Page for civil use, later becoming G-EAAE.* (Handley Page Association)

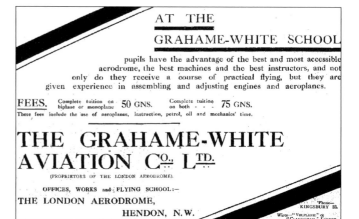

The Fairey Aviation Co. Ltd – the influential Fairey Fox with its Curtiss engine and Reed propeller first flew here unregistered on 3 January 1925, Northolt being too waterlogged at the time.

The Grahame-White Aviation Co. Ltd was formed in August 1911 to take over the London Aerodrome, Hendon and Grahame-White's other aviation interests. The advertising slogans used by the company included 'Hendon, Britain's greatest flying centre', 'Speed with Safety', and (from 1919) 'Manufacturers and designers of all types of pleasure aircraft'. The company's telegraphic address was: 'Volplane', Hyde, London.

Claude Grahame-White was one of Britain's earliest pilots, making his first flight at Issy-les-Moulineaux on 6 November 1909 in a Blériot. Grahame-White flew both Blériot and Farman types in many flying meetings and pageants and set up a British Flying School at Pau in France. Grahame-White's early activities did much to publicise aviation, and were also highly successful financially. In the Boston meeting of 1910, he earned no less than £6,420. His total prize money for the year was £10,280, a considerable fortune that assisted in the financing of The Grahame-White Aviation Co. Ltd.

Grahame-White purchased the assets of the Aeronautical Syndicate from Handley Page in 1912, J.D. North of the Aeroplane Syndicate becoming the Chief Designer for Grahame-White at the age of only twenty years. Training was carried out by The Grahame-White School of Flying, which trained seventy-one pilots in the years prior to the outbreak of the First World War.

The Hendon meetings of 1912-1914, which did so much to popularise aviation, were inseparably associated with Grahame-White. The company designed and produced a number of notable early machines for pleasure and school flying, promotional and exhibition work. Perhaps the most famous of these was the large Type 10 *Charabanc*, designed by J.D. North. This machine was basically of Farman configuration, with a 120hp Austro-Daimler engine, and was used for passenger joy flights carrying up to seven passengers. On 2 October 1913, no less than nine passengers, weighing a total of 1,371.5lb, were carried for nearly twenty minutes! The *Charabanc*, which had a wing span of 62ft 6in and weighed 3,100lb, was also used to make the first parachute descent in Great Britain from an aeroplane.

Another successful type at the opposite end of the size and weight scale was the *Lizzie* of November 1913. This was a diminutive sesquiplane with a (top) wing span of 28ft 6in, and a lower wing span of 14ft. Used extensively for aerobatic display and exhibition flying, it was said to fly well despite its rather startling appearance. Power was provided by a 50hp Gnome rotary. The machine's odd appearance was partly due to the very large gap (more than 6ft) between the wings. Later, the lower wings were extended to produce a more or less conventional two-bay configuration.

The Lizzie, with its sesquiplane configuration was reminiscent of an earlier J.D. North design for Grahame-White, the Type 7 *Popular* of January 1913. The *Popular* was a pusher biplane (resembling a slightly crude Farman Shorthorn), also with a 28ft span upper wing and 14ft lower wing span. The prototype was underpowered with a 35hp Anzani, and production aircraft were to be fitted with the 50hp Gnome.

Other Grahame-White designs built before the First World War included the *Baby* and *New Baby* school biplanes (of Boxkite configuration), the Type 8 seaplane, the Type 9 monoplane, the Grahame-White *Boxkite* of 1912 (distinguished by its twin rudders), and the Type 11 *Warplane* of 1914. The *Warplane* was of 'Gunbus' configuration, the gunner being in the front seat of the nacelle of a pusher biplane.

In May 1913 Grahame-White obtained the agency for manufacture of Morane Saulnier monoplanes and began building the Morane Saulnier G and H monoplanes under contract. Service deliveries included twelve built for the Army (serial numbers 587-598), three Morane H (623, 627, 629), a Morane Saulnier G for the Navy (serial 1242), and a further batch of twenty-four Morane H monoplanes built in 1915.

Above: *Grahame-White modified four Blackburn Kangaroo aircraft for joy-riding purposes after the First World War. This example was later registered as G-EADG.* (Miltary Aircraft Photographs)

Left: *The historic Grahame-White factory and hangar at Hendon are not looking at their best in this 1994 photograph.* (Author)

The Type 13 two-seat scout was one of a number of experimental Grahame-White types that did not enter production. (Miltary Aircraft Photographs)

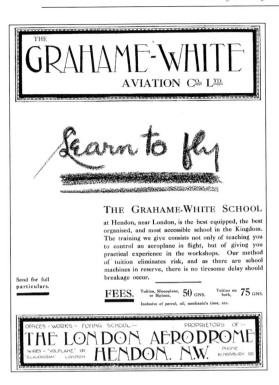

A number of Grahame-White pre-war machines were taken into service with the Army and Navy. Of Grahame-White's own designs, the most significant was to prove to be the Type 15 (or Admiralty Type 1600), which was a training machine developed from the Grahame-White *Boxkite*. Some 136 Type 15 were built for Service use.

Further wartime production included the Royal Aircraft Factory BE2, the first order for which was placed with the company on 29 September 1914, twenty-four being built. The company became an important producer, particularly of the AIRCO DH6 and the Avro 504, employing a workforce of nearly 3,000. Production included:

- Ten Grahame-White Type 19, a British built version of the Breguet BM5 *Concours*, twenty further aircraft were cancelled.
- 100 Henry Farman F.20 under sub-contract from AIRCO.
- 700 DH6 (ordered on 13 January 1917) – see further comments below.
- Some 900 Avro 504K.

Further orders for forty Handley Page V/1500 bombers, and for 500 Sopwith Snipe were cancelled. During the First World War, the Grahame-White School trained 560 pupils without a single fatality. J.D. North left Grahame-White in mid-1915, moving to Austin Motors, and later became the Chief Designer of Boulton Paul.

The DH6 caused significant financial difficulty to Grahame-White. Due to a shortage of suitable timber, the company was instructed to manufacture a large number of these machines using 'swamp cypress'. The timber shortage was caused by the fact that, once the USA entered the war, their production of aircraft-quality timber was diverted to supply their own production needs. A number of DH6 machines were built using this unsatisfactory timber. These aircraft were promptly declared unfit for use, leaving Grahame-White with great difficulty in obtaining payment for the work completed, whilst still having to meet his wage bill.

In February 1917, the War Office took over full control of the aerodrome, including a number of The Grahame-White Aviation Co. Ltd buildings. Toward the end of the First

World War, the contracting situation became chaotic and Grahame-White ended in bitter dispute with the Government over contractual issues, Excess Profit Duty, and compensation for the loss of commercial use of Hendon Aerodrome. These matters were not finally resolved until ownership of the aerodrome passed to the Air Council in 1926. Grahame-White did not receive his final compensation payment until August 1929.

In 1918 Grahame-White held 500 acres of property and fifty acres of buildings. An attempt was made to re-enter aircraft production with the Grahame-White *Bantam* (a sporting biplane rather like a Sopwith Pup which appeared at Hendon at Easter 1919 registered K-150), and the Grahame-White E7 *Aero Limousine*, a twin-engine, five-passenger biplane flown in August 1919. By January 1919, Grahame-White was manufacturing cars, producing a two-seater called the Duckboard, reconditioning war surplus vehicles and making furniture. Unfortunately, the enterprise proved unsustainable and the Grahame-White factory was later occupied by **Angus Sanderson (1921) Ltd**.

The Grahame-White factory and hangar still stand close to the site of the RAF Museum at Hendon. By the mid-1990s, the buildings were looking very forlorn. In 1997 it was announced that the RAF Museum planned to incorporate the factory into its display. National Lottery funding will be used to assist this project which includes moving the factory building and a bay of the 1910 Grahame-White hangar onto the Museum site, allowing development to take place on the actual factory site.

The **Hall Aviation Co.** produced the Hall Aviation school biplane, and a number of other machines for use by the Hall School of Flying. The School of Flying was active at Hendon from late 1913 with Blériot, Avro and Caudron machines. The founder of these concerns was J. Lawrence Hall, himself a keen sporting pilot. By August 1914, the fleet also included the Deperdussin monoplane, and the company was advertising its capability for 'Aeroplane Constructions'. By January 1915, the company had their new school biplane – a Caudron-like machine powered by a 45hp Anzani – flying at Hendon. Several Hall tractor biplanes were also in use.

In June 1915, a new design, the Hall No.6 tractor biplane, was produced by fitting a new conventional fuselage to a set of Caudron wings. The resultant tractor biplane, powered by a 50hp Gnome, proved to be very successful. The James Brothers moved from Ruffy-Baumann to Hall Aviation Co. at the same time. In April 1916 the company was advertising: 'Hall Tractor biplanes. These machines are fitted throughout with standard controls, are safe, speedy and well maintained.' There is little doubt that this text was intended to 'knock' the old-fashioned Beatty Wright machines with which Hall was competing for business at Hendon.

Handley Page Ltd. Monoplanes built by Handley Page Ltd were flying from Hendon by October 1912, following the move of the parent company to Cricklewood. Twenty-eight passengers were thus flown in the Handley Page monoplane during the first two weekends of October 1912. Their flying characteristics were highly praised by Wilfred Parke in comments (*Aviaticanda*) published after his death. Of the 50hp Handley Page monoplane, he said, 'for pure pleasure of flying it is miles ahead of anything else I have ever been in as pilot or passenger. She is an extremely safe and excellent machine.' He also praised its light rudder control and draught-free seating.

The prototype Handley Page O/100 bomber (RNAS serial 1455) first flew at Hendon on 17 December 1915, having been moved by road to Hendon by night on 9 December. This move provided yet another saga of telephone wires, trees and lamp posts being moved and replaced, it taking five hours to complete the 1½ mile journey. Handley Page subsequently created his own airfield alongside his Cricklewood Works allowing him to avoid such inconveniences.

The **Handley Page Flying School** operated as an adjunct to the manufacturing operation until it was taken over by the G.W. Beatty school in February 1914.

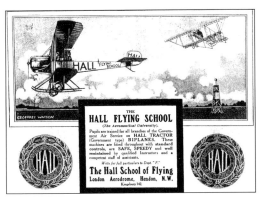

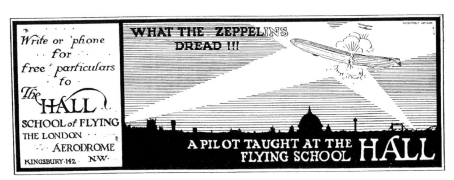

The Handley Page Flying School

From Monday, Feb. 16, the Handley Page Flying School will be under the control of Mr. G. W. Beatty.

Pupils of the School will be trained on the Handley Page Monoplanes with which the School is equipped.

Lt Parke with the 80hp Handley Page Type F Military Trials monoplane at Hendon. (Handley Page

Hart Aeroplanes & Waterplanes Ltd – Howard Wright was a director of this company which built a set of wings of novel design. These were fitted to a Blériot and successfully flown at Hendon in autumn 1912. Howard Wright then moved on to J. Samuel White & Co. at Cowes.

Hewlett & Blondeau Ltd. After Hewlett & Blondeau moved to Leagrave near Luton, their aircraft were sometimes test flown at Hendon. Thus in April 1916, Sydney Pickles was carrying out production testing at Hendon of 100hp BE2c aircraft constructed by Hewlett & Blondeau.

The **London & Provincial Aviation Co.** of Edgware is mainly associated with Stag Lane rather than Hendon. However, in 1915, the company was advertising as follows: 'London & Provincial Aviation Co., School of Flying, The Aerodrome, Hendon. Be prepared to serve your country by learning to fly. Pupils trained quickly and thoroughly for Naval and Military Services by experienced instructors. TRACTOR MACHINES in sole use.'

The London & Provincial School of Flying was formed at Hendon in October 1913. By November 1914, the company had their own school biplane flying at Hendon. In January 1915, they were reported to have a new Anzani-powered biplane at Hendon. In the *Flight* edition of 7 May 1915, the 45hp London & Provincial biplane was described as flying exceptionally well and was a 'splendid climber'. London and Provincial machines powered by 50hp Gnome, and 60hp Anzani engines are pictured in *Jane's All the World's Aircraft* of 1919.

One 100hp Anzani-powered aircraft (later registered G-EAQW) was used during the First World War for parachute experiments. This machine was built in 1916 and set a series of looping records at Hendon at that time. This machine was designed by Mr A.A. Fletcher (Tony Fletcher), who joined London & Provincial in 1916. Mr Fletcher was later chief designer of **Central Aircraft**, and had previously been designer at Martinsyde, where he was responsible for the Martinsyde G100.

After the move from Barking to Cricklewood, Handley Page aircraft were flown from Hendon. Here Rowland Ding is at the controls of the Type G biplane. Handley Page opened their own airfield at Cricklewood in 1918. (Handley Page Association)

Handley Page Ltd used Hendon as its airfield from 1912 until the creation of its own airfield at Cricklewood. The O/100 was first flown at Hendon, this being the fourth prototype. (Handley Page Association)

Five London & Provincial tractor biplanes were later used at Stag Lane, which was owned by the London & Provincial Aviation Co.; a hangar was erected there in January 1916. London & Provincial also manufactured the Caudron GIII and in December 1915, two Caudron machines were under construction for the Bournemouth Aviation Co.

Mann & Grimmer. (See also Surbiton.) Test-flying of the Mann & Grimmer M1 was carried out at Hendon from 19 February 1915, the first pilot being Mr Rowland Ding (who was also associated with the Lakes Flying School of Windermere). The aircraft was a two-bay biplane with a 100hp nose-mounted Anzani engine driving twin, chain-driven, pusher propellers behind the wings. The gunner was located in the extreme nose for maximum field of fire. By August 1915, a change of engine had increased power to 125hp.

In November 1915, as the aircraft was showing promise, Mann & Grimmer advertised the design rights, with the machine and works also for sale. With an unfortunate sense of timing, the machine crashed in the same month (on 16 November) due to gearbox failure, causing breakage of the propeller drive chains at the end of a long climb to more than 8,000ft. Subsequently, a question was raised in Parliament as to whether extra time would be allowed to repair the machine and conduct War Office tests. A typically political reply was given – 'the matter is under consideration.'

Martin & Handasyde carried out initial (unsuccessful) experiments with a monoplane that was built in 1908 at the Old Welsh Harp public house at Hendon.

The **McCardle & Drexel** School was an early tenant of Hendon before moving to Bournemouth.

F.C. Nestler Ltd, was registered in August 1913 at 49 Bond Street, London, with offices and works at 9 Greycoat Street, Westminster. This company built the Nestler Scout, the new Nestler machine being reportedly under test at Hendon, flown by Mr J.B. Fitzsimons, in March 1917. The aircraft bore a passing resemblance to the Bristol Scout and was powered by a 100hp Gnome. Unfortunately it was destroyed in an accident on 26 March 1917. The company's advertising ran: 'Contractors to HM Admiralty and War Office, Aeroplane Manufacturers'; 'Aeronautical Engineers and constructors'; 'Makers and patentees of Howard-Nestler collapsible Hangars' (this latter from November 1916).

Nieuport (and related companies). In January 1913, **Nieuport (England) Ltd** was advertising 'Flying grounds at Hendon and Southampton [waterplanes]'.

Aircraft constructed by **Nieuport & General Aircraft Co. Ltd** (also known as British Nieuport – a style they adopted in their advertising) were assembled and test flown at Hendon. An example of this is found in the case of the Nieuport Goshawk G-EASK, in which Harry Hawker was tragically killed on 12 July 1921. The official accident report states that the aeroplane was built at the Nieuport Works, Hendon, and first flown on 17 June 1920. (See also Cricklewood.)

In October 1911, the **Compton Paterson** biplane was tested 'in a field near the Welsh Harp', where it took off in a twenty-yard run. This machine, unlike Mr Paterson's Liverpool-based designs (flown at Freshfield), was constructed by Messrs Lawton Motor Body Works at Cricklewood.

The **Ruffy School of Flying**, Hendon, was advertising in November 1914, and was 'previously the Prosser school'. This company became the **Ruffy-Baumann School of Flying** in February 1915. The Welsh James Brothers (who had previously flown at Narbeth) were associated with the school from December 1914, before moving on in June 1915 to the Hall

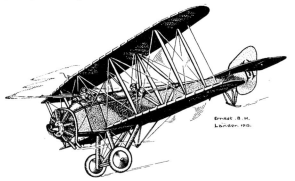

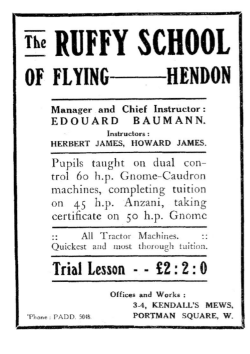

Aviation Co. In 1915, the company built their first aircraft, a small single-seat biplane powered by a radial engine, and designed by C.M. Poulsen of *Flight* magazine. In October 1915, Ruffy-Baumann was flying a tractor biplane which, like the Hall School Biplane, was Caudron-derived. The company was again reformed into the **Ruffy, Arnall & Baumann Aviation Co. Ltd**, which was registered in January 1917. This company built the RAB 15, this type being taken over by the **Alliance Aeroplane Co. Ltd** as the Alliance P1 when Alliance took over Ruffy, Arnall & Baumann in 1918 (see also Acton). Ruffy-Baumann had offices and works at Portman Square. In April 1916, auxiliary works were in use at 'The Burroughs, Hendon'.

Savage Skywriting Co. Ltd. Major J.C. Savage converted no less than twenty-nine SE5As for sky-writing; many of these were sold abroad, notably to the USA and Germany. The company operated at Hendon from 1921 until 1935.

In January 1912 a **Sommer** biplane was being tested at Hendon that had been constructed by Hyermann & Warren. The all-steel biplane was of generally Boxkite configuration, but with unequal span wings. The overhung upper outer wing panels were used differentially for lateral control. The designer, Roger Sommer, was originally a felt manufacturer.

The American-designed **Thomas** T2 Scout was tested at Hendon, see also Bickley.

Heston

Heston Airport was a centre for 'Society' aviation in the 1930s, with such august occupants as the Household Brigade Flying Club. Airwork Ltd was formed in 1928 to establish Heston as a centre of sporting and social flying. Airwork Ltd and Heston Air Park were both founded by Alan Muntz and Sir Nigel Norman. The airfield was constructed during 1928 and officially opened in July 1929, on the occasion of the 1929 King's Cup Air Race. Heston was the first British airfield to have a concrete apron and an all-concrete hangar (which was used by Airwork Ltd and is still standing today).

The large central hangar had an arched roof of 100ft span and 19ft-high doors. A further hangar was constructed within which twenty lock-up 'garages' were provided for private-owners' machines. Three showrooms were provided for aircraft sales, these being initially occupied by A.V. Roe & Co. Ltd, Malcolm Campbell Ltd, and The Blackburn Aeroplane Co. Ltd for sales, respectively, of the Avian, Moth and Bluebird.

The airfield was closed at the end of 1947; the control tower and most other buildings were demolished at the end of 1978.

Airwork Ltd built the prototype Cierva C.30 fuselage, and constructed a single C.30P, G-ACKA, which was flown in April 1933. This was effectively the pre-production version of the C.30A, which was then produced in large numbers by A.V. Roe & Co. Ltd in Manchester. After the Second World War, Airwork Ltd reconditioned a number of Mosquito aircraft at Heston prior to their export to Turkey.

Auto Auctions Ltd. This company was clearly a dealer rather than manufacturer. It was, however, reported to be 'World distributors of the Blackburn Bluebird IV', and had offices at Heston and Burlington Gardens, Old Bond St.

Carden-Baynes Aircraft Ltd was formed at Heston on 3 April 1936. This company produced the sole Carden-Baynes Bee – G-AEWC. The Bee was a two-seat, side-by-side, twin-engine pusher monoplane with Carden Ford engines; it flew on 3 April 1937. Its most striking feature was that its wing could be swivelled through ninety degrees around a vertical axis to reduce the aircraft's width for hangarage. Its single test flight revealed inadequate engine cooling. The project was abandoned and Carden-Baynes Aircraft Ltd went into receivership at the end of June 1937. The Bee was scrapped in 1939, L.E. Baynes becoming the Chief Designer of Alan Muntz & Co. Ltd.

Chrislea Aircraft Co. Ltd was registered at Crescent Works, Mornington Terrace, London NW1 on 2 October 1936 by R.C. Christophorides and R.V. Leak, the first syllables of their surnames being used to form the company name. The first Chrislea product was the LC1 Airguard G-AFIN, which was built at Heston. The Airguard was a Mikron-powered low-wing two-seat cabin monoplane, which flew in the late summer of 1938. The Airguard somewhat resembled the Tipsy Belfair, although lacking the latter's elliptical wing planform. In 1939, the sale price quoted for the Airguard was £350.

The post-war Chrislea CH3 Ace (prototype G-AHLG) first flew at Heston in early September 1946. Initial advertising in 1946 emphasised affordability: 'The Chrislea "Ace" – It's the UNIVERSAL Plane. The lowest priced four seater aircraft in the world.' This four-seat high-wing monoplane was characterised by its tricycle undercarriage and (after initial flying with a single fin) twin fins. Most notably, the Ace also featured a novel control system in which there was no rudder bar, all controls being provided by a steering wheel control mounted from the dashboard. A universal joint at the base of the 'steering column' allowed control inputs to be provided in all axes. Pitch control required vertical translation of the wheel, side-to-side motion-controlled yaw and steering wheel-like rotation generated roll. A floor-mounted foot throttle was provided as well as a normal hand throttle. Perhaps not surprisingly, there was muted enthusiasm for this degree of novelty and production aircraft were fitted with a conventional rudder bar.

In April 1947, Chrislea moved to Exeter, this move being enforced by the closure of Heston Airport. Development of the Chrislea Ace, Super Ace and Skyjeep was continued at Exeter, where the company built a total of thirty-two aircraft.

The **Comper Aircraft Ltd** factory moved to Heston from Hooton Park in March 1933. The Heston factory produced the Mouse, Streak and Kite: low-wing monoplanes, which shared

SE5A F904 was built by Wolseley Motors and was subsequently part of the Hendon-based Savage Skywriting fleet. (Author)

This attractive sign demonstrates that Hounslow Council is keen to recognise the aviation heritage represented by the Heston Airport site. (Author)

The uniquely configured Bee suffered from inadequate engine cooling. (Ken Ellis Collection)

The Comper Mouse G-ACIX. After the successful Swift, and the move of Comper Aircraft Ltd to Heston, Comper struggled to find a successful product. (Military Aircraft Photographs)

The Super Ace was the final production form of the Chrislea Ace, which was first flown at Heston in September 1946. The Super Ace was developed and built at Exeter. (Author)

The attractive Comper Streak resembled a low-wing Comper Swift with a retractable undercarriage. Although showing great promise, only a single example was built. (Military Aircraft Photographs)

the elegance of design of the lovely Swift. Comper also took out a Cierva license and built an experimental single-seat autogiro, the C.25, based on a Swift fuselage.

The Mouse G-ACIX was a three-seat low-wing aircraft, a concept that was later to be adopted by the similar BA Eagle. The Mouse was first flown on 10 September 1933. The Streak G-ACNC was a single-seat Gipsy Major-powered racing aircraft which was first flown at Heston on 12 April 1934. The Streak was entered for the prestigious Coupe Deutsch de la Meurth. Although capable of speeds over 170mph, the Streak's racing performance was ruined by a retractable undercarriage that refused to stay retracted! The two-seat Kite (G-ACME) first flew in May 1934, and was essentially a two-seat Pobjoy-powered Streak.

Comper Aircraft Ltd became **Heston Aircraft Co. Ltd** (see below) on 10 August 1934. After the formation of Heston Aircraft, Nick Comper and F.R. Walker formed a new company, **Comper Aeroplanes Ltd** (address: 2 The Ridgeway, Walton on Thames) which designed and began construction (at Brooklands) of a twin-boom high-wing pusher single-seat design known as the Comper Fly. The Fly was intended to prove the concept of the Comper Scamp, a two-seat version of the design, intended to be Mikron II-powered. The Fly had not yet been completed when Comper met a most regrettable and tragic death in Hythe on 17 June 1939. The Fly failed to live up to its name when tested in 1940 by Heston Aircraft, and the prototype was taken over by Gerard Fane, see below.

The Fairey Aviation Co. Ltd operated a flight test organisation at Heston from January 1945 whilst Heathrow Airport was being developed. Aircraft tested here included the Spearfish and Firefly. The first Spearfish RA356, designed to Specification O.5/43, was flown on 5 July 1945, to be followed by RA360 (11 April 1947) and RA363 (23 September 1947). The main Firefly marks which were flown at Heston were the Mk 4, Mk 5 (352 built) and Mk 6 (133 built).

In a convoluted process, components for these aircraft were manufactured at Hayes; the aircraft were then assembled at White Waltham; flown to Heston for paint and equipment fit-out; and finally flown back to White Waltham for continued flight-testing. Heston ultimately proved unsuitable for air traffic reasons and the Fairey Aviation flight test activity was moved to White Waltham. The Fairey Gyrodyne G-AIKF was first flown at Heston on 7 December 1947, shortly before Fairey moved to White Waltham. The Fairey Aviation Research and Armament Division (later renamed the Weapon Division) was based here to carry out missile research, this eventually leading to the Fireflash air-to-air missile.

Capt. Gerard Fane was a collaborator of Nicholas Comper, and set up **Comper Fane Aircraft Ltd** (also known as C.F. Aircraft Ltd) on 9 August 1939, the company subsequently trading as **Fane Aircraft Ltd**. This company took over the unsuccessful Comper Fly and subsequently developed the Fane F.1/40 Flying Observation Post G-AGDJ/T-1788. This was a competitor to the General Aircraft GA47 (G-AGBL/T-47/T-0224), and had a configuration (other than the side-by-side seating), similar to the modern Quad-City Challenger ultralight.

The requirement for these two designs was to operate from small fields and roads, have a steep climb angle, be easy to fly, carry two occupants plus a radio, provide an excellent view (it was essential that the configuration be a pusher), and be easy to maintain. A tricycle undercarriage was seen as an advantage. Many elements of this specification would appeal to the present-day pilot looking for a practical aeroplane to base on a farm strip. The Fane F1/40 was built at Norbury and flown at Heston in March 1941.

The **Hafner** R2 was tested at Heston in 1932. The successful ARIII Gyroplane G-ADMV was first flown at Heston in September 1935. Raoul Hafner was also active at Hanworth; Denham, Bucks; and at Filton/Weston-super-Mare with the Helicopter Division of The Bristol Aeroplane Co. Ltd.

The **Helmy** Aerogypt was built at Heston by an Egyptian national, S. Helmy, in 1938 and flown in February 1939. The type was a small low-wing cabin monoplane powered initially by three 22hp Douglas Sprite engines. The Aerogypt featured a patented high-lift surface mounted above the cabin roof, which was intended to be raised in flight to provide additional lift and reduce approach and landing speeds. This feature was unsuccessful, and was later removed.

The single aircraft built, G-AFFG, was subject to progressive development to eventually become the Aerogypt IV, which was test flown from White Waltham.

Heston Aircraft Co. Ltd took over the assets of Comper Aircraft Ltd on 10 August 1934, changing its title to **The Heston Aircraft Co. Ltd** on 8 November 1935. The company's first product was the Heston Phoenix, a Gipsy Six-powered five-seat high-wing aircraft with a retractable undercarriage. The Phoenix was first flown on 18 August 1935 (G-ADAD). Heston Aircraft advertised the type with the slogan: 'Britain's most silent aeroplane'. The price quoted in *Flight* for a Phoenix was a very up-market £2,050 and a total of only six Phoenix were built. The first production aircraft VH-AJM was sold to C.J. Melrose. After only three hours' test flying, Melrose set off from Lympne to Adelaide on 9 April 1936, arriving successfully on 25 April.

Other work undertaken by Heston Aircraft included the pre-war construction of Wellesley II bomb containers and SARO London floats. The company designed and built the unsuccessful T.1/37 trainer prototype L7706, which flew in late 1938 but exhibited poor handling. During the Second World War, Heston Aircraft designed the naval modifications for the Sea Hornet. The prototype Sea Hornet was PX212, and the modifications required included new undercarriage legs, folding wings, arrester hook, '3 point accelerator fittings for assisted take-off', plus specific naval role equipment. The changes resulted in weight growth of 550lb, 280lb of which was contributed by the wing fold. PX212 was first flown on 19 April 1945, and was followed by two further Heston-built development aircraft. The first deck landing of a Sea Hornet was carried out on *HMS Ocean* on 10 August 1945.

Other products and development activities at Heston Aircraft included:

The Aerogypt is seen here in its initial form, powered by three Douglas Sprite engines. The aircraft was subject to further development at White Waltham. (Ken Ellis Collection)

- Heston Type 5 Racer G-AFOK (see below).
- P.92/2 V3142, a half-scale Boulton Paul F.11/37. The P.92/2 was built by Heston Aircraft under the designation Heston JA8 and flew for the first time in Spring 1941. The aircraft was a twin-engine monoplane with a mock-up of a large diameter faired cannon turret mounted over the centre fuselage.
- Conversion of Seafire IIC to Merlin 32 power.
- Installation of dive brakes on Spitfire BR372.
- Production of camera installation sets for the Seafire PR/FR variants.
- Rocket-assisted take-off trials of Spitfire, Swordfish, Seafire (144 Spitfire IIB RATOG kits), Barracuda and Chesapeake.
- Modification of a wide range of US aircraft for British use.
- Extensive component manufacture (Walrus floats, Spitfire wings, Wellington leading edges and engine nacelles, parts for Warwick, Sea Otter, Lerwick, Mosquito and Hornet).
- Six hundred and fifty repaired Spitfires.
- One hundred twelve-gun noses for Douglas Havoc aircraft (modification designed by Martin-Baker).
- Experimental radar and searchlight installations on the Douglas Boston.
- Fifty Mosquito aircraft modified in twenty days in early 1944 with nitrous oxide injection systems to boost performance.
- Secret modifications to allow a Mosquito to drop Barnes Wallis' 'Highball', rotating bouncing bomb.
- Heston JC6 AOP: VL529 and VL530 to Specification A.2/45, competing with the Auster Type N and the Scottish Aviation Prestwick Pioneer.

To support this diverse range of activity, additional factory capacity was opened at Slough, and the Penguin Book works on Bath Road were also used.

The Napier-powered Heston Type 5 Racer G-AFOK crashed on its first flight on 12 June 1940. Its pilot, G.L.G. Richmond wrote (in *The Aeroplane Spotter*) in 1943 describing that flight as follows:

Adaptation of the Hornet for naval use was the responsibility of Heston Aircraft Ltd. (BAE SYSTEMS)

The Heston JC6 AOP aircraft was an unsuccessful competitor to the Prestwick Pioneer. (BAE SYSTEMS)

Elevator control was effective up to the point of take off, but was then insufficient to cope with trim changes due to change in power. Reductions in rpm caused the nose to fall, and vice versa. Within 30 seconds of take-off the engine coolant reached its maximum temperature and was still rising. With considerable effort, the aircraft was positioned for a landing that was made harder by the control difficulties, resulting in a heavy landing which led to the aircraft breaking its back.

An important wartime activity at Heston was the development of photographic reconnaissance versions of the Spitfire, many of the required modifications being implemented by Heston Aircraft Ltd. This arose as an extension of F.S. Cotton's clandestine pre-war activities in which he used a company known as The Aeronautical Research & Sales Corporation as cover for illegal SIS controlled photographic sorties over pre-war Germany. These civilian missions continued into wartime, and culminated in F.S. Cotton being asked to set up a RAF specialised photographic unit at Heston. The 'Heston Flight' as it was initially known, became the No.2 Camouflage Unit in November 1939, the RAF Photographic Development Unit in January 1940, and was eventually regularised in July 1940 as the PRU – Photographic Reconnaissance Unit. This unit in its various guises used Hudson and Blenheim aircraft, and was directly responsible for the development of the Spitfire PR1A, 1B, 1C, 1D, 1F and 1G.

Hordern-Richmond Autoplane: this was a three-seat, twin-engine low-wing design which was built by The Heston Aircraft Co. Ltd. E.G. Hordern was a test pilot for British Aircraft Manufacturing Ltd, and subsequently for Heston Aircraft Ltd. The Richmond portion of the name refers to the Duke of Richmond and Gordon who collaborated in the design.

The prototype G-AEOG was first flown on 28 October 1936, but is described (by Harald Penrose) as being so heavy (and underpowered with its two Continental A40 engines) that it could do little more than glide if one engine stopped. The name Autoplane referred to the unusual control arrangements: A central joystick was provided which branched, the top of each stem being equipped with a wheel that was turned to control the rudder. The usual movements of the control column displaced the elevators and ailerons.

Hordern-Richmond Aircraft Ltd was set up at Denham in April 1937 to manufacture the type. No production took place, and the company turned to the production of laminated compressed wood products and, particularly, propellers. Hordern-Richmond subsequently moved to Haddenham (near Thame) and was taken over by Rotol in 1945.

The **Luton** LA3 Minor prototype, G–AEPD, made its first flight here on 3 March 1937. The LA3 was the forerunner of the highly successful LA4, which was developed at Gerrards Cross, near Denham.

Martin–Baker Aircraft Co. Ltd. The Martin–Baker MB2 P9594 was operated at Heston, where Capt. Baker was Chief Flying Instructor, and was publicly demonstrated here on 26 May 1939. The aircraft first flew at Harwell on 3 August 1938.

Mignet *Pou de Ciel*. Heston has an association with the *Pou de Ciel* as the location where the first British 'Flying Flea' G–ADMH was built and flown. Heston therefore is a convenient point at which to summarise this popular, but ultimately unsuccessful flying movement.

The Flea craze was created following the publication of the first English translation of *The Flying Flea* by Henri Mignet, the first edition of 6,000 copies selling out within a month in 1935. By April 1936, eighty-one Fleas had been registered; by the time the type was banned this number had risen to 121. Some estimates suggest that construction of as many as 1,000 Fleas may have been started in the United Kingdom, although Ord-Hume gives a probably more realistic figure of about 350, in addition to the 121 that were allocated a registration.

It is tragic that due to its unforeseen design flaw, the Flea proved unsafe and, instead of ushering in an age of relatively unrestricted popular aviation, proved to be the catalyst for today's restricted and regulated skies. The first British Flea was built by S.V. Appleby who later built others under the name, **Puttnam Aircraft Co.** This aircraft, G–ADMH, first flew on 14 July 1935, albeit with a flying life of only two weeks. A number of **E.D. Abbott**-built Fleas were also flown at Heston. A.E. Clouston tells in his autobiography *The Dangerous Skies* of flight testing three Fleas at Heston, and two more at Gravesend.

Navarro Safety Aircraft Ltd (also The Aircraft Construction Co. of Feltham). Mr Joseph Navarro designed and built the three-engine, three-seat Navarro Chief, which was reported to be nearing completion at Heston during 1930. ABC Scorpion engines were used, and the general configuration resembled that of a small Westland Wessex or Ford Tri-motor. The safety features referred to in the company name consisted of an extraordinary empennage,

Heston has an association with the Flying Flea. G-ADMH, the first example to fly in the UK, was built by S.V. Appleby and flown at Heston in July 1935. (Flying Flea Archive)

The Youngman Baynes research aircraft displays the centre portion of its high lift flap system. (Ken Ellis Collection)

which incorporated a rudder that could be split as an air-brake, and differentially moving elevators, linked to the ailerons. The aircraft was not registered, and is generally thought to have remained unflown. Ord-Hume suggests that it is possible that a single flight test was accomplished before the aircraft was abandoned. The Navarro Chief and other assets of the company were sold at auction at Heston in May 1932. The company had offices at Finsbury House, Blomfield Street, London, EC2.

Robinson Aircraft Co. Ltd, manufacturers of the Redwing, established a sales office at Heston from 2 December 1931. For further details see Croydon and Thornton Heath. The company also spent a period operating from Colchester, Essex.

The **Taylor Watkinson** Dingbat G-AFJA was a single-seat, low-wing monoplane with a deep fuselage, and was powered by a Carden Ford engine. The Dingbat was built at Teddington and was flown at Heston on 2 August 1938 (note that other sources indicate a June first flight). G-AFJA was briefly restored to flying condition at North Weald in 1959, and again in 1974, but was again damaged in an accident in 1975.

Incidentally, although the name Dingbat has been widely adopted when referring to this machine, Ord-Hume indicates that the type should be known as the Ding-Bat; certainly its name was clearly painted in this form on the aircraft's fin when it flew at Heston.

The **Youngman Baynes** experimental high-lift research aircraft was a one-off design combining an extensively modified Proctor IV fuselage with a special wing designed by R.T. Youngman. The wing incorporated full-span double-slotted flaps of 25% chord across the inner wing and centre section, and outboard slotted flaps with inset drooping ailerons. The flap and control surface installation was exceptionally clean aerodynamically and free from the usual array of flap hinge and track fairings. The aircraft, VT789, was constructed by **Heston Aircraft Ltd**, having been designed by the Aircraft Section of **Alan Muntz & Co. Ltd**, under the direction of L.E. Baynes. VT789 was first flown on 5 February 1948, and was later registered G-AMBL.

Highbury

Deperdussin (also **The British Deperdussin Aeroplane Syndicate** and **British Deperdussin Co. Ltd**). The company were advertising in November 1911 that 'British built

Deperdussin are being manufactured in our London works, Mildmay Avenue, Newington Green'. This may have been at **Ogilvie & Co.** who have the same address. In July 1913 the British Deperdussin 'Seagull' was based at Osea Island in the Blackwater estuary, near Millbeach. Related entries can be found under Hendon, London (Central) and Upper Holloway. The company also operated a flying school at Brooklands, Surrey.

The **Falcon Aircraft Co. Ltd** of 28 Kelvin Road, Highbury, was registered in September 1918, acquiring the business of F.S. Engineering Co. with £11,000 capital. Nothing else is known.

Hoods & Bodies Ltd of Northampton Grove, Canonbury, N1, is listed in *The Aviation Pocket-Book, 1919-1920* as an aeroplane manufacturer.

The **Leconfield Aircraft Works Ltd** was registered in April 1918 with offices at 345 City Road, E1, taking over Leconfield Works, Canonbury, N1, to carry out the business of 'aircraft manufacturers, sheet metal workers, etc'.

Ogilvie & Co., of Mildmay Ave, Newington Green Road, London, N1, is listed in *The Aviation Pocket-Book, 1919-1920* as an aeroplane manufacturer with propeller branch. The company is also referred to as Ogilvie & Partners by H. Penrose.

The origins of **C.G. Spencer & Sons Ltd**, of 56a Highbury Grove, London N5, date back to 1835. The real speciality of the firm was balloons, kite balloons and parachutes. C.G. Spencer, his father Edward, and his son Stanley were all enthusiastic aeronauts. Stanley Spencer was the builder of the first successful British Airship in 1902.

The company was the manufacturer of the Spencer Stirling monoplane shown at the 1910 Olympia Exhibition, which was designed by Herbert Spencer. In July 1913, typical advertising ran: 'Manufacturers of Aeroplanes, Airships, Balloons and aeronautical apparatus of every description, fabric, propellors and accessories'; 'Airships, Balloons. Aeroplanes, Biplanes or Monoplanes built to order under Client's personal supervision'. Herbert Spencer subsequently designed and flew a series of Farman-like biplanes at Brooklands, Surrey.

In October 1915, *Flight* reported the registration of C.G. Spencer & Sons Ltd, with capital of £3,000 as constructors of balloons, airships, aeroplanes, airships and appliances of all kinds. The company was 'acquiring the stock of partly built aircraft of A.C. Spencer' of Highbury, balloon and aircraft manufacturer. Shortly afterwards, the company was advertising 'Planes built to Specifications. Highest workmanship & material'.

Witton, Witton & Co., of 13 Goodwin Street, Fonthill Road, Finsbury Park, N4, advertised their comprehensive capabilities thus: 'Aircraft – Fuselages, Chassis, Tails, Cowlings, Airscrews or Complete Machines'; 'Manufacturers of the Witton Piano'.

Robert Young Construction Co. Ltd of Canonbury Works, Canonbury Street, Essex Road, London, N1, advertised as 'Aeroplane Makers'. Nothing else is known.

Highgate

The Highgate Aircraft Co. Ltd, Offices and Works, Pauntley Street, Archway Road, Highgate N19. This company was registered in January 1917 as taking over the business of Highgate Aircraft Co. Its advertising of May 1917 indicated that the company were 'Designers and Manufacturers of Aircraft, Contractors to HM War Office'; 'Metal parts manufacture – pressings and blanks for A-W, RE, DH and other types'. The company's telegraphic address was 'Hygaircraf, Uphol, London'; presumably Uphol indicates that the origin of the company was in the upholstery trade.

The Thames Aviation Works (Burtons Ltd) previously of London Fields Station (Great Eastern Railway), Hackney, E8, moved to 30A Highgate Road, NW5, in April 1919 'as a result of London Fields station being re-opened'. For further details, see Hackney and Homerton,

Ilford

In June 1917, an advertisement was placed for an aeroplane woodworker 'required at once' at Ilford Aeroplane Works, Ilford. This was almost certainly for Oakley Ltd.

Oakley Ltd, of 28 Duke Street, Piccadilly, built three Sopwith Triplanes (N5910 – N5912) at Ilford from an order for twenty-five aircraft. The first aircraft work by this firm was associated with the installation of Curtiss engines in BE2C aircraft. The third and last Triplane built by the firm is preserved in the RAF Museum at Hendon, having been completed on 19 October 1917.

Islington

Dove Bros Ltd, of Cloudesley Place, Islington, N1, is listed in *The Aviation Pocket-Book, 1919-1920* as an aeroplane manufacturer with propeller branch.

Kenley

Kenley Common was taken over for use as RFC Acceptance Park No.7 in June 1917, giving rise to questions in Parliament on the subject of destruction of trees. Aircraft handled included large numbers of Sopwith Camel, together with the RE8, SE5 and Sopwith Dolphin.

Kensal Green

Broughton Blayney Aircraft Co. The Broughton Blayney Brawny, a development of the Perman Parasol, was built from 1936 by **T.H. Gill & Son**, of 75 Kilburn Lane, London, W10. Mr Blayney was a director. See Hanworth for further details.

Rolls-Royce Ltd set up a repair works in September 1917 at Barlby Road, W10, using a factory site previously occupied by the Clement-Talbot motor works. This factory repaired more than 600 engines.

Kensington

The **ARIII Construction Co. Ltd** had offices at 2 Airlie Gardens, Kensington, W8, before moving to Feltham. Autogyro development activities were carried out at Hanworth, Heston and Denham.

Wm Cole & Sons Ltd had offices at 92 High Street, Kensington, London, W8, and works at 235 Hammersmith Road, W6. The company advertised as 'Aircraft Contractors to HM Government'. For further details, see Hammersmith.

Croplease plc of 58-60 Kensington Church Street, W8, was formed in April 1989 and acquired the rights to the Fieldmaster/Firemaster designs from **Croplease Ltd**, which was based at Shannon. Croplease Ltd had taken over these rights after the receivership of **Norman Aeroplane Co. (NAC)** in October 1988. Related activities were undertaken at Bembridge, Sandown, Barry, Shannon and Old Sarum.

It is remarkable that, of the total of three aircraft built by Oakley Ltd at Ilford, one has survived. This is Sopwith Triplane N5912, displayed in the Royal Air Force Museum. (Author)

Kilburn and Maida Vale

Central Aircraft Co. Palmerston Works 179 High Road, Kilburn, NW6: This company was set up in September 1916 as a subsidiary of **R. Cattle Ltd**, a joinery firm of 27 Wybert Street, Stanhope Street, London, NW. In November 1917 the company was advertising thus: 'War Office & Admiralty Contractors. Planes, Ailerons, Elevators, Spars, Struts, Ribs, etc'. Aircraft were flown from a small field next to the factory, before the company transferred its flying to Northolt; see Northolt for further details. The last aircraft constructed by this firm was the Sayers monoplane that competed in the 1922 Itford Hill gliding competition.

The company's Chief Designer was A.A. (Tony) Fletcher, former assistant to George Handasyde, and previously with London & Provincial at Stag Lane.

Weston Hurlin Co. (WHC), of 2 Edbrooke Road, Marylands Road, Harrow Road, W9, advertised in April 1912 that they 'have undertaken several important contracts for military machines [...] are prepared to accept further orders for Aeronautical work of any description – propellers, spare parts, complete machines'. Weston Hurlin constructed a biplane of unusual configuration in 1911, with the upper wing being of half the span of the lower. The design was unsuccessful and the company was wound up in October 1912.

Kingsbury

In February 1917, Messrs. Borningham purchased 150 acres at Kingsbury for aerodrome purposes and were reported to be 'erecting a splendidly equipped factory', which featured particularly generous hangarage. **Kingsbury Aviation Co. Ltd**, was registered in May 1917 and built 150 DH6 from C5126, thirty Sopwith Snipe (from J6493), and were contracted for twenty Vimy which were subsequently cancelled. Mr Warwick Wright was a director of Kingsbury Aviation Co. Ltd, which was a subsidiary of The Kingsbury Engineering Co. Ltd. After the First World War, Kingsbury Aviation offered tuition and joy-riding from nearby Stag Lane. The aircraft used included a Hewlett & Blondeau-constructed Armstrong Whitworth FK3 B9612/G-EAEU, and Avro 504K D6217/G-EAGT.

Early flight testing by **The Fairey Aviation Co. Ltd** was carried out from a field at Kingsbury, two miles south of Stag Lane on the west side of Watling St. The aircraft involved were Sopwith 1½ Strutters from the batch of 100 built by Fairey Aviation.

Fraser's Flying School. This establishment was set up in 1922, advertising 'Dual control Avros, Sopwith Scout. Among our machines is the famous Austin 'Kestrel'. Exhibition flights given, machines erected and tested'. They were based at 64 Haymarket SW1 and Kingsbury Aerodrome. It is not thought that any machines were actually constructed, however.

Hooper & Co. Ltd had a factory at Kingsbury during the Second World War, which was subsequently taken over by **Vanden Plas Ltd**. Vanden Plas manufactured Vampire and Venom fuselages here under sub-contract from The de Havilland Aircraft Co. Ltd.

King's Cross

Courtney Pope & Co. Ltd had the following addresses: 6-9 Alpha Place, Caledonian Road, Kings Cross, London N1; and 8a Caledonian Road, N1. Although listed in *The Aviation Pocket-Book, 1919-1920* as an aeroplane manufacturer, the company is thought to have made propellers as its primary business.

Kingston upon Thames and New Malden

The Kingston entry lists first the activities of Sopwith, Hawker, Hawker Siddeley and British Aerospace before presenting a review of the work of other companies that were based in this area.

T.O.M. Sopwith started work at Kingston at the end of 1912 in the Central Hall roller-skating rink 'adjoining Cinema Palace and Kingston Railway Station' at Canbury Park Road, this move being prompted by the lack of space available at Brooklands. In December 1912 *Flight* reported that 'Mr Sopwith has leased a skating rink in the Richmond Road, Kingston on Thames, to establish his works under the management of Mr Sigrist.' **The Sopwith Aviation Co.** was renamed **The Sopwith Aviation Co. Ltd** in December 1913 following re-financing, the authorised capital being £26,000 (however, this is also reported as taking place in March 1914). Seaplane flotation tests took place on the River Thames, making use of the facilities and slipways at R.J. Turk & Sons boatyard. The factory was extended in 1917, and a lease taken out on the Richmond Road factory at Ham.

Sopwith created many outstanding designs, both as a pioneer, and for military use in the First World War. Outstanding examples include the following:

- The Bat Boat, the first successful British flying boat. The Bat Boat was the first truly practical amphibian, this being proven by its success in winning the Mortimer Singer Prize. This was achieved by performing twelve alternate land and sea landings in three hours and twenty-five minutes, out of an allotted maximum of five hours.
- The Sopwith Three Seater biplane, which was piloted by H.G. Hawker to break several height records in 1913, including the carriage of a single passenger to 12,900ft, two to 10,600ft, and three to 8,400ft.

- The Tabloid which, in floatplane form as the Sopwith Schneider, won the Schneider Trophy race of 1914 at a speed of 85.5mph on 20 April 1914, and continued on to set a 300km world speed record for seaplanes of 92mph.
- The famous Sopwith designs of the First World War: Pup, Camel, 1½ Strutter, Snipe and Cuckoo. The Camel was Sopwith's most famous product, and proved to be an effective and highly manoeuvrable fighter once its handling quirks had been mastered.

Production histories of the main Sopwith types are summarised in the table below, noting that the numbers built are, in some cases, the subject of conflicting data:

Type	First Flight	Comments
Three Seater	7 February 1913	Eleven built, used for setting height records in May, June and July 1913.
Bat Boat	1913	Hull constructed by S.E. Saunders Ltd. Used to win the Mortimer Singer Prize.
Tractor Seaplane	Mid-1913	Three built. Two-seat tractor biplane seaplane. Serial numbers 58, 59, 60.
Type 807 Naval Seaplane	1913	At least twelve aircraft built, the type being a folding-wing seaplane developed from the 1914 Circuit of Britain entry.
Gunbus	1913	Large two-seat three-bay pusher biplane of 50ft span. Six were built by Sopwith, and a further thirty by Robey & Co. Ltd as the Sopwith Admiralty Type 806. At least thirteen of these were delivered as spares.

The Sopwith company offices and factory in Canbury Park Road, Kingston are still well preserved, as shown by this 1994 photograph. (Author)

RECORDS.

BRITISH Duration Record - -   8 hours 23 minutes.
  ,,   Height Record for Pilot alone -   11,450 feet.
  ,,   ,,   ,,   ,, and 1 Passenger, 12,900 ,,
  ,,   ,,   ,,   ,, ,, 2 Passengers, 10,600 ,,
  WORLD'S ,,   ,,   ,,   ,, 3 ,,   8,400 ,,

Winner Mortimer Singer Competition for first British
Machine to rise from and alight on LAND AND WATER.

SOPWITH AVIATION CO.

OFFICES & WORKS—KINGSTON-ON-THAMES.

Telephone 1777 Kingston.   *Telegrams "Sopwith, Kingston."*

SOPWITH AVIATION CO.

MANUFACTURERS OF

AEROPLANES & HYDRO-AEROPLANES.

**British Altitude Record captured at Brooklands last
Saturday by SOPWITH 80 H.P. BIPLANE.**

The Sopwith 80 h.p. Tractor Biplane, in its War Office Test at Farnboro',
gave a speed variation of 40·6 m.p.h. to 73·6 m.p.h., Climbing Test 1,000 ft.
2 minutes 22 seconds, and accomplished the Rolling Test with great
success, landing and getting off the test ground.

**ALL these performances were accomplished with a
Passenger and four hours' fuel on board.**

Telegrams "Sopwith, Kingston."
Telephone 1777 Kingston.   Offices & Works: **CANBURY PARK ROAD,
KINGSTON-ON-THAMES.**

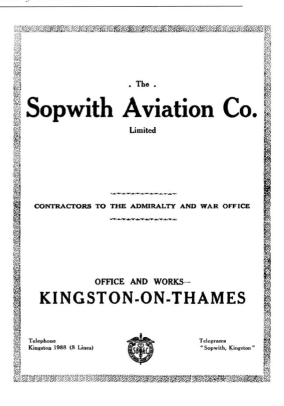

. The .

Sopwith Aviation Co.

Limited

CONTRACTORS TO THE ADMIRALTY AND WAR OFFICE

OFFICE AND WORKS—

KINGSTON-ON-THAMES

Telephone
Kingston 1988 (8 Lines)   Telegrams
"Sopwith, Kingston"

Type	First Flight	Comments
Tabloid	Autumn 1913	Small single-seat tractor biplane. Thirty-six built. Outstanding performance included 1,200ft/min climb rate and 92mph maximum speed.
Schneider	1914	Modified Tabloid used for the 1914 Schneider Contest at Monaco. Subsequently adopted for production. About 136 production aircraft built. Developed into Sopwith Baby.
Two Seat Scout	1914	Twenty-four built for RNAS, serials 1051 to 1074. Known as the 'Spinning Jenny'.
Admiralty Type 860	Late 1914	A large two-seat seaplane similar to the Short 184, of which eighteen were built with Serial Nos 851-860, 927-932, 935, 938.
Baby	September 1915	Light bomber-based on Schneider. 286 built: split between The Sopwith Aviation Co. Ltd (100) and Blackburn Aeroplane & Motor Co. Ltd. Developed into Fairey Hamble Baby.
1½ Strutter	December 1915	5,466 built, at least 1,513 in UK (other figures for UK production can be found). In addition to The Sopwith Aviation Co. Ltd (246), contractors included The Fairey Aviation Co. Ltd, Hooper & Co. Ltd, Mann, Egerton & Co. Ltd, Morgan & Co., Ruston Proctor & Co. Ltd, Vickers Ltd, Wells Aviation Co. Ltd and Westland Aircraft Works. Initially flown as Sopwith A1 or Admiralty type 9400. Prototype serial 3686.

Type	First Flight	Comments
Pup	Spring 1916	A total of six Sopwith Pup prototypes and 1,770 production aircraft is normally quoted, although some sources give 1,847 aircraft. Of these, The Sopwith Aviation Co. Ltd built only ninety-seven. Contractors comprised William Beardmore & Co. Ltd, The Standard Motor Co. Ltd, Whitehead Aircraft Ltd. First flown in early February 1916 as Admiralty Type 9901, prototype serial 3691.
Triplane	28 May 1916	This type served with distinction with the RNAS. Perhaps among the most famous were the aircraft of B Flight 10 Sqn. RNAS – the Black Flight – '*Black Maria, Black Death, Black Roger, Black Prince* and *Black Sheep*'. Some 152 were built, the prototype N500 being flown in early June 1916. The main contractor in addition to The Sopwith Aviation Co. Ltd (103) was Clayton & Shuttleworth Ltd, with three aircraft being built by Oakley Ltd at Ilford.
Camel	22 December 1916 (cleared for flight)	Wide variations can been found in total production numbers. A figure of 5,747 (F.1 and 2F.1 Camel) is given in the Sopwith biography *Pure Luck*, but a figure of 5,490 is documented by J.M. Bruce. Francis Mason in *The British Fighter Since 1912* states 5,695 plus a total of 230 2F1 (grand total 5,925), of which at least 100 were cancelled. Total orders for 5,497 Camel, plus 250 2F1 are also cited by Bruce Robertson, this figure being consistent with that given in *Pure Luck*. J.M. Bruce states that 1,325 Camel were built in 1917, and 4,165 in 1918.

Only around 10% of the total were built by The Sopwith Aviation Co. Ltd (503 Camel and fifty Ships Camel), with Boulton & Paul Ltd and Ruston, Proctor & Co. Ltd the major sub-contractors. Other contractors were: Arrol-Johnson Ltd; William Beardmore & Co. Ltd (2F.1); British Caudron Co.; Clayton & Shuttleworth Ltd; Hooper & Co. Ltd; March, Jones & Cribb Ltd; Nieuport & General Aircraft Co. Ltd; and Portholme Aerodrome Ltd. In October 1918, 2,648 Camel were in service with the RAF, equipping thirty-eight squadrons. The prototype 2F.1 with 150hp Bentley rotary was N5. This variant was mainly used for naval service and first flew in March 1917. |
| T1 Cuckoo | Mid-1917 | 233 built, prototype N74 built by The Sopwith Aviation Co. Ltd. Production carried out by Blackburn Aeroplane & Motor Co. Ltd (162 aircraft, including thirty of a batch of fifty aircraft ordered from Pegler & Co., Doncaster), Fairfield Shipbuilding & Engineering Co. (fifty from an order for 100) and Pegler & Co. (twenty). Blackburn-built aircraft manufactured at Sherburn-in-Elmet. |

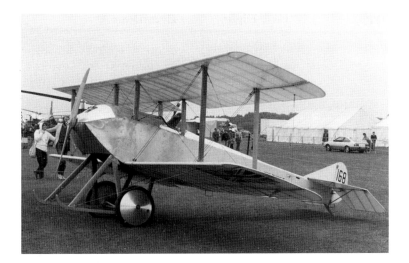

The clean Tabloid was the progenitor of the Sopwith series of single-seat fighters. '168' is a replica (G-BFDE) built by Don Cashmore at Ravenshead. (Author)

The Sopwith Baby at Yeovilton is painted as a Blackburn-built example, N2078. It is actually a composite of two Sopwith-built machines: 8214 and 8215. (J.S. Smith)

The widespread use of the Sopwith 1½ Strutter by Allied nations is reflected by this French example in the Musée de l'Air at Le Bourget. (Author)

Relatively few examples of the Sopwith Pup were built by the parent company, the main sub-contractors being Beardmore, Standard Motor Co. and Whitehead. (Author)

This Sopwith Triplane replica at the Champlin Fighter Museum, Mesa, Arizona, poses as Black Prince. (Author)

This Sopwith Camel is another of the excellent replicas displayed at the Champlin Fighter Museum. (Author)

*The powerful
Sopwith Schneider
G-EAKI flew in the
abortive 1919
Schneider Trophy
contest at
Bournemouth.*
(Rolls-Royce)

Type	First Flight	Comments
Dolphin	May 1917	Production numbers for the Sopwith 5F.1 Dolphin range from 1,532 to 2074, dependent upon source. Robertson's *Sopwith – The Man and His Aircraft* indicates the following production: over 1,043 built by The Sopwith Aviation Co. Ltd, with Darracq Motor Engineering Co. Ltd contributing 300 from orders for 400 and Hooper & Co. Ltd 216 from orders for 350 (a grand total of 1,559 aircraft). *British Military Aircraft Serials* by the same author indicates a slightly higher figure (e.g. 331 from Darracq).
Snipe	November 1917	The Snipe production prototype B9962 followed a number of experimental Camel derivatives fitted with BR1 and BR2 rotary engines. Large production orders followed, with delivery totals quoted as low as 1,100, and as high as 2,178 (including six prototypes). Robertson's *British Military Aircraft Serials* indicates the following production: The Sopwith Aviation Co. Ltd (544, plus thirty-four Dragonfly-powered Sopwith Dragons); Boulton & Paul Ltd (420 of 500); Coventry Ordnance Works Ltd (150 from 300 ordered); The Kingsbury Aviation Co. (thirty from J6493); D. Napier & Son Ltd (150); Nieuport & General Aircraft Co. Ltd (about forty from order for 100); Portholme Aerodrome Ltd (144 aircraft from orders for 900 aircraft, some 556 of which were diverted to Ruston, Proctor & Co. Ltd). This justifies a Snipe production total of 2,038. Robertson's *Sopwith – The Man and His Aircraft* indicates total production as 2,103; 560 by Sopwith. See additional comments below.

Type	First Flight	Comments
3F.2 Hippo	13 September 1917	Two only, X11 and X18, competitor to Bristol F.2B. Also reported as X10 and X11, with X18 being cancelled.
Salamander	27 April 1918	The TF.2 Salamander was heavily armoured for trench strafing. The prototype E5429 was first flown on 27 April 1918. The Sopwith Aviation Co. Ltd built some 163 from orders for 500. Additional contracts were placed with: ANEC (107 from an order for 150, other sources suggest none were completed); The Glendower Aircraft Co. Ltd (twenty-two from order for 100, some sources state fifty were built), National Aircraft Factory No.1 (400, all believed cancelled), Palladium Autocars (100, all believed cancelled) and Wolseley Motors (150, all believed cancelled). The Salamander was very much affected by the mass cancellation of orders which occurred after the Armistice, leaving considerable uncertainty over actual production numbers. (Production totals of 175, 183+, 210, 292 (as above) and 419 can be found).

Total production of the Sopwith Snipe has been the subject of some debate, with totals cited between 1,100 and 2,178. Production was widely sub-contracted, one source giving the numbers of aircraft being built as The Sopwith Aviation Co. Ltd (560); Boulton & Paul Ltd (415 from 500 ordered); Coventry Ordnance Works Ltd (150 of 300); D. Napier & Son Ltd (150); Nieuport & General Aircraft Co. Ltd (100); Ruston, Proctor & Co. Ltd (498 of 800); Portholme Aerodrome Ltd (144), some jointly between Ruston and Portholme; possibly 100 (of 150 ordered) by March, Jones & Cribb Ltd (delivered to store); and thirty by The Kingsbury Aviation Co. (delivered to store). It is likely that some of these aircraft were delivered without engines, and that others may have not been completed. This list also differs from other figures found in researching this book, including references elsewhere to Snipe production by Barclay, Curle & Co. Ltd; The Daimler Co.; and Portass & Son. These figures illustrate some of the difficulties encountered when examining the production details of aircraft types that were in large-scale production at the time of the Armistice.

The company was renamed **The Sopwith Aviation & Engineering Co. Ltd** in May 1919, advertising its war record as follows:

> *The Sopwith Aviation & Engineering Co. Ltd has designed a larger number of types, which have been accepted and standardised by the British Government, than any other aircraft manufacturer. Its enormous works have been devoted entirely to the production of its own machines, which have also been made in huge quantities by sub-contractors.*

> *During the war there were constructed to the exclusive designs of The Sopwith Aviation and Engineering Co. Ltd 11,237 complete aeroplanes for the British Government. In addition to upwards of 5,000 Sopwith machines manufactured in France and Italy.*

The peak production rate achieved was ninety aircraft per week (British Aerospace data).

After the First World War, Sopwith attempted to replace its lost aircraft contracts with manufacture of ABC motorcycles, advertising in January 1920: 'The outstanding excellence of the Sopwith war and peace aeroplanes characterises another of its productions: the ABC

DURING THE WAR

there were constructed

to the EXCLUSIVE DESIGNS of the

SOPWITH AVIATION & ENGINEERING Co., Ltd.

11,237

complete aeroplanes for the British Government

· including ·

SCOUTS, FIGHTERS, ARMOURED FIGHTERS, RECONNAISSANCE MACHINES, BOMBERS, SEA-PLANES, TORPEDO-PLANES, SHIP-AEROPLANES, Etc., etc.

In addition to upwards of

5,000

Sopwith Machines manufactured in France by the French Government for French and American needs, and also manufactured in Italy for the Italian Government.

THERE IS NO AIRCRAFT FIRM IN THE WORLD BACKED BY SUCH EXPERIENCE AND SO WELL EQUIPPED FOR THE PRODUCTION OF CIVIL AEROPLANES.

THE

Sopwith
AVIATION & ENGINEERING C? L?

Registered Offices and Works:

KINGSTON-ON-THAMES.

Telephone: Kingston 1988 (8 lines).
Telegrams: "Sopwith, Kingston."

London Offices:

65, SOUTH MOLTON ST., W. 1.

Telephone: Mayfair 5803-4-5.
Telegrams: "Efficonomy, Phone, London."

Australia : THE LARKIN-SOPWITH AVIATION COMPANY OF AUSTRALASIA, LTD., 18, GURNER STREET, ST KILDA, MELBOURNE, also ABERDEEN HOUSE, 94, KING STREET, MELBOURNE, and LONDON BANK CHAMBERS, CORNER OF PITT AND MOORE STREETS, SYDNEY.

Below: *The Hawker Tomtit was one of the less numerous types produced by H.G. Hawker Engineering Co. Ltd alongside its prolific Hart family: thirty-six Tomtits were built.* (Author)

L7180 is a Hawker Hind. Many aircraft from this particular batch were subsequently converted to Hind Trainers by General Aircraft Ltd. (J.S. Smith)

The Hurricane is represented here by G-HURI, a Canadian-built Mk XIIa. (Author)

The outstanding Fury I was noted for its elegance, crisp controls and excellent rate of climb. (Hawker Siddeley)

motorcycle – *The best of its kind'*. In practice, the company only manufactured fifteen aircraft in the two years between the Armistice and September 1920.

Ultimately there came a financial crisis, and Sopwith entered voluntary liquidation, on 11 September 1920, eventually paying off all their creditors. The financial difficulties were communicated to the employees by a notice circulated on 10 September 1920, which stated, 'We must regret that we find it impossible to reopen the works as the difficulties by restricted credit prevent the Company from finding sufficient working capital to carry on the business, and it will therefore be wound up.' The creditors meeting (reported in October 1920) were told that the company had 6,000 employees at the end of the war. Production of motorcycles had been undertaken, but the company had been hit by a slump. At the same time, problems had arisen over disputed Excess Profits Duty. Liquidation by means of sale as a going concern was now sought.

The **H.G. Hawker Engineering Co. Ltd** was registered on 15 November 1920 with capital of £20,000. Formed after The Sopwith Aviation & Engineering Co. Ltd went into voluntary liquidation, Hawker Engineering took over all Sopwith patent rights, and the support business for the Sopwith aircraft then in RAF service. Like Sopwith, they also supplemented the aircraft business by the manufacture of motorcycles, and also the manufacture of aluminium bodies for sports cars and racing cars, including work for AC Motors.

The Hawker concern ultimately grew into one of Britain's greatest aircraft manufacturers, whose Kingston and Dunsfold design and manufacturing teams formed a key component of British Aerospace. The Kingston design team moved to Farnborough, and the manufacturing activity transferred to Dunsfold, following the closure of the Kingston site. Under BAE SYSTEMS, the Farnborough design activity continues, but Dunsfold was closed at the end of 2000.

H.G. Hawker Engineering Co. Ltd received initial contracts for the overhaul and refurbishment of Snipe and other Sopwith aircraft, before moving on to build their own designs,

The Sea Fury was the last British piston-engined fighter to see service, and the type is regarded by many as the pinnacle of development of this class of aircraft. (Author)

Hawker's classic jet fighter, the clean and versatile Hunter, is seen here displaying to the SBAC Show crowd. (Via Author)

The latest version of the single-seat Harrier to see RAF service is the Harrier GR.5/7, fuselages for which were built at Kingston prior to the transfer of production to Dunsfold. (Author)

starting with the Woodcock. As with Sopwith, Hawker retained production premises in Kingston and flight test facilities at Brooklands, aircraft being moved by road to Brooklands for final assembly and test. (Hawker is used here to refer to both **H.G. Hawker Engineering Co. Ltd**, and **Hawker Aircraft Ltd** which succeeded it in May 1933.) Like Sopwith, Hawker was to specialise in fighter and light bomber aircraft. The main production types were as follows:

- **Woodcock** – sixty-four built by Hawker, together with fifteen of the similar Danecock, twelve of which were constructed by the Royal Danish Navy Dockyard factory at Copenhagen.
- **Cygnet** – notable as Sidney Camm's first design. Two built (G-EBJH and G-EBMB) and entered in the 1924 and 1926 Two-seat Light Aeroplane Trials, being the clear winners of the latter competition.
- **Horsley** – 138, all built by Hawker.
- **Hart** – 1,042 day bombers, of which Hawker constructed 246. The Hart was also built under sub-contract by Gloster Aircraft Co. Ltd (seventy-two), Sir W.G. Armstrong Whitworth Aircraft Ltd (456), Vickers (Aviation) Ltd (226), together with forty-two aircraft under licence at Trollhäten, Sweden. The Hart was an outstanding design, which first flew in June 1928 and was produced in many variants. Developments included the Demon, Audax, Osprey, Nimrod, Hind, Hardy, Hector and Fury. From 1931 onward, Hart (and Hart variant) production was extensively sub-contracted – halving its price in the process, much to Hawker's anguish. Including all subsequent variants, the Hart and Fury accounted for a total production run of nearly 3,300 aircraft. The Hart was also extensively used for engine testing, various examples being host to various versions of the Napier Dagger, Bristol Perseus, Mercury, Pegasus and Jupiter, and the Rolls-Royce PV12 and Merlin.
- **Tomtit** trainer for the RAF and civil use – prototype, five civil machines, twenty-four RAF aircraft, two aircraft for the RCAF, and four aircraft for the RNZAF – total of thirty-six aircraft. These figures are given by F.K. Mason in *Hawker Aircraft Since 1920*, but he also cites a production total of forty-five.
- **Fury I** – 146 fighter aircraft which, although bearing a close family resemblance to the Hart and its derivatives, is distinguished by its single-seat configuration.
- **Nimrod** – eighty-seven naval single-seat fighter.
- **Demon** – 298 aircraft: 192 by Hawker, the remainder by Boulton Paul Aircraft Ltd – fifty-nine at Norwich, and forty-seven at Wolverhampton.
- **Osprey** – 144 aircraft: 136 by Hawker, and eight at Trollhäten, Sweden.
- **Audax** – 718 aircraft: 265 by Hawker, plus A.V. Roe & Co. Ltd (244), Bristol Aeroplane Co. Ltd (141), Gloster Aircraft Co. Ltd (twenty-five) and Westland Aircraft Ltd (forty-three).
- **Hartbees** – designed especially for South African use; four were built by Hawker, and a further sixty-five by Roberts Heights Artillery & Aircraft Depot, Zwartkop, Pretoria.
- **Hind** – 592 Army co-operation and general purpose aircraft, all by Hawker.
- **Fury II** – 118 aircraft: forty-three by Hawker and seventy-five by General Aircraft Ltd.
- **Hector** – 179 aircraft: one only by Hawker, and the remainder by Westland Aircraft Ltd.
- **Hurricane** – 14,553 in total: 10,030 by Hawker, together with Gloster Aircraft Co. Ltd (2,750), The Austin Motor Co. Ltd (300), Avions Fairey (two), and Canadian Car & Foundry Corporation (1,451). The Hurricane was the most successful aircraft in the Battle of Britain in terms of enemy aircraft destroyed. Peak Hurricane production was seventy-seven in a single week in March 1942, and 279 in a single month in March 1943. Other production totals can also be found.

The British Aerospace factory at Ham Road, Kingston, in its heyday. (BAE SYSTEMS)

The cleared Sopwith/Hawker/ British Aerospace site at Ham Road, Kingston, shortly after its closure. This area is now given over to executive housing. (Author)

- **Henley** – 202 aircraft: all but two built by Gloster Aircraft Co. Ltd.
- **Typhoon** – 3,300 aircraft: all but seventeen built by Gloster Aircraft Co. Ltd (other sources also give a total of 3,315).
- **Tempest** – 1,395 in total: 1,359 by Hawker, and thirty-six (Tempest II) by The Bristol Aeroplane Co. Ltd.
- **Fury** – sixty-five aircraft: all at Hawker with the exception of a single example constructed by Boulton Paul Aircraft Ltd.
- **Sea Fury** – 860 aircraft: all by Hawker.
- **Sea Hawk** – about 555 aircraft: all but thirty-five of the production aircraft by Sir W.G. Armstrong Whitworth Aircraft Ltd.
- **Hunter** – 1,972 aircraft, including trainer variants, of which Hawker built 957 at Kingston and 318 at Blackpool, the remaining construction being split between Sir W.G. Armstrong Whitworth Aircraft Ltd, Avions Fairey and Fokker. Arguably Britain's most successful post-war military aircraft, the Hunter is justifiably famous for its good looks, superb handling and robust longevity. The last flight of a Hunter in British military service took place at Boscombe Down on 10 August 2001, the

aircraft being a Hunter T. Mk 7 of the Empire Test Pilots School, XL612. Export customers (including both new-build and sales of converted ex-RAF aircraft) included Abu Dhabi, Chile, Denmark, India, Iraq, Jordan, Kenya, Kuwait, Lebanon, Peru, Qatar, Rhodesia, Saudi Arabia, Singapore, Sweden and Switzerland, in addition to construction in Belgium and the Netherlands.

- **P.1127** and **Kestrel** development aircraft for the Harrier. Six P.1127 and nine Kestrel were built.

Note that alternative production figures can be found for some of the above designs.

Sidney Camm (later Sir Sidney) was Hawker's famous Chief Designer from 1925 to 1959 when he was appointed Chief Engineer. Camm was to oversee the design of a succession of incomparable fighters including the Fury, Hurricane, Typhoon, Tempest, Sea Fury, Hunter and the Harrier. Camm joined Hawker from Martinsyde, with whom he had been employed since 1914.

In 1928 the Ham factory was leased to Leyland Motors. In June 1929, the H.G. Hawker Engineering Co. Ltd was accurately advertising itself as 'Specialists in Military Aircraft. Contractors to HM Air Ministry and Foreign Governments'.

Hawker Aircraft Ltd was registered on 18 May 1933, and purchased the shares of Gloster Aircraft Co. Ltd in February 1934. **Hawker Siddeley Aircraft Co.** was formed in July 1935 – the merger was made public during the first week of July 1935, the press announcement stating that:

> Shares in the new company the *Hawker Siddeley Trust Ltd* are to be offered to the public with authorised share capital of £2,000,000. The Trust is to acquire all the ordinary shares of the Armstrong Siddeley Development Co. Ltd, and 1,000,000 (half the total) of the shares in Hawker Aircraft Ltd, so that it will control both concerns. The Armstrong Siddeley interests cover Sir W.G. Armstrong Whitworth Aircraft Ltd, Armstrong Siddeley Motors Ltd, A.V. Roe & Co. Ltd, Air Service Training Ltd, together with other ancillary and auxiliary concerns.

The Aeroplane commented that 'the prospects of the various parties in the merger seem very bright'. Most of the remaining shares of Hawker Aircraft Ltd were transferred to Hawker Siddeley Aircraft during 1937.

In 1948 when the Leyland Motors lease expired, Hawkers progressively moved from Canbury Park Road to the Richmond Road site at Ham, with the move being completed by 1960. The Hawker Hunter was built at Richmond Road, Ham, with the first aircraft flying at Boscombe Down, Wiltshire, on 20 July 1951. The magnificent Design Office fronting on to Richmond Road was occupied in 1958.

Further changes in identity included **Hawker Siddeley Group Ltd** (1955) and **Hawker Siddeley Aviation Ltd** (1963). The headquarters remained at Kingston, with eleven operating sites around the United Kingdom. Nationalisation in 1977 then created **British**

Aerospace with its corporate headquarters at Farnborough. Kingston was the lead site for the development of the Hawk, and also led Harrier developments with the Harrier GR3, Sea Harrier and Harrier II. At the beginning of 1989, **British Aerospace plc** was formed, with the Kingston site being part of **British Aerospace (Military Aircraft Ltd)**. From 1990 the site was progressively run-down, leading to closure at the end of 1992, after which the site was cleared of all buildings (including the Design Office), and sold for housing. During the time that the Kingston factories were in being, Sopwith, Hawker and BAe constructed a total of 43,313 aircraft, many of them at this historic site. In 1998, it was announced that a memorial to Kingston's aviation heritage was planned, and that a suitable site had been located by the local council.

The **Aerial Construction Co.** of Hampton Court Road, Middlesex was registered in December 1917 to carry out the business of Aeronautical Engineers. Nothing else is known.

T.W.K. Clarke & Co., 14 Union Street, and Crown Works, High Street, Kingston on Thames. This company was established in 1906, and built two gliders in 1909 and 1910, the first of which was a Wright glider built in August 1909 for Alec Ogilvie. Something of the development of the company, which had the telegraphic address, 'Flyers, Kingston on Thames', can be traced from its advertising: 'Our gliders hold World's records'; 'Contractors to HM Government – Hydro-aeroplane floats'. In February 1913, the company moved to new works at High St, Hampton Wick. Later on the company concentrated on supplies for the model aircraft movement, although in 1915, their works included a propeller department turning out both two and four-blade designs with 'Workmanship & accuracy guaranteed'. At this time, they were also advertising as 'Contractors to the Admiralty and War Office'.

The **EBORA Propeller Co. Ltd** had a business address at 11/12 Surbiton Park Terrace, Kingston on Thames.

May, Harden & May, an AIRCO company, had experimental works at Kingston Bridge Boathouse, Hampton Wick. Two Phoenix P5 flying boat fuselages were built here. The Linton Hope-designed hull for the AD flying boat (serial number 1412) was also built here in mid-1915. The company also had works on Southampton Water.

The **Minchin Engineering Co. Ltd**, Penrhyn Road, Kingston, advertised their ability to supply 'complete units, undercarriages, spar boxes, empennages, elevators, rudders'.

Navarro Co. Southsea Road, Kingston on Thames. In July 1919 Mr J.G. Navarro was reported to have severed his connection with **Navarro Wellesley Aviation Ltd**, of Kingston upon Thames. In October 1920 **Navarro Aircraft & Automobiles**, designed the Navarro Bullet which featured a monocoque fuselage and bore a resemblance to the German Albatross.

Reid & Sigrist Ltd was formed in February 1928 had its Head Office at Shannon Corner, Kingston By-pass, New Malden. The RS1 Trainer (or 'Snargasher') was designed at New Malden. The main activities of the company were conducted at Desford, Leicestershire.

The **Swift Aeronautical Engineering Co.**, later the **Swift Aviation Co.** of 41-43 Richmond Road, Kingston on Thames advertised that they were 'specialists in Sopwith machines'. They appear to have been a parts supplier supporting the Sopwith factory, and other sub-contract producers.

Leyton

Shenstone & Co., Aircraft Department, Grange Road, Leyton, E10, advertised its capabilities as 'Aircraft production with modern methods'.

London (Central)

The following listing consists mainly of registered offices, and is complemented by a further list under 'City'. The list is not likely to be comprehensive and the information presented is often limited to the street address of the relevant office. Where relevant, advertising slogans are included to give some indication of the companies' business interests. **London (Central)** is bounded by Victoria, Marble Arch, Marylebone, King's Cross, Blackfriars (stations), and Embankment between Blackfriars Bridge and Vauxhall Bridge.

The Aero Mechanical Co. Ltd, of 60-66 Rochester Row, SW1, were advertising in December 1917 as: 'Contractors to the Air Board. Metal fittings a speciality. Complete DH6 fittings and dies in stock, also most fittings for DH4, DH5 and Handley Page. Our name has been built up by our ability to effect deliveries on time.'

Aeros Ltd, 39 St James's Street, Piccadilly, SW. In February 1913 this company was the British representative for Donnet Leveque hydro-aeroplanes. Franco-British Aviation (FBA) was registered in November 1913 to take over this role.

The Aircraft Company Ltd/The Aircraft Manufacturing Co. Ltd/AIRCO, 47 Victoria Street, London, SW, and (from December 1917) 27 Buckingham Gate, London, SW1. This company, founded by George Holt Thomas was the ancestor of The de Havilland Aircraft Co. Ltd. Its early business was based upon its being the British licensee for Farman aeroplanes. Flying operations were at Hendon, which see for further details.

In 1915 it was advertising:

> *Henry Farman biplanes and monoplanes of all types. Identical machines with those being delivered daily to the French Army. Maurice Farman biplanes, on which Officers are doing so much work in all sorts of weather. The Farman machines are easy to learn and easy to pilot after learning. Farman Hydro-Aeroplanes – The Finest.*

Aircraft Consolidated Ltd, of 97 New Bond Street, W1, was registered in September 1918. Nothing else is known.

The Aircraft Disposal Co. Ltd, Regent House, Kingsway, London WC2 (later known as ADC Aircraft Ltd). This company was formed by Handley Page Ltd to take over and manage the resale of surplus aircraft, engines and components purchased from the Government at the end of the First World War. Initially the company had a major depot in Regent's Park, before centring its operations at Waddon, Croydon. For further details, see the entry for Croydon.

Aircraft Exchange & Mart Ltd of 7 Park Lane, W1, had its origins with Light Aircraft Ltd, and was a distributor rather than an aircraft constructor. The company operated from Hanworth, and acquired the interests of the **Hendy Aircraft Co.** which it later sold to **Parnall Aircraft Ltd.** It was advertising in July 1935 as sole concessionaires for the Blackburn B2, Monospar and Hendy Heck. The company also acted as distributor for the Airspeed Courier. A further slogan from 1936 was, 'We sell, buy, exchange all types of aircraft, aero engines, accessories and instruments. Sole concessionaires for Parnall Heck, Blackburn B2 Trainer, Aeronca Aircraft.'

The Aircraft Supplies Co., of 17 John Street, Theobald's Road, London, WC, advertised, 'Every metal part for aircraft of all kinds supplied.' See also **M&L Aviation Works**, below.

Airwork Ltd, 15 Chesterfield Street, London, W1. In September 1954, it was announced that Airwork Ltd had been appointed to carry out storage, overhaul, maintenance and repair of RCAF Canadair Sabre aircraft in service in Britain. The company also operated at Heston, Hurn, St Davids, Pembrokeshire, and at many other locations around Britain.

The Alliance Aeroplane Co. Ltd, 45 East Castle Street, London W1 and Cambridge Road, Hammersmith, and Noel Road, Acton: 'Contractors to Ministry of Munitions of War Air Board'. For further details, see the entries for Acton and Hammersmith.

Sir W.G. Armstrong, Whitworth & Co. Ltd, 8 Great George Street, Westminster (and Newcastle). Later to be merged with the interests of John Siddeley to form Sir W.G. Armstrong Whitworth Aircraft Ltd.

Associated Aircraft Ltd of 97 New Bond Street, W. This company was registered in November 1917 as 'manufacturers of and dealers in aircraft and components'.

The Austin Motor Co., (Head Office) 479 Oxford St, W1. The main operational activities of the company were conducted at Longbridge, Birmingham.

Aviation Traders Ltd operated from a number of addresses including 21 Wigmore Street, W1; 15 Great Cumberland Place; and Portland House, Stag Place, SW1. The main operational activities of the company were conducted at Southend and Stansted.

A.V. Roe & Co. Ltd used a number of business addresses in London, including: Avro House, 44a Dover Street, W1; aircraft works, Newton Heath; experimental works Hamble (early 1920). The office address in October 1920 was 166 Piccadilly, W1 (The Royal Aero Club). Additional addresses: 1 West Halkin Street, Belgrave Square, W1; and 18 St James' Square, W1 (as part of Hawker Siddeley).

British Aircraft Corporation Ltd (**BAC**), 100 Pall Mall, SW1. BAC was formed on 12 January 1960 by merging the aviation interests of **The Bristol Aeroplane Co. Ltd**, **The English Electric Co. Ltd**, **Hunting Aircraft Ltd** (BAC taking a controlling interest) and **Vickers Ltd**. The operating subsidiaries when BAC was formed were **Bristol Aircraft Ltd**, **English Electric Aviation Ltd** and **Vickers-Armstrongs (Aircraft) Ltd**. (Note that other dates for the formation of BAC are quoted, including 1 January 1960, February 1960, and 1 July 1960.) Hunting Aircraft Ltd was fully absorbed into BAC from 1 January 1964, but was closed in December 1966, Jet Provost work moving to Warton. Control (as of 1971) was split as follows: GEC Ltd 40%, Vickers Ltd 40% and Rolls-Royce 20% (Rolls-Royce having acquired The Bristol Aeroplane Co. in 1966). The corporate offices in London were those previously occupied by **Vickers-Armstrongs (Aircraft) Ltd**. BAC's main operating sites were at Filton, Hurn, Luton, Preston, Samlesbury, Warton, Weybridge and Wisley.

Barker & Co. Ltd, of 66-68 South Audley Street, W1, is listed in *The Aviation Pocket-Book, 1919-1920* as an aeroplane manufacturer with propeller branch.

BAT (British Aerial Transport Co. Ltd), of 38 Conduit Street, London W1 was founded by Sir Samuel Waring in June 1917 with offices at 90 Cannon Street, EC, experimental works at 5a Hythe Road, Willesden, London, NW10, and flying from Hendon. See Hendon and Willesden for further details.

Beagle Aircraft Ltd (British Executive & General Aviation Ltd), 75 Victoria Street, SW1, also (November 1961) Sceptre House, Regent Street, London, W1. This company was formed on 7 October 1960 and was a subsidiary of Pressed Steel Ltd. Beagle produced two main designs: the Beagle 121 Pup, and the twin-engine Beagle 206. Beagle's main operating bases were Rearsby and Shoreham.

Beardmore Aero Engineering Co. Ltd; Beardmore Aero Engines Ltd; William Beardmore & Co. Ltd: offices at 36 Victoria Street, London SW1 and 112 Great Portland Street, W1. Manufacturing locations at Dalmuir and Inchinnan.

Benoist Aeroplane Co., of 54/55 Piccadilly, W. This American company built early flying boat designs. The British licensee was R.F. Wells & Co. of Chelsea.

F.W. Berwick & Co. Ltd, of Park Royal, London, NW10, and 18 Berkeley Street, W1, advertised as 'Aeroplane and Aero Engine Manufacturers to the Air Board'. The main production types were the DH4, DH9 and DH9A. Aircraft were delivered to the No.2 Aircraft Acceptance Park at Hendon for testing. The company also made the ABC Dragonfly engine and were 'proprietors and manufacturers of the Sizaire-Berwick Car'. For production details, see Park Royal.

Blackburn. The following addresses provided the London offices of the various incarnations of the Blackburn concern, whose main production facilities were in Leeds, Brough, Dumbarton and Sherburn-in-Elmet.

Blackburn & Co., 1-3 Stephen Street, Tottenham Court Road, London, W. Offices and warehouse (November 1916).

Blackburn Aeroplane & Motor Co. Ltd, Amberly House, Norfolk Street, Strand WC2. (1923 through the 1930s).

Blackburn Aircraft Ltd, Stafford House, Norfolk Street, London SW2. The company announced the transfer of offices to 11 Upper Grosvenor Street, London, W1, on 22 March 1946.

Blackburn & General Aircraft Ltd, 42 Berkeley Square, W1.

Blériot Ltd, 53-54 Long Acre, London, WC2. The main activities of **L. Blériot Aeronautics**, **Blériot & SPAD Manufacturing Co.** and **ANEC** were conducted at Fairoaks/Addlestone.

Louis Blériot Aeronautics, Belfast Chambers, 156 Regent Street, W1, and at Brooklands/Weybridge. This company was later to become **ANEC**, via an intermediate stage as **Blériot & SPAD Manufacturing Co.** Another clearly related firm was **Blériot Manufacturing Aircraft Co. Ltd**, of Clun House, Surrey Street, Strand. This company was in breach of its registration when it failed to publish its results in May 1915, and paid just over 15/- in the pound in liquidation in January 1919.

John Brinsmead & Sons Ltd, of 18-22 Wigmore Street, W1, is listed in *The Aviation Pocket-Book, 1919-1920* as an aeroplane manufacturer with propeller branch. The company is thought to have had additional works in Hampstead, as indicated by its telephone numbers: Mayfair 1243 & 3524, and Hampstead 6095.

The Bristol Aeroplane Co. Ltd, Bristol Aircraft Ltd, 6 Arlington Street, St James', SW1.

British Aerospace plc had its head office at 11 Strand, London WC2, this being later moved to Warwick House, Farnborough Aerospace Centre. Offices were retained at Brewers Green, Caxton Street, St James's. **BAE SYSTEMS** maintains offices at Stirling Square, Carlton Gardens.

British Aircraft Ltd, of 32 Charing Cross, Whitehall, was registered in September 1916 as 'Manufacturers and dealers in aeroplanes'.

British Breguet Co. of 1 Albemarle Street, Piccadilly, London, W, also had works and offices 5 Hythe Road, Cumberland Park, Willesden, NW. This company was established in 1912 and 'constructs Breguet models in England', these differing in their detailed construction from the original French designs. For further details, see Willesden.

The **British Wright Co. Ltd**, of 33 Chancery Lane, WC2, was set up in March 1913 by Mr Griffith Brewer, who was the first British person to fly (with the Wright brothers), and held the Wright United Kingdom patents. The company agreed a lump sum settlement with the Crown for the use of Wright patents, and then developed a business manufacturing aircraft flight instruments.

Britten-Norman Sales Ltd, 26 Dover Street, London, W1. The main business of the company was conducted at Bembridge, Isle of Wight.

R. Cattle of 27 Wybert Street, Stanhope Street, NW. This joinery firm and cabinet makers was advertising 'wood for use in aircraft construction' in May 1913, and 'spars, struts, and ribs to pass Government inspection' in March 1915. The amount of aircraft construction work undertaken during the First World War led to the decision by the firm to set up a new subsidiary, **The Central Aircraft Co.**, as indicated by the following announcement from November 1916: 'Owing to the large increase in aircraft business, this is now being conducted under the style **The Central Aircraft Co.**, Palmerston Works, 179 High Road, Kilburn.' For further details, see Kilburn and Northolt.

The Cierva Autogiro Co. Ltd, Bush House, Aldwych, WC2 and The Aerodrome, Hamble. The Cierva design team was located at Bush House during 1932. Development of new aircraft (e.g. Cierva C.19 Mk V) was carried out at Hamble with sales activity at Hanworth Air Park. After the Second World War, The Cierva Autogiro Co. Ltd began helicopter manufacture at Thames Ditton, and then at Eastleigh, Southampton, before being absorbed into Saunders-Roe Ltd.

H.C. Cleaver Ltd, of 35 Berners Street, W1, is listed in *The Aviation Pocket-Book, 1919-1920* as an aeroplane manufacturer. The company is also believed (based upon its telephone numbers) to have had works at Wembley.

Comper Aircraft Co. Ltd, 39 Grosvenor Place, London, SW1, and at Hooton Park, Merseyside and Heston, which see for further details.

Coventry Ordnance Works Ltd, 28 Broadway, Westminster. The main business of the company took place at Coventry, with flying operations at Brooklands.

Cravens Ltd, of 68 Victoria Street, SW1, is listed in *The Aviation Pocket-Book, 1919-1920* as an aeroplane manufacturer with propeller branch. The company is also believed (based upon its telephone numbers) to have had works in Sheffield.

Croydon Aviation & Engineering, Effingham House, Arundel Street, Strand, WC2. This business was acquired by **Croydon Aviation & Manufacturing Co. Ltd**, of 2 Gresham Buildings, Guildhall, EC in March 1919, with the considerable capital of £20,000.

John Dawson & Co. (Newcastle) Ltd: offices at 20 Victoria St, SW1; works at St Lawrence Road, Newcastle on Tyne.

Delacombe & Marechal of 166 Piccadilly, London, W, (The Royal Aero Club) held the sole rights in the United Kingdom for the sale and construction of Borel aeroplanes and hydro-aeroplanes. In July 1913, the company was advertising as 'Contractors to the Admiralty and War Office'. The company also advertised the Clement-Bayard single-seat armoured monoplane in 1914.

The British Deperdussin Aeroplane Syndicate used the address of 30 Regent Street, London, SW1 in July 1911 and moved to 39 Victoria Street, Westminster, in November 1912. The company works were at Holloway Road, N19. A final move (in liquidation) took place in October 1913 to Clun House, Surrey Street, Strand, WC. The company operated at Hendon, Brooklands, Highbury and Upper Holloway.

Dudbridge Iron Works Ltd had offices at 87 Victoria Street, SW1 and works at Stroud. The company was the sole United Kingdom agent for (and manufacturer of) Salmson engines, and was also a founder member of the SBAC.

G.M. Dyott, 1 East Chapel Street, Mayfair. This address was given when the Dyott Monoplane was offered for sale in December 1913.

The **East Anglian Aviation Co. Ltd**, of 26 Shaftesbury Avenue, built the Westlake Monoplane in 1913, the aircraft being flown at Clacton, Essex.

Engineering & Aircraft Construction Co. Ltd, 329 High Holborn, WC1. It is not known if this company, registered in late 1917, was successful. Its authorised capital of £5,000 suggests a reasonably serious enterprise, however.

The English Electric Co. Ltd, Queen's House, Kingsway, WC2, and Marconi House, Strand, WC2. Queen's House was used as a design office in the 1920s, after the company moved from its initial registered office at Abchurch Yard, EC. Marconi House was later re-named English Electric House. the company's main activities were conducted at Bradford, Preston, Samlesbury and Warton.

W.G. Evans & Sons, of 1-5 Williams Mews, Stanhope Street, Euston Road, London, NW1, was advertising in 1916 and 1917:

> *Wings & Ailerons, Tails and Rudders.*
> *You need only assemble the parts.*
> *WE MAKE THEM.*
> *Wood parts machined accurately for Fuselage, Chassis, etc.*

The Fairey Aviation Co. Ltd, of 175 Piccadilly, W1 and 24 Bruton Street, W1. C.R. Fairey (later Sir Richard Fairey) was active as Chief Engineer for the Short Brothers during their pioneering days, and set up **The Fairey Aviation Co. Ltd** on 15 July 1915 with 175 Piccadilly as its registered address. The company's main operating sites were Hayes, Hamble, Harmondsworth, Heston, Northolt, Heaton Chapel/Stockport and White Waltham.

Farringdon Engineering Co. Ltd, of 39 Victoria Street, SW1, is listed in *The Aviation Pocket-Book, 1919-1920* as an aeroplane manufacturer with propeller branch.

The Ford Motor Co. Ltd, Aircraft Department had its headquarters at 88 Regent Street, London, W1, and operated at Ford Aerodrome (Yapton) and Hooton Park.

Fraser's Flying School had offices at 64 Haymarket, SW1, and operated at Kingsbury Aerodrome. The company advertised, 'Among our machines is the famous Austin 'Kestrel'. Machines erected and tested.'

General Aeronautical Co. Ltd, of 30 Regent Street, SW1, was registered in May 1918, as taking over the company of the same name incorporated in 1914. The company aims on registration were to continue business as 'manufacturers and dealers in aeroplanes, parts thereof, and in particular propellers and airscrews'. It was also reported that this company took over the BAT Works after the end of 1919. The firm is listed in *The Aviation Pocket-Book, 1919-1920* as an aeroplane manufacturer with propeller branch.

W. Villa Gilbert & Co., of 7 Princes Street, Westminster, SW1, is listed in *The Aviation Pocket-Book, 1919-1920* as an aeroplane manufacturer.

The **Gosport Aircraft Co.**, had offices at 15 George Street, Hanover Square, W1, with its main operations conducted at Gosport and Southampton.

The Grahame-White Aviation Co. Ltd used the following addresses: March 1912 – 166 Piccadilly, (The Royal Aero Club); and from February 1915, 32 Regent St. The company advertised as 'Aeronautical Engineers and constructors. Contractors to the Admiralty and War Office'. By 1920, the company address was 12 Regent Street, Pall Mall, SW1. In 1911, **C. Grahame-White** had the address of 1 Albemarle Street, W1. The history of the Grahame-White concern is presented under Hendon.

Hall Aviation Co., 118 New Bond Street, W1, and at Hendon, see which for further details.

Handley Page, 72 Victoria Street, SW1; works at 110 Cricklewood Lane. The company was established at the end of 1908, becoming **Handley Page Ltd** in June 1909. For details, see Barking and Cricklewood. The company later established assembly and flight test activities at Radlett, Herts.

Handasyde Aircraft Co. Ltd, Carlton House, 110 Regent Street, W1. This company was formed by G. Handasyde and F.P. Raynham after the collapse of Martinsyde, but folded in turn in 1924. The company works were at Woking, Surrey.

Hart Aeroplanes & Waterplanes Ltd, of 6 Holborn Viaduct, EC, issued a prospectus in November 1912 to seek funds to exploit a new design of wing which was tested on a 35hp Blériot under the supervision of Grahame-White Aviation Co. Ltd. One of the directors was Howard Wright. See also Hendon.

Hawker Siddeley Aviation Ltd had office addresses at 18 St James' Square, W1; Duke Court, Duke Street, St James', SW1; and 55-56 Pall Mall, London SW1. The **Hawker Siddeley Aircraft Co.** was formed in 1935 and became, in the form of **Hawker Siddeley Aviation Ltd**, one of the 'big two' companies (the other being the British Aircraft Corporation) following the consolidation of the industry in the 1960s.

The contribution of the Hawker Siddeley companies to victory in the Second World War was enormous, with the combined production of the companies (Sir W.G. Armstrong Whitworth Aviation Ltd, Armstrong Siddeley Motors Ltd, Gloster Aircraft Co. Ltd, Hawker Aircraft Ltd, A.V. Roe & Co. Ltd, A.V. Roe Canada Ltd, Air Service Training Ltd and High

Duty Alloys Ltd) including more than 40,000 aircraft and over 38,500 engines; more than 11,000 aircraft were repaired. Peak annual aircraft production was 8,795 in 1943-1944. Between 1938 and 1944 factory space increased more than seven-fold and aircraft production increased from sixty per month to more than 600 per month.

For further details on the development of the company, please refer to the introductory chapter: Evolution of the Industry. The main operating sites of the company included Baginton, Bitteswell, Brough, Chadderton, Chester (Broughton/Hawarden), Dunsfold, Hamble, Hatfield, Hucclecote, Kingston upon Thames, Moreton Valence and Woodford.

Heaton Aldam & Co. of 156 New Bond Street, W1, is listed in *The Aviation Pocket-Book, 1919-1920* as an aeroplane manufacturer. Nothing further known.

Helliwells Ltd had headquarters at Kingsbury House, King Street, St James, SW1, and works at Walsall Airport.

Hewlett & Blondeau Ltd had offices at 55 St James' Street, SW1; and 77 King's Road, SW3, with works at Omnia Works, Vardens Road, Clapham Junction. The Omnia Works extended to nine acres. For further details, see Battersea, Clapham Junction and Hendon. The company also operated at Leagrave, near Luton, Bedfordshire, and at Brooklands, Surrey.

The **Highbury Aircraft Co.** of 1a & 45 Rosebery Ave, EC1, and 17-25 Laystall Street, EC1 is listed in *The Aviation Pocket-Book, 1919-1920* as an aeroplane manufacturer. Its advertising suggests a rather more restricted role, however: 'Manifolds, Cowlings and all classes of sheet metal work'.

Hooper & Co. had offices at 54 St James Street, London W1 and works at 77 King's Road, Chelsea. In December 1916 the company was advertising as 'Aircraft Contractors to the War Office' and 'Aeroplane Builders to HM Air Council'.

The heritage of the company was also made clear as follows: 'Royal Warrant coachbuilders', 'Motor body builders and coachbuilders to the King, Queen, Queen Alexandra, King of Spain, King of Norway. Coachbuilders to Queen Victoria and King Edward'.

The company was a significant manufacturer of Sopwith machines. For further details, including production quantities, see the entry for Chelsea.

Ikaros Aircraft & Manufacturing Ltd, of Effingham House, Arundel Street, WC2, was registered in September 1918. Nothing else is known.

C.F. Kearley Ltd, of 4 Gt Marlborough Street, W1, is listed in *The Aviation Pocket-Book, 1919-1920* as an aeroplane manufacturer with propeller branch. In addition to its London office, the company had other offices and works, to judge from its telephone numbers: Hammersmith 467, Gerrard 4412 and City 8742.

The Kingsbury Aviation Co. had offices at 175 Piccadilly, W. For further details see the entry for Kingsbury.

The **Lancashire Aircraft Corporation Ltd**, with offices at 11 Berkeley Street, London, W1, was a company which specialised in aircraft engineering and modification, and which operated a freight and charter airline based at Blackpool and elsewhere. It, together with its subsidiary Samlesbury Engineering Ltd, was involved in the development and production of the Edgar Percival EP9 as the Lancashire Aircraft Prospector.

Lane's British Aeroplanes Ltd, of 31 Foley Street, London, W1, built at least two successful monoplanes. The first, which resembled a Blériot with a biplane tail, was tested at Brooklands and Edinburgh, and was entered by H.J.D. Astley in the 1910 Dunstall Park meeting. A single-seat Farman-style biplane was also constructed in 1910.

W. Turner Lord & Co. of 20 Mount Street, W1, is listed in *The Aviation Pocket-Book, 1919-1920* as an aeroplane manufacturer. In addition to its central London office, it is assumed to have had works in North London, having the telephone numbers Gerrard 5273 and North 2454 (which indicates the Islington area).

Macfie & Co. Ltd, of Hampden House, Kingsway, WC, is listed in *The Aviation Pocket-Book, 1919-1920* as an aeroplane manufacturer with propeller branch. The company was registered in November 1915 and may have had connections with R.F. Macfie, who flew from Brooklands and Fambridge.

Mann, Egerton & Co. Ltd had offices at 379-381 Euston Road, N, and advertised as 'Manufacturers of proved efficiency of all types of aircraft'. The company had works at Norwich and, in November 1917, an accessories department at 177 Cleveland Street, London, W1.

Maple & Co., of 149 Tottenham Court Road, W1, is listed in *The Aviation Pocket-Book, 1919-1920* as an aeroplane manufacturer with propeller branch. Nothing else is known.

Martin Hearn Ltd had offices at 41 Oxford Street, London, W1, and works at Hooton Park, Cheshire. The company was involved in aircraft assembly and modification, and glider manufacture.

Martinsyde Ltd had offices at 17 Waterloo Place, Regent Street, SW1; an alternative address being given (in 1920) as Carlton House, 11d Regent Street, (Waterloo Place), SW1. Martinsyde Ltd conducted its flight test activities at Brooklands, Surrey.

Messenger & Co. Ltd, of 122 Victoria Street, SW1, is listed in *The Aviation Pocket-Book, 1919-1920* as an aeroplane manufacturer with propeller branch. Nothing else is known.

Metropolitan-Vickers Electrical Co. Ltd, 1 Kingsway, London, WC2. The company was contracted to build Manchester, Lancaster and Lincoln aircraft at Trafford Park, Manchester.

M&L Aviation Works Ltd, 17 John Street, Theobald's Road, WC1. This company was registered in September 1916 as 'Manufacturers and dealers in aeroplanes, seaplanes, airships and aircraft of all kinds, component parts, accessories and fittings'. The company shared its address with The Aircraft Supplies Co.

Morgan & Co. Ltd, of 10 Old Bond Street, W1, built more than 500 aircraft at their Leighton Buzzard factory.

Morrisons Engineering Ltd, **Morrisons Aircraft Services**. 'Morrisons – Croydon and Peterborough, Aircraft Construction, Maintenance and Repair.' Offices at 11 Upper Grosvenor Street, London W1.

D. Napier & Son Ltd, of 14 New Burlington Street, W1, built some 600 aircraft at Acton during the First World War. They are better known for their aero engine products, particularly the Napier Lion and Napier Sabre. The company operated at Acton and Luton (engine flight test department).

National Aircraft Manufacturing Co. Ltd, of 15 Drummond Crescent, Seymour Street, Euston Road, NW1, was registered in October 1917 to take over the business of **National Aircraft Manufacturing Co.** of 15a Hackney Road, London, NE. The company advertised: 'Aircraft components – planes, spars, struts, elevators, ribs, fuselages, nacelles, undercarriages, etc., etc. – assembly and erection.'

The **Navarro Aircraft Syndicate** had offices at 86 Gray's Inn Road, and at Burton upon Trent. A clearly related company, the **Navarro Aviation Co. Ltd**, of 5 Victoria Street, SW was registered with £35,000 capital in September 1918. The later **Navarro Safety Aircraft Ltd** (see Heston) designed the three-engine, three-seat Navarro Chief, which featured a radically unconventional control system. This company had offices at Finsbury House, Blomfield Street, London, EC2.

F.C. Nestler Ltd was registered in August 1913 at 49 Bond Street, London, W, with offices and works at 9 Greycoat Street, Westminster, SW. This company built the Nestler Scout, the new Nestler machine being reportedly under test at Hendon, flown by Mr J.B. Fitzsimons, in March 1917. The company advertised as 'Contractors to HM Admiralty and War Office, Aeroplane Manufacturers'; 'Aeronautical Engineers and constructors'; and 'Makers and patentees of Howard-Nestler collapsible Hangars' (this latter from November 1916).

Nieuport (England) Ltd, of 45 Gt Marlborough St., London, W1, was registered in November 1913 and advertised as 'Makers of all types of aeroplane: Armoured destroyers for fighting airships, fast monoplane scouts, two-seat military monoplanes, Nieuport Dunne biplanes'. **The Nieuport & General Aircraft Co. Ltd** operated from the same offices.

The Norman Thompson Flight Co. Ltd of Dewar House, 11 Haymarket, SW1, and Middleton on Sea specialised in the design and manufacture of flying boats.

Oakley Ltd of 28 Duke Street, Piccadilly (also quoted at 83 Regency St) built three Sopwith Triplanes at Ilford.

H. & D.J. Oyler Ltd of 35 New Cavendish Street, W1, were the constructors of the 1911 Fritz monoplane to the designs of Fritz Goetze. Trials were conducted at Brooklands.

Parnall & Sons had offices at 8 South Street, London, W1, and N. Circular Road, Neasden (the company's main production activities were conducted at Bristol and Yate).

Patey & Co. Ltd was initially registered in February 1917 at 4 Gt Marlborough Street, SW, and later at 45 Horseferry Road, SW1. The company aims on registration were to be 'manufacturers and designers of aeroplanes, automobiles, etc.' In August 1918 the company was advertising as: 'Contractors to the Air Board.'

Pegasus Aircraft Co. Ltd of Totterdown Street, Tooting, SW17, and 1 Albemarle Street, W1, used the grandiloquent slogan, 'The Cavalry of the Clouds', and were 'Designers and Manufacturers of Aeroplane Propellers'.

Percival Aircraft Co. Ltd was formed in 1933 at 81 St George's Square, London, SW1, later moving to other addresses which included: 20 Grosvenor Place, SW1 and 72 Chesterfield House, Curzon Street, W1. On 8 August 1934, the company was re-named **Percival Aircraft Ltd**. The company's main production activities were conducted at Gravesend and Luton.

E.G. Perman & Co., of 24 Brownlow Mews, Guildford Street, Grays Inn Road, London, WC1, was an offshoot of G.A. Puttnam and constructed at least eleven *Pou de Ciel*. This activity led to the development of the Perman Parasol, a single example G-ADZX being built. A further development of the Perman Parasol was the **Broughton Blayney** Brawny, three of which were built. Mr Broughton was an employee of Perman & Co. who had been involved in the production of the *Pou*, but the Brawney itself was built by T.H. Gill & Son of 75 Kilburn Lane, W10. See also Kensal Green, Heston (*Pou*) and Hanworth.

The Peterborough Aircraft Co. Ltd was an offshoot of The Aeronautical Corporation of Great Britain Ltd, and had London offices at 7 Park Lane, W1. The company had works in the former Sage factory in Peterborough and manufactured an Aeronca derivative, the Peterborough Ely.

Sydney Pickles and **Clifford B. Prodger** undertook freelance testing of all types of land machines and seaplanes. Trading as **The Sydney Pickles Aviation Co.**, the company office address was 166 Piccadilly, London, W (The Royal Aero Club). Initial advertising included 'official acceptance tests on all standard land machines and seaplanes a speciality' (1915/1916).

In 1917, the **Prodger-Isaac Aviation Co.** was formed (at the same address) to continue this work.

Official Acceptance Tests. Delivery and experimental flights, on land machines and seaplanes. Private aerodromes surveyed and pilots reports furnished. Special arrangements with sub-

contractors for Handley Page type land machines and 'America' type flying boats. Rates on application to The Prodger-Isaac Aviation Co. (C.B. Prodger & Bernard Isaac)

Clifford B Prodger, J Lankester Parker and other pilots. Approved. ADMIRALTY PILOTS for acceptance trials. INSURANCE: We are now in a position to quote low rates, through our brokers at Lloyd's, for the Insurance of Aircraft during Acceptance Trials and Delivery Flights with an excellent and most comprehensive policy. (November 1917).

Planet Aircraft Ltd of 29 Clarges Street, London, W1, were promoters of the unsuccessful Planet Satellite. The aircraft used magnesium alloy extensively in its construction and was advertised as 'embodying a major development in aircraft design and construction'.

Pobjoy Airmotors & Aircraft Ltd maintained a London office at 20 Berkeley Square, London, W1.

Power Jets (Research & Development) Ltd of 8 Hamilton Place, London, W1, and also at Whetstone, Leicester, was formed as a state-owned enterprise in 1944, taking over **Power Jets Ltd** and their research and development activities in the field of jet engine propulsion for aircraft.

W.A. Rollason Ltd, Terminal House, Grosvenor Gardens, London, SW1 – 'WA Rollason for aircraft services including maintenance, reclamation, sales and repairs'. The company operated at Croydon, Eastleigh, Hanworth, Redhill and Shoreham.

Rolls-Royce Ltd of 14-15 Conduit St, W1, is, of course, not an aircraft manufacturer. Rolls-Royce have, however, made such an important contribution to the development of the British aircraft industry that mention of their work is surely justified.

Rolls-Royce Ltd was registered on 16 March 1906, with works in Manchester and Derby; the Derby works were opened on 9 July 1908. Other main works were later established at Crewe and Glasgow in support of the expansion schemes prior to the Second World War. The Crewe works were set up as a shadow factory and delivered their first engine on 20 May 1939, eleven months after the start of factory construction.

The first aircraft engine produced was the Eagle (used by the Royal Aircraft Factory FE2D), this being followed by the Falcon which was used by the Bristol F2B Fighter. The 600hp Condor was intended for use by the Handley Page V/1500 and subsequently used in several inter-war types including the Horsley and Short Singapore.

The most significant family of Rolls-Royce piston engines originated with the Rolls-Royce F of July 1925. This engine was named Kestrel from 1931, and its development led, via the Buzzard, Rolls-Royce R racing engine and PV12, to the Merlin and Griffon.

The Schneider Trophy proved to be a huge stimulus for engine development. The Rolls-Royce R engine was developed under intense pressure from 1,545hp in May 1929 to 1,900hp by mid-September for the 1929 race itself. A balance of fuel chemistry, engine design, component development, carburation and supercharging resulted in a power level of 2,350hp being available from essentially the same engine when used in the 1931 competition.

More than 150,000 Merlin engines were built during the Second World War (including US production). A key contributor to the war effort, the Merlin-powered many types, including the Spitfire, Hurricane, Defiant, Battle, Fulmar, Halifax, Wellington, Whitley, Beaufighter, Mosquito, York, Lancaster, Mustang, Seafire and Barracuda. By 1944, Rolls-Royce had seven million square feet of factory space devoted to Merlin construction, with 350 companies acting as sub-contractors. Engine development flight testing conducted by Rolls-Royce is described under the entry for Hucknall.

In a post-war industrial coalescence almost mirroring that of the airframe sector, Rolls-Royce has emerged as almost the sole source of British aircraft engines, and Britain's component of a number of important international collaborations in this field. This is a story to be told elsewhere, perhaps.

The Ruffy School of Flying (later **Ruffy-Baumann Aeroplanes**, later **Ruffy Arnall & Baumann Aviation Co. Ltd**), had offices and works at 3-4 Kendall Mews, Portman Square, W1, and operated from the London Aviation Ground, Acton, which see for further details. Initial flying (from late 1914) was at Hendon, and then at Acton. In November 1917, the company was advertising 'Ruffy-Baumann. School Machines. Immediate Deliveries.' The firm was ultimately absorbed into The Alliance Aeroplane Co. Ltd.

Fdk Sage & Co. Ltd, of 58-62 Grays Inn Road, London, WC1, 'and at Peterborough, Paris (5 Boulevard des Italiens), Brussels, Buenos Aires, Valparaiso & Johannesburg'. The Sage company was an old established firm of shopfitters whose aircraft department was set up under the control of E.C. Gordon England. The company announced in January 1919 their return to shopfitting.

In the Second World War, the associated company **Fdk Sage & Co. (SA) Ltd**, shopfitters of Johannesburg, undertook the repair of Anson and Oxford airframes.

Saunders-Roe Ltd, had offices at Bush House, Aldwych, WC2 (1930), and also at 45 Parliament Street, SW1. In 1945, the company was advertising 'Supreme for Ocean Travel – The British Flying Boat. Saunders-Roe Ltd – Designers and Constructors of Large Flying Boats'. It is hard to think of a more concise description of the company's business. The company's main operating base was at East Cowes, Isle of Wight, with helicopters activities at Eastleigh.

Major J.C. Savage of 7-8 Norfolk Street, Strand, WC2, specialised in the adaptation of the SE5A for skywriting. In 1922, Major Savage was advertising 'Skywriting – each demonstration rivets the attention of everyone within an area of 100 square miles'. For further details, see Hendon.

Scottish Aviation Ltd had offices at 2 Cockspur Street, SW1 and 60 Buckingham Place, SW1. The company works was located at Prestwick.

The Selsdon Aero & Engineering Co. Ltd, of 1 Albemarle Street, London, W1, was advertising in August 1918 their ability to supply 'Engine components & parts, gun synchronizing gear, air, oil, water and petrol pumps'. The company is listed in *The Aviation Pocket-Book, 1919-1920* as an engine and parts manufacturer.

Shapland & Petter, of 62 Oxford Street, W1, is listed in *The Aviation Pocket-Book, 1919-1920* as an aeroplane manufacturer with propeller branch. The company probably also had works at Barnstaple in the light of their telephone numbers of Museum 1434 and Barnstaple 9.

Short Brothers (Rochester and Bedford) Ltd made use of a number of London addresses including: Whitehall House, 29/30 Charing Cross, SW1; 25 Cockspur Street, SW1; Berkeley Square House, Berkeley Square, W1; and 17 Grosvenor Street, W1. The main operational activities of the Short Brothers companies were conducted at the Isle of Sheppey, Rochester and Belfast.

Short Brothers (Rochester and Bedford) Ltd was formed under this title in June 1919, acquiring **Short Brothers Ltd**. Contemporary advertising ran: 'Contractors to HM Admiralty, Air Ministry and leading Governments of the world'. In 1946, the company advertising material featured the following copy: 'Shorts, established 1908, The First Manufacturers of Aircraft in the World'. London telegraphic address: 'Seaplanes, London'. The final manifestation of the company (prior to its acquisition by Bombardier Inc. in 1989) was **Short Brothers plc**, of 14 Queen Anne's Gate, SW1.

The Sopwith Aviation & Engineering Co. Ltd made use of 65 South Molton Street, W1, from February 1919, the premises being used as a show room for Sopwith-manufactured ABC motorcycles. Aircraft were constructed at Kingston upon Thames, and flown at Brooklands, Surrey.

The **Herbert Spencer** 1910 biplane, of boxkite configuration was built at 40 Sackville Street, London, W1, and tested at Brooklands. See also **C.G. Spencer & Sons Ltd**, Highgate.

Standard Aircraft Manufacturing Co. Ltd, of Effingham House, Arundel Street, London, WC2, and 28 Bow Common Lane, London, E3, advertised 'Aircraft and parts to official specifications' and as 'Contractors to the War Office'. Types and quantities are unknown, although the company is listed as an aircraft manufacturer in *The Aviation Pocket-Book, 1919-1920*. The firm was registered in May 1916, with capital of £100.

The **Standard Aviation Co. Ltd** of 39 St James's Street, London, SW1, was registered in July 1911 as 'manufacturers and dealers in aeroplanes'.

Staples & Co. of Chitty Street, Tottenham Court Road, W1, is listed in the *Flight* directory pages of December 1917 as an aeroplane manufacturer. Nothing else is known.

Sunbury Aviation Co. Ltd, of 32 Charing Cross, SW1, was registered with capital of £10,000 in May 1918. Nothing else is known.

The Supermarine Aviation Works Ltd had London offices at Donnington House, Norfolk Street, Strand, WC2, but conducted its main business at Southampton.

Tamworth, Hindley & Co., of 26 Buckingham Gate, SW1, is listed in *The Aviation Pocket-Book, 1919-1920* as an aeroplane manufacturer with propeller branch.

W.G. Tarrant, of Byfleet, had offices at Clock House, Arundel Street, WC2 and were the contractors for the construction of the giant Tarrant Tabor. In their advertising they, like many others, refer to their status as 'Contractor to the Air Board'.

Trollope, Son & Colls, of 77 Grosvenor Road, SW1, are listed in *The Aviation Pocket-Book, 1919-1920* as an aeroplane manufacturer with propeller branch. This company still exists and were very surprised to learn of their purported connection with aviation. Trollope & Colls Ltd (the present firm) did indeed have an office at 77 Grosvenor Road at the time, where there was a joinery shop. The company had, and retains, a reputation for fine joinery work and state that they could easily have made laminated wood propellers.

The **United Aircraft Co. Ltd**, of 4 Great Marlborough Street, W1, advertised in August 1918 as 'Contractors to the Air Board' and also had activities at Gosport, Hants, and South Road, Southall.

Vickers Ltd, Aviation Department, Vickers House, Broadway, SW1, and (from April 1916) Imperial Court, Basil Street, Knightsbridge, London, SW3. One of Britain's earliest aircraft manufacturers, Vickers were advertising in 1913 their test facilities and training school: 'Testing Ground Joyce Green, near Dartford. Aviation School Brooklands – thorough tuition from slow biplanes to fast monoplanes. Special terms to Naval and Military officers';

VICKERS LIMITED,

Contractors to the
WAR OFFICE & ADMIRALTY.

Aviation Department,
Imperial Court, Basil Street,
KNIGHTSBRIDGE, S.W.3

Telephone: No. 6810 Kensington (2 lines).   Telegraphic Address: Vickerfyts. Knights. London

'Contractors to the War Office and Admiralty'.

The company operated at many sites (and under a range of identities) before its absorption into the British Aircraft Corporation. Its most important operations were conducted at Blackpool, Brooklands/Weybridge, Chester (Broughton/Hawarden), Chilbolton, Crayford, Erith, Hurn, Joyce Green, South Marston and Wisley.

Waring & Gillow Ltd. This famous and long-established furniture manufacturer expanded into aircraft manufacture during the First World War at the instigation of Sir Samuel Waring. The company were keen to state their origins in their advertising, a typical example being: 'Furnishers and Decorators to HM the King. Contractors to the War Office and Admiralty. Aviation Department, Cambridge Road, Hammersmith, and 164-180 Oxford St'. For further details, refer to the entry for Hammersmith.

Wellesley-Brown Aircraft Ltd, of 23 Suffolk Street, Pall Mall, was registered with £5,000 capital, in September 1918. Nothing else is known.

Westland Aircraft Ltd and **Westland Helicopters Ltd** maintained London offices at 8 The Sanctuary, Westminster, SW1. The company's main operating base has been at Yeovil, Somerset, throughout the firm's existence. Other works include Weston-super-Mare, taken over from Bristol Helicopters; Hayes, taken over from Fairey Aviation; and Cowes, taken over from Saunders-Roe.

J. Samuel White & Co. Ltd maintained London offices at 28 Victoria Street, London, SW1, and conducted its main operations at Cowes, Isle of Wight.

White, Allom & Co. Ltd, of 15 George Street, Hanover Square, W1, is listed in *The Aviation Pocket-Book, 1919-1920* as an aeroplane manufacturer. The company was involved (through Sir Charles Allom and Sir Charles Nicholson, of Camper & Nicholsons) in the formation of the Gosport Aircraft Co. Ltd.

Whiteman Manufacturing Co. Ltd, of 15 Bateman Street, SW, was registered in January 1918, with capital £1,000, as 'Manufacturers and dealers in aeroplanes, airships, life saving devices'.

Wm Willett, of Sloane Square, SW1, is listed in *The Aviation Pocket-Book, 1919-1920* as an aeroplane manufacturer with propeller branch. Nothing else is known.

Wolseley Motors of Adderley Park, Birmingham, had London offices at York Street, Westminster, London, SW1. The company, which was best known for its car manufacture, was a subsidiary of Vickers Ltd and advertised as: 'Manufacturers of aero engines and aircraft'. Wolseley manufactured the Royal Aircraft Factory BE2 and SE5A during the First World War.

The **Worms Aircraft Construction Co.**, of 4 Sackville Street, Piccadilly, advertised 'complete metal and wood components for all types of aircraft' with works at Twickenham and Chelsea. In April 1918, the company changed its name to **Worms Aircraft Construction Co. Ltd**, with works at Bournemouth.

Howard Wright/Warwick Wright Ltd, Battersea Railway Arches, and 110 Marylebone High Street, NW1. This firm was originally a partnership between Howard Wright and J.T.C. Moore Brabazon, which was set up on 28 November 1906 for motor car construction, with a workshop at Battersea, underneath the arches of the London, Brighton & South Coast Railway. In 1907 aircraft construction was started, with the designers being Howard Wright and W.O. Manning.

Warwick Wright Ltd was taken over by **The Coventry Ordnance Works** (COW) at the end of 1911 with COW aircraft being tested at Brooklands.

Maylands (Romford)

This airfield was the home of Hillman Airways and is described by Harald Penrose as 'merely a big field'. The ultimate fate of the airfield was to be converted into Maylands Golf Course.

Gordon Dove – this pretty single-seat monoplane was strongly reminiscent of the Tipsy S2. Three aircraft were built in 1937, with the later aircraft having a modified undercarriage. The construction was undertaken by **Premier Aircraft Constructions Ltd** at Harold Wood. The Dove prototype G-AETU was first flown on 3 March 1937.

Merton

It was reported in June 1913 that **The Aircraft Manufacturing Co. Ltd** (AIRCO) had acquired the Merton skating rink (High Street, Merton) for the construction of Farman aircraft. AIRCO operated from The Hyde, Hendon, but the catalogue of the Aero & Marine Exhibition at Olympia in March 1914 refers to The Aircraft Manufacturing Co. of 47 Victoria Street, London, SW, as having works at Hendon and Merton. A subsidiary company, **Airships Ltd** was formed in February 1914 and was also based in Merton.

Mortlake and Kew

The **Glendower Aircraft Co. Ltd** of South Kensington built a factory at Mortlake Road, Kew, on land originally used for market gardening. The majority of the aircraft built were delivered directly to store. These comprised 101 AIRCO DH4, and a number of Sopwith Salamander aircraft from an order for 100 aircraft. Robertson indicates that twenty-two aircraft were completed, but information from Barry Abraham suggests that a total of fifty were delivered to store. Eight DH4A cabin conversions were also completed.

After the failure of the company, its Kew works were used by the car industry, initially by the Maxwell Motor Co., and subsequently by the Chrysler-Dodge Co.

The **Mortlake Aircraft Co. Ltd**, of 37 Sheen Lane, Mortlake, was registered at the end of October 1917, replacing the **Mortlake Aircraft Co**. Nothing else is known.

North Finchley

The Whitworth Engineering Co. Ltd, High Road, North Finchley, London, N12. When registered, this company described its activities as: 'Manufacturers of aircraft for all purposes, pleasure cars, commercial vehicles, and gas producers for lorries'. Nothing else is known. See also South Kensington.

Northolt

In February 1912 negotiations were in hand for an aerodrome at Northolt of 260 acres extent. The aerodrome was opened as the Central Aircraft Aerodrome in July 1919.

The mighty 300hp **Alula** wing Semiquaver G-EAPX was flown here on 27 August 1921, the aircraft having been assembled at Addlestone. See also **The Varioplane Co. Ltd** and **The Commercial Aeroplane Wing Syndicate Ltd** of Gresham Street, City of London.

The Central Aircraft Co. This firm, formed in September 1916, was a subsidiary of **R. Cattle**, a joinery firm of 27 Wybert Street, Stanhope Street, London, NW. Central Aircraft had works at Palmerston Works, 179 High Road, Kilburn, NW6, and was advertising in November 1917: 'War Office & Admiralty Contractors. Planes, Ailerons, Elevators, Spars, Struts, Ribs, etc'.

The company set up the Central Aircraft Flying School at Northolt which advertised:

> *The fee for the whole course is £125, for which a pupil is guaranteed the Royal Aero Club's Certificate and not less than 10 hours actual flying.*

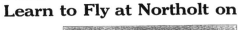

Learn to fly at Northolt on the machine which holds all training records. Special terms to qualified pilots requiring flying practice. The aerodrome is within a few minutes walk of Northolt junction (served by GWR Paddington and GCR Marylebone). It is also within a short walk of Ruislip station – Metropolitan Railway.

These advertisements were placed in January 1920, and were illustrated by photographs of Centaur IV aircraft G-EAHS and G-EABI.

The company used its own Centaur IV design for instruction, the type being a conventional tractor biplane of docile handling qualities. Central Aircraft's designer was A.A. (Tony) Fletcher, former assistant to George Handasyde, and previously with London & Provincial at Stag Lane. Eight Centaur IV were built in either two-seat or three-seat versions, all except the prototype (K-108/G-EABI) being powered by a 100hp radial engine.

Central went on to build two twin-engine, nine-seat machines. The first (Central Centaur IIA K-170/G-EAHR) flew in July 1919, but crashed in July 1920 due to crossed elevator cables. Although a second Centaur IIA G-EAPC was built and flown in May 1920, this also crashed fatally in September 1920. Central Aircraft built the Sayers-designed glider that competed in the 1922 Itford Hill Trials. On 18 March 1924, **The Central Aircraft Co. Ltd** was registered, but this had only a brief existence before the appointment of receivers in January 1927, and the subsequent closure of the firm.

The Fairey Aviation Co. Ltd carried out flight testing at Northolt prior to 1929, during which year they were given notice to quit. This forced the move of Fairey flight test activities to their own Great West Aerodrome at Harmondsworth. Fairey's initial use of Northolt was probably the flight testing of some of the 100 Sopwith 1½ Strutter aircraft built by Fairey Aviation. Other aircraft of this order were tested at Kingsbury, south of Stag Lane. The Fairey F.2 twin-engined fighter (RNAS serial 3704) was the first aircraft of Fairey's own design to be built. The F.2 was a three-bay biplane of 77ft wingspan, and first flew at Northolt on 17 May 1917. A selection of other Fairey aircraft to make their first flights at Northolt is given below:

- Fairey IIIA: first production N2850, first flown on 6 June 1918. Fifty were ordered but many were delivered straight to store.
- Fawn J6907, first flown on 8 March 1923.
- Ferret N190, first flown on 5 June 1925. Only three examples built, but notable as the first all-metal aircraft to be built by Fairey.
- Fox I: first production aircraft J7941, and first flown on 10 December 1925.
- Fairey IIIF: prototype N198, and first flown on 19 March 1926. The first ten IIIF were produced as production line conversions from the Fairey IIID, the first true production IIIF S1168 flying on 18 February 1927. The first IIIF Mk II was flown at Northolt on 18 August 1927.
- The private venture Curtiss D-1-powered Firefly I biplane was first flown at Northolt on 9 November 1925. The Firefly I was essentially a single-seat fighter equivalent of the Fox.
- The Fairey Long Range Monoplane was a clean cantilever design with a wingspan of 82ft. The first of two built, J9479 was first flown at Northolt on 14 November 1928, although it is reported to have just became airborne during taxi trials on 30 October 1928. This aircraft was successfully flown non-stop to Karachi, a distance of 4,130 miles, but crashed on 16 December 1929 during a second record attempt, killing the crew.
- The Firefly I was followed by the Firefly II, another private venture prototype designed to meet specification F.20/27; this being flown on 5 February 1929. Further development led to the all-metal, Rolls-Royce F.XIS (Kestrel IIS)-powered, Firefly IIM, which was flown on 6 January 1930. This aircraft was later registered as G-

The Fairey Fawn was a day bomber for the RAF, derived from the Pintail amphibian. The type first flew in 1923. (Ken Ellis Collection)

ABCN. (See also Hayes and Harmondsworth for details of Firefly II production at Hayes and in Belgium). The last private venture prototype of this series was the single naval Firefly III which competed against specification N.21/26. The unregistered prototype was first flown on 17 May 1929 and later received the civil registration G-ABFH and the military serial S1592.

- The single Fleetwing N235 (an unsuccessful competitor to the Hawker Osprey against specification O.22/26) was first flown on 15 May 1929. The Fleetwing was a most elegant sesquiplane.
- The first Fox IIM, J9834, was first flown at Northolt on 25 October 1929. Having competed unsuccessfully with the Hawker Hart against specification 12/26, the Fox II was then offered for export, attracting significant orders (and production) in Belgium. For further details, refer to the entry for Harmondsworth.

Northolt was still used intermittently by Fairey Aviation after the Second World War, examples of such use being the first flights of the first production Gannet WN339 on 9 June 1953, and of Gannet T. Mk 2 WN365, on 16 August 1954.

Kennedy Aeroplanes Ltd. The Kennedy Giant was designed by J.S. Mackenzie Kennedy and built by The Fairey Aviation Co. Ltd and The Gramophone Co. (later to become HMV). Kennedy had worked in Russia with Igor Sikorsky, and the Kennedy Giant was much influenced by Sikorsky's ideas for large aircraft design and construction. The Giant was powered by four 200hp Salmson radial engines and was erected in the open, there being no hangar in the country large enough to house it. This edifice had a wingspan of 142ft and was 80ft long. It is believed to have only 'hopped' once in late 1917.

Martin–Baker Aircraft Co. Ltd. The Martin-Baker MB1 G-ADCS was first flown at Northolt during March 1935. The company's main operating base is Denham, Bucks, with other activities (past and present) at Wing, Buckinghamshire; Harwell, Oxfordshire; and Chalgrove, Oxfordshire.

D. Napier & Son Ltd. The Napier Experimental Engine Installation Unit was based at Northolt (convenient to the company's Acton factory), but moved to Luton from Northolt in 1940.

The sole example of the Martin-Baker MB1 was flown at Northolt in March 1935. The company later produced superlative fighter prototypes before becoming the world's best known supplier of aircraft ejection seats. (Martin-Baker)

Park Royal

Claude **Grahame-White** used the abandoned Royal Agricultural Society showground at Park Royal as the starting point for his famous race from London to Manchester with Louis Paulhan. Grahame-White first took off on 23 April 1910, but this attempt ended in an accident at Lichfield. A second attempt from the same site began on 27 April, leading to a close and dramatic race which was eventually won by Paulhan.

The Park Royal site was immediately to the north of the Aviation Ground later established at Acton, on the opposite side of the A40, in the area now occupied by the Northfield Industrial Estate.

F.W. Berwick & Co. Ltd, of Park Royal, London, NW10, and 18 Berkeley Street, W1, were advertising vacancies in October 1917. The company were 'Aeroplane and Aero Engine Manufacturers to the Air Board', the main production types being the AIRCO DH4 (100 from B2051), DH9 (180 from orders for 230) and DH9A (at least 140 aircraft from an order for 170). The aircraft were delivered to the No.2 Aircraft Acceptance Park at Hendon for testing. The company also manufactured the ABC Dragonfly engine and were 'proprietors and manufacturers of the Sizaire-Berwick Car'.

The **Park Royal Coach Works Ltd** formed part of the **London Aircraft Production Group** during the Second World War, and were responsible for the manufacture of outer wings and engine cowlings for the 710 Halifax aircraft constructed by the group. These aircraft were assembled, test flown and delivered from Leavesden.

Pimlico

Mann & Overton, coachbuilders of 15 Commercial Road, Pimlico, SW1, displayed a monoplane of Santos Dumont configuration at the 1910 Olympia show. This aircraft was tested at Dunstall Park, Wolverhampton, in late 1910.

Prestige & Co. Ltd, of Cambridge Wharf, Grosvenor Road, SW, is listed in *The Aviation Pocket-Book, 1919-1920* as an aeroplane manufacturer with propeller branch. Nothing else is known.

Richmond

The **DFW German Aircraft Works**, of Streatham Hill, SW, promoted its 'Works at Richmond, flying from Brooklands'. It was announced in May 1914 that it was intended that the works should begin the British manufacture of the DFW design from 1 July 1914. The outbreak of the First World War prevented these plans from coming to fruition.

L. Howard Flanders Ltd opened works at Richmond in March 1912, at 31 Townshend Terrace, Sheen Road. Richmond, Surrey, advertising: 'Flanders monoplanes and biplanes for land or water. L. Howard Flanders Ltd.' A series of monoplanes and biplanes were built, these aircraft being test flown at Brooklands.

PDV Aircraft Spares, Princes Street, Richmond: although this company is listed as an aeroplane manufacturer in the *Aviation Pocket-Book 1919*, it seems to have been mainly a components business to judge from its name and its advertising.

Whitehead Aircraft Co. Ltd, of the Old Drill Hall, Townshend Road, Richmond, and Lily Road, Fulham, advertised as: 'Aeroplane Manufacturers, Contractors to HM Government'. The company was founded in May 1915 and was advertising vacancies in that month. A summary of the aircraft built by this important manufacturer at Richmond and Feltham is as follows:

Type	Comments
BE2a/b	Six aircraft; the first, serial number 2884, being completed in November 1915.

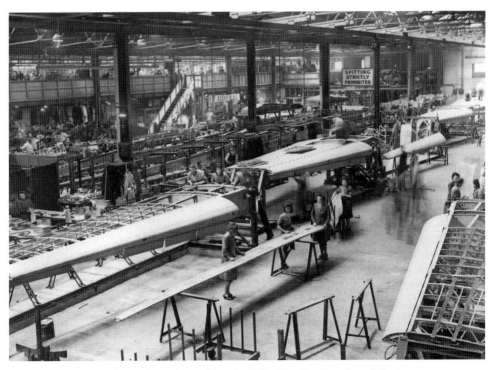

Halifax outer wing production by Park Royal Coach Works. (Handley Page Association)

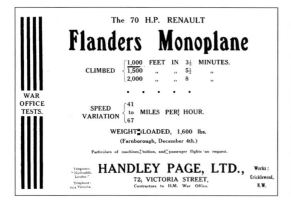

Type	Comments
MF.11 Shorthorn	100 aircraft built at Richmond; the first being A2176.
Sopwith Pup	Orders received for 820 machines; the first being A6150. The precise number completed is not clear as many of the later batches were completed as spares.
SE5A	An order for 100 aircraft was placed but cancelled.
DH9/9A	500 aircraft, made up of 100 DH9 and 400 DH9A.

In 1916, the company was taken over by **Whitehead Aviation Construction Co. Ltd** (which was registered in April 1916), to be absorbed in turn by **Whitehead Aircraft (1917) Ltd.** Following disputes, the company entered a claim on the Government in excess of £400,000. A petition for the winding up of the company was lodged in June 1919 and the company went into liquidation as a result of an extraordinary general meeting held on 11 July 1919. Its founder, Mr J.A. Whitehead of Hanworth Park House, Feltham, subsequently found himself in Bankruptcy Court facing contingent liabilities in November 1920.

Whitfield Aviation Ltd, of 14 Paternoster Row, EC, and 10 Dane Street, High Holborn, WC (offices), was registered in September 1918 and reported in November to be acquiring Pulvo Engineering Co. Ltd. The address of the works was given in March 1919 as Friars Lane, Richmond, Surrey.

STANLEY PROPELLERS
BY THE STANLEY AVIATION CO.
Telephone:
CITY 8347.
:: 67, Kingsland Road, London, E. 2. ::
GOVERNMENT CONTRACTORS.

Shoreditch and Surrounding Area

Brown Brothers Ltd, of Great Eastern Street, EC2, advertised their ability to deliver 'Metal fittings for aircraft – RE8, BE2d, FE8, FE2b, DH4, etc.' In October 1917 they were offering: 'Sopwith F1 fittings, immediate deliveries.' The company is listed in *The Aviation Pocket-Book, 1919-1920* as an aviation accessories supplier.

B. Cohen & Sons Ltd, of 1-19 Curtain Road, EC2, is listed in *The Aviation Pocket-Book, 1919-1920* as an aeroplane manufacturer with propeller branch. Their own advertising suggests that they were propeller specialists and in late 1918 they announced their return to furniture manufacture. That this was the original nature of their business can be inferred from their telegraphic address – 'Sideboard, London'.

The London Aviation Co. Ltd had its Head Office and Works at 24, and 27-30 Charlotte Road, Great Eastern Street, EC2, with a dope shop at 96 Old Street, EC; other works were at New Inn Yard, Shoreditch and 126 Gossett Street, Bethnal Green, EC2. The company advertised in December 1916 as 'Manufacturers of Aircraft'; and 'Contractors for all descriptions of Aeroplane woodwork, planes, nacelles, fuselages, etc.' Another attribute was the company's 'Special facilities for handling large contracts'.

The **National Aircraft Manufacturing Co. Ltd**, of 15 Drummond Crescent, Seymour Street, Euston Road, NW1, and Printing House Yard, 15a Hackney Road, London, NE, was run by Mr F. Norman, who had flown the Scottish Aviation Caledonia monoplane in 1911. The company's advertising offered a comprehensive capability, including (in November 1916) the following: 'Aircraft components – planes, spars, struts, elevators, ribs, fuselages, nacelles, undercarriages, etc., etc. – assembly and erection'; 'Aircraft components in wood and tube work. Planes, Empennages, Fuselages, Nacelles, Struts'.

The **South Wales Aviation Works Ltd**, of 141 Curtain Road, EC, was formed in May 1918 with the limited capital of £100. The company had the same address as the **Thames Aviation Works** (Burtons Ltd), see below.

The **Stanley Aviation Co.** had addresses at Chatham Place, Morning Lane, Hackney, E9; Stanley Works, Langton Road, Cricklewood; and 67 Kingsland Road, E2 (Shoreditch). This company was registered in April 1916 and was advertising as 'Government Contractors' in July 1917. Other advertisements running through to August 1918 refer to the company as 'Manufacturer of Stanley Propellers' and supplying: 'Propellers, fuselages, planes, rudders, fins, skids, etc'.

The **Thames Aviation Works (Burtons Ltd)** of 141 Curtain Road, EC2 (Shoreditch) was registered in April 1917. This was clearly a significant enterprise involving as it did three sawmills, and six other works. In October 1917 the firm was advertising employment vacancies. The text of one of its contemporary advertisements ran: 'Three years experience, Constructors of complete aircraft.' One of its slogans ran, rather charmingly: 'Specialities – Big Stuff and Best Work.'

The company address changed to London Fields Station (Great Eastern Railway), Hackney, E8, and it appears literally to have occupied the station buildings. This can be inferred by the announcement of a further change of address in April 1919, the company moving to 30A Highgate Road, NW5 'as a result of London Fields station being re-opened'.

Southall

The **United Aircraft Co.**, of 4 Great Marlborough Street, W1, was advertising in August 1918 as 'Contractors to the Air Board'. In addition to its head office, the company indicated that it also operated at Gosport, Hants, and at South Road, Southall.

South Hampstead

Cierva Rotorcraft Ltd, 265 Finchley Road, South Hampstead, NW3 (company address in 1968). This company was formed to construct and develop the Rotorcraft CRLTH-1 Grasshopper III at Redhill Aerodrome.

The **Frank Hucks Waterplane Co. Ltd**, of 2 Adelaide Road, Hampstead, NW, was established in 1912 and merged with **Eastbourne Aviation Co.** to form **Eastbourne Aviation Co. Ltd** in early 1913.

South Kensington and Knightsbridge

The **Glendower Aircraft Co. Ltd**, of 3 Glendower Place, South Kensington, was registered in November 1916. The company telegraphic address was 'Glenacelle'. Subsequent company addresses, all in South Kensington, included 54 Sussex Place, Queensbury Mews, and 12-14 Harrington Road. The company is also reported to have had premises at Kew, North Sheen and Mortlake. In May 1917, the company was advertising as 'Manufacturers of Aircraft, Contractors to HM War Office'. Other advertising from 1917 catalogued the following capabilities and experience: 'Aircraft Manufacturers, Contractors to the Air Board'; 'Contractors to HM Air Ministry'; and 'Manufacturers of aircraft and seaplanes of all descriptions'.

In February 1918, Glendower announced that they had acquired eleven acres of land three miles from South Kensington on which they were erecting a large factory. The company also advertised as part of 'The "Entente" Companies' which comprised **The First British International & Aerial Navigation Co.**, **Glendower Aircraft Co. Ltd**, and **The**

Whitworth Engineering Co. Ltd, of High Road, North Finchley. The Entente Companies supplied everything 'from the smallest nut to the finished machine'. Glendower Aircraft Co. Ltd built 101 DH4, the first being F2633, supplying all but the wings and ailerons. Further production included about twenty-two Sopwith TF2 Salamander from an order for 100; the company also being responsible for eight DH4A cabin versions, the first being F5764. In 1919, Glendower took over the **Sceptre Aviation Co.** By July 1920, the company had encountered financial difficulties and it ceased to trade shortly thereafter. See also the entry for Mortlake and Kew.

Kennedy Aeroplanes Ltd, of 102 Cromwell Road, South Kensington, London W7, were responsible for the design of the Kennedy Giant. For details, see Hayes and Northolt.

Nieuport (England) Ltd, of 28 Milk Street, EC, was registered in January 1914 and moved almost immediately (in February 1914) to 45 Marlborough St, South Kensington. The company listed its flying grounds as Hendon and Southampton (waterplanes). Mr G.M. Dyott was retained as pilot.

Vickers Ltd. The head office was at Imperial Court, Basil Street, Knightsbridge, London, SW3.

Stag Lane

The de Havilland Aircraft Co. Ltd, Stag Lane Aerodrome, Edgware: 'Contractors to the Air Ministry, Designers and manufacturers of "DH" aircraft.' Stag Lane became the production base of the new de Havilland company from 5 October 1920, and remained so during

Stag Lane at its earliest stages of development – an unbelievable contrast to the present day site. (BAE SYSTEMS)

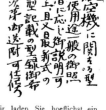

The aptly named Giant Moth dominates this Stag Lane scene. (BAE SYSTEMS)

The oldest de Havilland-built aircraft still flying is this DH51 Miss Kenya. (Author)

the heyday of the Moth, until production moved to Hatfield in 1934. Early advertising featured the slogan: 'During the War, over 30% of the total number of machines built for the British and USA forces were de Havilland aeroplanes.'

The DH18, six of which were built, marked the transition between AIRCO, at the Hyde, and de Havilland at Stag Lane. Construction of at least the first aircraft, G-EARI, was completed at the Hyde, and at least two fuselages were taken from the Hyde to Stag Lane and completed there. The DH18 flew in March 1920 and featured an enclosed passenger cabin ahead of the pilot's open cockpit, a configuration which de Havilland later returned to with the DH83 Fox Moth.

The de Havilland company started its occupation of the Stag Lane site with four huts on the aerodrome, one of these huts being preserved at Hatfield as the de Havilland museum. The de Havilland flying school was offering dual tuition in the DH6 for £6 per hour in 1923. The company was also advertising in *Flight* in no less than seven languages. The early business of de Havilland was dominated by the refurbishment of DH4 and DH9 aircraft for export sale, or for RAF use. In 1922 two DH27 Derby twin-engine day bombers were ordered, the first flying in September of that year, but de Havilland remained unable to obtain significant military orders for new designs. A summary covering the main types subsequently constructed in the de Havilland factory at Stag Lane is provided by the following table:

Type	First Flight	Prototype	Comments
DH34	26 March 1922	G-EBBQ	Ten-passenger biplane; twelve built.
DH50	30 July 1923	G-EBFN	Seventeen built in Britain: eleven in Australia, three in Belgium and seven in Czechoslovakia. Alan Cobham flew 28,000 miles to Australia and back in a DH50 G-EBFO between 30 June and 1 October 1926. Cobham had previously flown the same aircraft to Rangoon and back (during the winter of 1924/1925), and to Cape Town and back (winter 1925/1926).
DH53 Humming Bird	2 October 1923	G-EBHX	Single-seat light monoplane for the 1923 Lympne Trials initially powered by a 750cc Douglas motorcycle engine. Fifteen were built, eight of which served with the RAF.
DH51	1 July 1924	G-EBIM	90hp RAF 1A or 120hp AirdisCo-powered two-bay biplane, widely regarded as a key stepping stone toward the development of the DH60 Moth.
DH60 Moth	22 Feb 1925	G-EBKT	The aircraft that revolutionised private aircraft ownership – see additional comments below. Production (including prototypes and pre-series aircraft) comprised about eighty-eight Cirrus Moth, 394 DH60X, eighty-nine DH60M/60T, 595 DH60G Gipsy Moth and 146 Moth Major with the inverted Gipsy III engine. Additional production in Canada, Australia, United States of America, Norway and France.
DH66 Hercules	30 September 1926	G-EBMW	This three-engine airliner subsquently saw service throughout the Empire on the long distance routes of Imperial Airways, having been designed for the Cairo – Karachi route. Eleven were built.
DH61 Giant Moth or Canberra	6 December 1927	G-EBTL	Single-engine six-passenger biplane with the same configuration as the DH18 and Fox Moth. Eight built, with a further two aircraft not completed.

RAF Gipsy Moth K1217. (Ken Ellis Collection)

The Puss Moth was used for many notable long-distance flights. The type introduced a clean modern appearance and cabin luxury to the British light aircraft market. (Author)

The DH83 Fox Moth is represented here by a Canadian-built DH83C G-AOJH. (Author)

Type	First Flight	Prototype	Comments
DH71 Tiger Moth	24 June 1927	G-EBQU	Single-seat racing monoplane. Two only built. Set a 100km closed circuit speed record of 186.47mph on 24 August 1927. Initially flown with a Cirrus II, but subsequently used for development of the Gipsy engine.
DH75 Hawk Moth	7 December 1928	G-EBVV	High-wing four-seat monoplane initially flown with DH Ghost V8 engine. Eight production aircraft (DH75A and B) with increased power Lynx or Whirlwind radial engines and increased wing area.

The DH84 Dragon was originally designed to the specifications of Hillman Airways. This example, EI-ABI, is preserved by the airline Aer Lingus. (Author)

G-ACOJ is an immaculately restored DH85 Leopard Moth which wears markings originally allocated to a Parnall Peto. (Author)

This road sign, adjoining Stag Lane, almost seems to be a commentary on the fate of the British aircraft industry. (Author)

Type	First Flight	Prototype	Comments
DH80 Puss Moth	9 September 1929	E.1/ G-AAHZ	Clean high-wing monoplane; production designation DH80A. 285 built including twenty-five in Canada; initially advertised as the Moth Three at the high price of £1,000, a standard Gipsy Moth being available for £595. The type was much used for long distance flights. A typical Puss Moth slogan from 1930 was: 'High speed travel de luxe'.
Cierva C.24 Autogiro	September 1931	G-ABLM	Single example of this Gipsy-powered cabin Autogiro built by de Havilland.
DH82 Tiger Moth	26 Oct 1931	E.6, later G-ABRC	The standard RAF basic trainer of the Second World War. Production numbers are somewhat uncertain, with nearly 5,500 built in the UK from a total of some 8,800. Outside the UK, production was undertaken in de Havilland factories in Australia, Canada and New Zealand, together with licence production in Portugal, Norway and Sweden. An additional 420 aircraft were built as Queen Bee target drones.
DH83 Fox Moth	29 Jan 1932	G-ABUO	Ninety-eight built by de Havilland in the UK, two in Australia, and a further fifty-two in Canada, characterised by its pilot's cockpit to the rear of the four-seat passenger cabin.

Type	First Flight	Prototype	Comments
DH84 Dragon	12 November 1932	E.9/ G-ACAN	A twin-engine six-passenger biplane originally built for Hillman Airways. The aircraft became the mainstay of a growing regional airline business, a role later to be continued by the DH89. 115 built (some sources 114), with a further eighty-seven in Australia for RAAF use.
DH85 Leopard Moth	27 May 1933	E.1/ G-ACHD	A successor to the Puss Moth which it resembled, other than its revised undercarriage and more tapered wing platform. 132 built at Stag Lane and Hatfield (some sources state 133).
DH86 Express	14 January 1934	E.2, later G-ACPL	The DH86 ten-passenger transport biplane powered by four Gipsy Six engines was the last de Havilland type to fly for the first time from Stag Lane. The aircraft received its Certificate of Airworthiness only fifteen days after its first flight. Sixty-two DH86 were built in a number of versions.

Inextricably associated with Stag Lane, the prototype DH60 Moth G-EBKT first flew on 22 February 1925. The availability of the Moth led to the rapid expansion of the Flying Club movement, and of private aircraft ownership. The Moth offered outstanding performance, illustrated not only by its many long-distance flights, but also by such flights as the light aircraft altitude record of 17,283.5ft set at Stag Lane by Lady Bailey and Mrs de Havilland in July 1927 using a DH60X Moth. Many other notable flights were made in the type.

Perhaps even more fundamental to the type's success than its practical design and good handling was that it exploited the 60hp Cirrus engine designed by the great engine designer Frank Halford and based upon half the cylinders of an Airdisco V8 engine. Frank Halford had been involved in the design of the Beardmore Halford Pullinger engine which entered large-scale production as the Siddeley Puma. Having developed the ADC Cirrus and Nimbus he produced the Gipsy engine in 1927. Halford moved to Napier, developing the H-type Napier Rapier, the Dagger and the Sabre, becoming Napier technical director in 1935. In 1944 Halford returned to de Havilland Engines as technical director, taking responsibility for the Goblin, Ghost and Gyron.

Transition from the Cirrus to the Gipsy engine from 1928 further accelerated the success of the Moth. Ever seeking new records in the interest of publicity, Mr and Mrs de Havilland used Gipsy Moth G-AAAA to break the Cirrus Moth altitude record set twelve months previously, with a new figure of 19,980ft on 25 July 1928. Whilst it is not the purpose of this book to dwell on flying exploits, the name of the Moth is inextricably linked with those of its famous pilots, including Capt. Stack, Amy Johnson, Lady Bailey, Capt. Hope, Capt. Bentley, Francis Chichester, Winifred Spooner, J.R.D. Tata, C.W.A. Scott and Jim Mollison. This record-breaking heritage was subsequently handed down (often featuring the same pilots) to the later Puss Moth, Dragon and Comet Racer.

This replica of G-ABAA is displayed at the Brooklands Museum. (Author)

A list of privately owned machines was published on 30 June 1930, demonstrating the dominant position of the Moth. Of 288 machines, 172 (60%) were de Havilland Moth aircraft. In fact, the only other types to reach double figures were the Avian (twenty-one), Puss Moth (seventeen) and Bluebird (twelve). The Moth gained a dictionary definition as 'a light aeroplane'. The success of the Moth was an extraordinary achievement by any standard, particularly as the entire production run was completed in peacetime and was thus primarily dependent upon sales to civilian pilots.

In 1930, de Havilland advertising was justifiably triumphant, as shown by the following unparalleled text: 'DH MOTH – The best light aeroplane in the world'. 'Today the Moth is used by:

- Royal Air Force, Royal Australian Air Force, Royal Canadian Air Force, South African Air Force, Irish Free State Army Air Corps, New Zealand Ministry of Defence, Chilean Military Air Force, Italian Air Force, Danish Air Force and Naval Air Service, Greek Naval Air Service, Spanish Air Force, Portuguese Air Ministry Naval Section, Yugoslav Ministry of War and Marine, Romanian Ministry of War, Norwegian Ministry of Defence.
- By the governments of India, Sweden, Finland, Japan, Poland, France, Italy, China, etc.
- At the majority of flying clubs and schools in: Great Britain, Australia, Canada, India, South Africa, Kenya, Sweden, Poland, Singapore, Switzerland, Spain, New Zealand, Finland, Colombia, Yugoslavia, Austria, China, Portugal, Ireland, Dutch East Indies.
- For private and commercial flying in all of the above countries and: Argentina, Brazil, USA, Germany, Straits Settlements, Nigeria, Tanganyika, The Bahamas, Rhodesia, New Guinea, Belgium, Peru, Mexico, Jamaica, Fiji, etc.'

In 1924 Stag Lane was still completely rural. This is hard to believe today, the site having been developed for housing. De Havilland Road (which adjoins Stag Lane) is, rather poignantly, a no-through road. A plaque commemorating the use of the Stag Lane factory was unveiled on 25 September 2000, the 80th Anniversary of the foundation of The de Havilland Aeroplane Co. Ltd.

G&H Aviations Ltd built up two Avro 504K from spares at Stag Lane in 1930, these being registered G-ABAA and G-ABAB.

London & Provincial Aviation Co. were the original proprietors of Stag Lane airfield, the land for which they acquired during October 1915. The company trained 550 pilots during the First World War with no accidents during wartime. London & Provincial announced their decision to cease flying in July 1919, when the Department of Civil Aviation refused to license the firm's post-war designs for passenger work.

The company regarded this decision as contentious and publicly announced that it 'has ceased aeroplane work, and does not intend to begin again until such times as Air Ministry officials alter their views as to what constitutes a safe aeroplane. It is to be noted that no L&P machine has ever broken in the air, and that no accidents have ever happened owing to defective L&P machines.' The problem was caused by the company's proposal to use the obsolete 50hp Gnome engine to power their training types.

The company stock was put up for sale on 14 January 1920, this comprising of three L&P fuselage type aeroplanes with 50hp Gnome engines, and fifteen Caudron biplanes without engines. Directions were given to Stag Lane Aerodrome: 'situated on the main Edgware Road, adjoining Burnt Oak Farm and opposite the Bald-faced Stag Public House.' London & Provincial subsequently produced furniture and chocolate.

Stag Lane was sold for housing development for £105,000 in 1933 (except for fifteen acres of factory and offices retained for use by The de Havilland Engine Co. Ltd). The last flight from the airfield was made by a Hornet Moth in July 1934.

Stoke Newington

British Aircraft Manufacturing Co. of Imperial Works, Belfast Road, Stamford Hill, Stoke Newington, N16, advertised their ability to supply 'Tailplanes, components, elevators, fins and rudders'.

In July 1917 it was announced that the Works at Belfast Road, formerly of the British Aircraft Manufacturing Co. had been acquired, and would be run as **Lindley's Aircraft Component Works**, Belfast Road, Stamford Hill, Stoke Newington, N16.

The **Hurlingham Aircraft Co.** of 91C Dynevor Road, Stoke Newington, N16, was registered at the end of October 1917 as 'Manufacturers of aircraft, designers'. It was announced in December 1918 that the company was now to be known as **Gerrard Engineering Works Ltd**.

The unlucky Taylor Watkinson Dingbat G-AFJA has been the subject of a sequence of accident/rebuild cycles. (Air Britain)

The airframe of the unsuccessful Planet Satellite was constructed by Redwing Ltd at their Thornton Heath factory. (Ken Ellis Collection)

Streatham Hill

The **DFW German Aircraft Works** of 41 Christchurch Road, Streatham Hill, SW, was set up in 1914, an announcement made in May 1914 stating: 'Flying at Brooklands aerodrome, Offices Streatham Hill, Works under construction to start manufacture at Richmond from July 1914'. The DFW company negotiated a production licence with Beardmore, who also built its Austro-Daimler engine. The outbreak of the First World War brought these plans to an abrupt end.

Surbiton

R.F. Mann and R.P. Grimmer were responsible for the design of the **Mann & Grimmer** M1 in 1915. The company address was the Arlington Aeroplane Works, 15 Arlington Road, Surbiton. Initially the company specialised in model aircraft supplies, having been set up in 1911 by a schoolmaster and one of his students. By March 1913 Mann & Grimmer were advertising as 'Aeronautical Engineers and aeroplane manufacturers'. Test flying of the M1 was conducted at Hendon, which see for further details. Later, Grimmer set up **The Aircraft Construction Co.** in London E16.

Teddington

Clarence Aviation Ltd, of 56 Walpole Road, Teddington, was registered in January 1918, with capital of £2,150. Nothing else is known.

The **Taylor Watkinson** Dingbat was a single-seat low-wing monoplane constructed by C.W. Taylor and E.T. Watkinson of Cromer House, Hampton Road, Teddington. See Heston for further details.

Thornton Heath and Wallington (see also Croydon)

Robinson Aircraft Ltd, Stafford Road, Wallington. The first two Redwing, G-AAUO and G-ABDO, were built at Stafford Road, adjacent to Croydon Airport, before the company took up premises on the airfield itself. The company also operated at Croydon, Gatwick Airport and Colchester. The Stafford Road site, and others in the locality remained in use for an extended period by Robinson Aircraft and its successors.

After the completion of Redwing production, the **Redwing Aircraft Co. Ltd** continued in the aeronautical engineering sector, receiving large contracts as part of the RAF expansion programme. The main factory was located in Bensham Lane, Thornton Heath, with many other premises in use in the Croydon area, including Stewart & Arden's Garage in Bensham Lane. One significant contract was the manufacture of new-build spare parts to support Fairey Battle aircraft which were being transferred to the massive Canadian pilot training programme. Differences in detailed build standard between Fairey and Austin-built machines considerably complicated this activity.

With effect from 31 August 1944, the company name was changed to **Redwing Ltd**. Shortly after the end of the Second World War, all of the Redwing sites were closed with the exception of that at Bensham Works, 340 Bensham Lane, Thornton Heath, and the company offices at Redwing House, Stafford Road. By the end of 1949, the latter was also closed.

The last aviation-related activity of the company was the manufacture, on behalf of Magnesium Electron, of the radical and unsuccessful Planet Satellite, which was erected, but not flown, at Redhill Aerodrome in 1948. A letter to *The Aeroplane* questioned whether the aircraft's configuration would allow rotation to achieve take-off incidence, and this may have contributed to the aircraft's difficulties. The fuselage of the Satellite was later used to provide the airframe for the equally unsuccessful Firth FH.1 G-ALXP. This was a helicopter with twin laterally disposed rotors mounted at the tips of a high-wing.

In August 1957, the company was advertising: 'Redwing Service to Industry – Redwing Ltd have been approved contractors for 28 years, specialising in the manufacture of high strength magnesium alloys.' The eventual descendant of this series of companies was Gaskell & Chambers Ltd of Thornton Heath.

Tooting

The **Pegasus Aircraft Co. Ltd**, of Totterdown Street, Tooting, SW17, and 1 Albemarle Street, W1, used the advertising slogans: 'The Cavalry of the Clouds', and 'Designers and Manufacturers of Aeroplane Propellers'. Nothing else is known.

Tottenham

Harris Lebus Ltd, Finsbury Works, Tottenham, N17, were well-known furniture manufacturers. During the First World War, Harris Lebus contributed, with The British Caudron Co. Ltd, components for fifty Handley Page O/400 aircraft in the D8301-50 series; the aircraft being assembled by Handley Page Ltd.

The company was responsible during the Second World War for large-scale glider production (including the Horsa (1,271), Hamilcar, and Hotspur (more than 1,000)). The company managed a group of companies including: **Birmingham Railway Carriage & Wagon Works**, **The Co-operative Society**, **AC Cars**, **Slazenger**, **Peerless Furniture** and others. A similar consortium including **Harris Lebus**, **Wm Lawrence & Co.** and **Waring & Gillow** constructed some 600 General Aircraft Hotspur.

Air Commodore Allen Wheeler CBE, MA, FRAeS, gives a generous tribute to the work of the company in his book *That Nothing Failed Them*:

> One name that comes to mind immediately is Harris Lebus who personally directed every detail of the manufacture of the gliders his firm made, achieved an almost incredible rate of production, and always seemed able and willing to incorporate modifications on his production lines however much trouble it gave.

J.A. Prestwich & Co. Ltd of Northumberland Park, Tottenham constructed a Blériot-derived monoplane (known as the **JAP-Harding** Monoplane) for Mr H.J. Harding, with an engine of their own design. The aircraft was first flown at Tottenham on 10 April 1910, and is preserved today in the collection of The Science Museum, London.

Twickenham

Mike Beach, a well-known constructor of superlative replicas of early aircraft, and a restorer of vintage gliders, has a workshop at Twickenham.

The **Jouques Aviation Works**, of Gould Road, Twickenham, and Willesden, London, NW, manufactured the BE2b/c/e/g, constructing some fifty-six aircraft, the majority being BE2c. Its Willesden works were taken over by **BAT (British Aerial Transport Co. Ltd)** in 1917. Jouques were advertising vacancies for tracers in March 1915.

Perry Aviation Co., Gould Road, Twickenham. This was the style used by Perry-Beadle from Summer 1914 in association with such advertising as: 'British built flying-boats and aeroplanes'. The works were for sale in October 1914. The Perry-Beadle 45hp tractor biplane was built at Twickenham following the less successful Perry-Beadle flying boat, and was flying at Brooklands in June 1914. This aircraft was taken into RNAS service with Serial No.1322.

The **Worms Aircraft Construction Co.**, of 4 Sackville Street, Piccadilly, had works at Twickenham and Chelsea and advertised 'Complete metal and wood components for all types of aircraft'. In April 1918, the company changed its name to **Worms Aircraft Construction Co. Ltd** with works at Bournemouth.

Upper Holloway

The British Deperdussin Aeroplane Syndicate Ltd had works at Elthorne Road, Holloway Road, N19, in 1912-1913. Among its imaginative advertisements was the offer of a '£15 prize for any pupil obtaining Royal Aero Cub Certificate without breakage and damage to machines. Our Brooklands School is the safest and best organised monoplane school in England.' The company was reported to have more work on hand than they could tackle in July 1912, with twelve monoplanes being constructed on shift work.

The **Puttnam Aircraft Co. Ltd**, of Victory Works, 407-9 Hornsey Road, London, N19, was much involved in the Flying Flea craze and built G-AEEC. The company had links to S.V. Appleby and E.G. Perman & Co. and was registered on 11 March 1936. By April, it was promoting the PAC *Pou* as 'The Flying Flea with all the guesswork taken out of it'. The same advertisement added that 'every machine made by PAC is test flown and passed by Stephen V Appleby'. By August 1936, the company was in receivership.

Further details are provided under the entry for Heston.

Vauxhall

Adam Grimaldi & Co. of Albert Works, Glasshouse Walk, Albert Embankment, Vauxhall, SE11, advertised as 'Aircraft Manufacturers. Contractors to HM Government'. This firm manufactured the fuselages of the enclosed DH4 biplanes used by Peace delegates when travelling between London and Paris. This activity included all interior fittings, petrol and oil tanks, ammunition boxes and chute for machine gun, and the top wing centre section. Grimaldi & Co. also fitted the undercarriage, wheels, joy-stick and rudder controls, tailplane and elevators. The origins of the company in coach-building are indicated by the telegraphic address 'Autocoach'.

Walthamstow

The **Gnome & Le Rhone Engine Co.** was an AIRCO company chaired by G. Holt Thomas. The firm occupied a 310,000sq.ft factory on a twenty-six-acre site at Blackhorse Lane, Walthamstow, E17. The company was later known as **Peter Hooker Ltd** (for which a prospectus was issued in August 1917). The head office was co-located with that of AIRCO at 47 Victoria Street, SW1. The projected annual turnover from the prospectus was no less than £600,000. After the First World War, Peter Hooker Ltd reverted to pump manufacture.

Wembley

The **A.V. Roe** Triplane I and II were tested at Wembley Park (the present site of Wembley Stadium) from November 1909, before A.V. Roe was invited back to continue testing at Brooklands from 1 March 1910. The second Roe I Triplane was flown at Wembley Park from

6 December 1909. During this period, Humphrey Verdon Roe provided financial assistance to A.V. Roe and the two men founded **A.V. Roe & Co.** on 1 January 1910, at Brownsfield Mills, Ancoats, Manchester.

H.C. Cleaver Ltd, of 35 Berners Street, W1, is believed to have had works at Wembley. The company is listed as an aeroplane manufacturer in *The Aviation Pocket-Book, 1919-1920*. Nothing else is known.

West Drayton

M.B. Arpin & Co. of Longford, West Drayton, built the sole Arpin A-1, G-AFGB, a twin-tail boom, low-wing pusher flown at Hanworth on 7 May 1938. When it was first flown, *Flight* reported that 'The Arpin Safety Pin' was the first British aircraft to be designed from the outset around the use of a tricycle undercarriage. See Hanworth for further details.

Willesden

A significant number of companies have constructed aircraft, engines and/or aircraft components in Willesden, many of them (including Arnott & Harrison, Breguet, Jouques, BAT and General Aeronautical) apparently using the same premises in Hythe Road. Another Hythe Road company in the aeronautical supplies business was the **British Emaillite Co.**, who were an important supplier of dope for aircraft use.

Arnott & Harrison Ltd, Aeronautical Engineers, of Hythe Road, Willesden, NW10, advertised as 'Manufacturers of all Aero Parts'; this was clarified in some advertising material as 'small aero parts'.

The pioneer pilot **H.J.D. Astley** flew from Brooklands. His first aircraft was the Astley Monoplane which was built in Willesden in 1909. Astley was an Old Etonian and was the first Old Boy to land his aeroplane on Eton playing fields. He was also closely associated with the **Universal Aviation** 'Birdling' monoplane, of 1911 which was visually very similar to the Blériot.

BAT (British Aerial Transport Co. Ltd) had experimental works at 5a Hythe Road, Willesden, London, NW10, and used Hendon as their flying field. The company was formed in June 1917 by Sir Samuel Waring and Major J.C. 'Jack' Savage of Skywriting fame. Its Chief Designer was F.K. Koolhoven, who had been works manager of the British Deperdussin Co.

After the failure of British Deperdussin, Koolhoven moved on to become designer for W.G. Armstrong Whitworth Aircraft, his FK1 design flying in August 1914. Koolhoven then moved to BAT in 1917.

The company is best known for its Bantam, a single-engine single-seat fighter/sporting aircraft which was built in a number of variants (the FK22, FK23, FK27). Six FK22 were ordered, although only two are known to have been completed. These were followed by a production batch of twelve FK23, seven of which were subsequently used for civilian flying. Three prototypes of a later design, the FK25 Basilisk, were built, the first aircraft F2906 flying on 10 January 1919.

The BAT FK26 first flew at Hendon in April 1919, and was like a giant Fox Moth with an enclosed four-seat cabin behind the enormous Eagle engine. The company's advertising ran: 'BAT: We are the first people out with a purely commercial model (not a modified war type), the BAT FK26.' For further details, see Hendon.

BAT was wound up after a BAT Bantam accident in March 1920, the remaining assets being sold in 1921 to C.P.B. Ogilvie & Partners of Willesden.

The **Birch Aircraft Manufacturing Co. Ltd**, of 169-171 High Street, Willesden Green, was registered in December 1917 with capital of £2,000. The company advertised in August 1918 its ability to supply: 'Avro type undercarriages from stock. Complete undercarriages to Air Board drawings and specification, ready for attachment to fuselage, with all bracing and towing cables, main skid and Palmer wheels. Also in a position to handle wood units, propellers, skids, etc. All work officially passed by resident AID before despatch.'

Breguet Aeroplane Ltd had works at 5 Hythe Road, Cumberland Park, Willesden, NW, in August 1912. The company evolved into the **British Breguet Co.** of 1 Albemarle Street, Piccadilly, London, W, having 'works and offices at 5 Hythe Road, Willesden'. This company was reported as 'constructing Breguet models in England', these differing in their detailed construction from the original French designs. Two Willesden-built Breguet aircraft received serial numbers, these being numbers 310 (110hp Canton-Unné), and 312 (85hp).

The **British Anzani Engine Co. Ltd**, of Scrubbs Lane, Willesden, NW10, advertised as 'Contractors to HM Government'.

The **General Aeronautical Co. Ltd**, of 30 Regent Street, SW1, is reported to have taken over the BAT Works after the end of 1919. This company advertised a variety of products, including propellers.

Jouques Aviation Works had their aforesaid works at Gould Road. Twickenham, and Willesden, London, NW. This company manufactured the Royal Aircraft Factory BE2b/c/e/g, constructing some fifty-six aircraft, the majority being BE2c. Its Willesden works were taken over by **BAT (British Aerial Transport Co. Ltd)** in 1917. Jouques were advertising vacancies for tracers in March 1915.

Miles Aircraft Ltd (of Woodley, Reading) used a 19,500sq.ft factory at Hythe Road, Willesden, for the dispersed production of Miles Master components, including empennage and spars.

R.G. Toms Aviation & Motor Co. Ltd had an address of 8 Hythe Road, but it is not known what aviation work was actually carried out by this company.

Scottish Aircraft & Engineering Co. Ltd. This company, which was registered on 18 June 1936, unsuccessfully attempted to build the lifting fuselage Burnelli UB14 under licence in Britain as the Clyde Clipper. Their Scotia Works were at Willesden, NW10. Later Burnelli developments were carried out by Cunliffe-Owen Aircraft Ltd at Eastleigh, Hampshire.

The Super Aviation Co. Ltd, of 154 Dalston Lane, London, E8, was registered at the end of October 1917 with works at Dollis Hill Works, Duddenhill Lane, Willesden, NW10. Its comprehensive capabilities were advertised as 'Aeronautical Designers, Constructors and General Engineers. Manufacturers of complete machines and spares. Seaplane and aeroplane manufacturers.'

The company changed its name in June 1918 to **Sceptre Aviation Co. Ltd**, to 'avoid confusion with a similarly named firm', this being, presumably, The Supermarine Aviation Works Ltd. Sceptre Aviation was an SBAC member and 'Contractor to the Air Ministry'.

Bibliography

50 Golden Years of Achievement, Hamble 1936-1986 (British Aerospace, 1986)

75 Years of Aviation in Kingston, 1913-1988 (British Aerospace, 1988)

Adventure with Fate, Harald Penrose (Airlife, 1984)

The Aeroplane Directory of British Aviation, Staff of *The Aeroplane* (Temple Press Ltd, 1953)

The Aerospace Chronology, Michael J.H. Taylor (Tri-Service Press, 1989)

Aircraft of the Fighting Powers, Vols 1-5, H.J. Cooper, Owen Thetford (Harborough Publishing, 1940-1944)

Aircraft of the Fighting Powers, Vol.6, Owen Thetford, C.B. Maycock (Harborough Publishing, 1945)

Aircraft of the Fighting Powers, Vol.7, Owen Thetford, E.J. Riding (Harborough Publishing, 1946)

Aircraft of the RAF – A Pictorial Record 1918-1978, Paul Ellis (Macdonald & Jane's, 1978)

The Aircraft of the World, William Green & Gerard Pollinger (Macdonald, 1953)

The Aircraft of the World, William Green & Gerard Pollinger (Macdonald, 1955)

The Aircraft of the World, William Green (Macdonald, 1965)

Airlife's General Aviation, R.W. Simpson (Airlife, 1991)

Armstrong Whitworth Aircraft since 1913, Oliver Tapper (Putnam, 1973)

Aviation Archaeology, Bruce Robertson (Patrick Stephens Ltd, second edition, 1983)

Aviation in Birmingham, Geoffrey Negus & Tommy Staddon (Midland Counties Publications, 1984)

Aviation in Manchester, B.R. Robinson (Royal Aeronautical Society, Manchester branch, 1977)

Aviation Landmarks, Jean Gardner (Battle of Britain Prints International, 1990)

The Aviation Pocket-Book, 1919-1920, R. Borlase-Matthews (Crosby, Lockwood & Son, seventh edition, 1919)

Avro, Harry Holmes (Chalford Publishing, 1996)

Avro Aircraft since 1908, A.J. Jackson (Putnam, 1965)

AVRO – The History of an Aircraft Company, Harry Holmes (Airlife, 1994)

Balloons to Buccaneers – Yorkshire's Role in Aviation Since 1785, Brian Catchpole (Maxiprint, 1994)

Boulton Paul Aircraft, Boulton Paul Association (Chalford Publishing, 1996)

Brassey's World Aicraft & Systems Directory, Michael Taylor (Brassey's (UK) Ltd, 1996)

Bristol Aircraft since 1910, C.H. Barnes (Putnam, 1964)

Bristol – An Aircraft Album, James D. Oughton (Ian Allan 1973)

'Britain's Air Strength', *The Air Defence of Great Britain,* Lt Cdr R. Fletcher, MP (Penguin, October 1938)

Britain's Motor Industry – The First Hundred Years, Nick Georgano, Nick Baldwin, Anders Clausager & Jonathan Wood (G.T. Foulis & Co., 1995)

British Aeroplanes, 1914-1918, J.M. Bruce (Putnam, 1962)

British Aerospace – The Facts, BAe Corporate Communications (British Aerospace, 1992 & 1996)

British Aircraft at War 1939-45, Gordon Swanborough (HPC Publishing, 1997)

British Aircraft Manufacturers since 1908, Günter Endres (Ian Allan Publishing, 1995)

British Aircraft of World War II, David Mondey (Chancellor Press, 1994)

British Aircraft, 1809-1914, Peter Lewis (Putnam, 1962)

British Aviation – Ominous Skies, Harald Penrose (HMSO, 1980)

British Aviation – The Adventuring Years, Harald Penrose (Putnam, 1973)

British Aviation – The Pioneer Years, Harald Penrose (Cassell Ltd, revised edition, 1980)

British Aviation – Widening Horizons, Harald Penrose (HMSO, 1979)

The British Bomber since 1914, F.K. Mason (Putnam, 1994)

British Civil Aircraft since 1919, A.J. Jackson (Putnam, second edition, Vol. 1: 1973, Vol. 2: 1973, Vol. 3: 1974)

British Commercial Aircraft – sixty years in pictures, Paul Ellis (Jane's Publishing, 1980)

The British Fighter since 1912, F.K. Mason (Putnam, 1992)

British Flight Testing: Martlesham Heath 1920-1939, Tim Mason (Putnam, 1993)

British Floatplanes, G.R. Duval (D. Bradford Barton, 1976)

British Homebuilt Aircraft since 1920, Ken Ellis (Merseyside Aviation Society, second edition, 1979)

British Light Aeroplanes – Their Evolution, Development and Perfection 1920-1940, Arthur W.J.G. Ord-Hume (GMS Enterprises, 2000)

British Military Aircraft Serials 1878-1987, Bruce Robertson (Midland Counties Publications, 1987)

British Prototype Aircraft, Ray Sturtivant (The Promotional Reprint Co. Ltd, 1995)

British Racing and Record Breaking Aircraft, Peter Lewis (Putnam, 1970)

Brush Aircraft production at Loughborough, A.P. Jarram (Midland Counties Publications, 1978)

Dangerous Skies The, A.E. Clouston (Pan Books, 1956)

Discover Aviation Trails, Paul Shaw (Midland Publishing, 1996)

Dizzy Heights – The Story of Lancashire's First Flying Men, Chris Aspin (Helmshore Local History Society, 1988)

English Electric Aircraft and their Predecessors, S. Ransom & R. Fairclough (Putnam, 1987)

Fairey Aircraft since 1915, H.A. Taylor (Putnam, 1974)

Fairey Aviation, J.W.R. Taylor (Chalford Publishing, 1997)

Fighters of the Fifties, Bill Gunston (Patrick Stephens Ltd, 1981)

Filton and the Flying Machine, Malcolm Hall (Chalford Publishing, 1995)

The First Croydon Airport 1915-1928, Douglas Cluett (editor), Bob Learmonth, Joanna Nash (Sutton Libraries and Arts Services, 1977)

First Through the Clouds, F. Warren Merriam (B.T. Batsford Ltd, 1954)

The Flight of the Mew Gull, Alex Henshaw (John Murray, 1980)

Flying Corps Headquarters 1914-1918, Maurice Baring (Buchan & Enright Publishers Ltd (reprint), 1985)

The Flying Scots – A Century of Aviation in Scotland, Jack Webster (The Glasgow Royal Concert Hall, 1994)

Forever Farnborough – Flying the Limits 1904-1996, P.J. Cooper (HIKOKI Publications, 1996)

The Forgotten Pilots, Lettice Curtis (Nelson Saunders, third edition, 1985)

Forty Years of the Spitfire – Proceedings of the Mitchell Memorial Symposium, I.C. Cheeseman (RAeS, Southampton Branch, 1976)

From Spitfire to Eurofighter, Roy Boot (Airlife, 1990)

Gloucestershire Aviation – A History, Ken Wixey (Alan Sutton, 1995)

Handley Page, Alan Dowsett (Tempus Publishing, 1999)

Hawker – A biography of Harry Hawker, L.K. Blackmore (Airlife, 1993)

Hawker Aircraft since 1920, F.K. Mason (Putnam, 1961)

Helicopters and Autogyros of the World, Paul Lambermont & Anthony Pirie (Cassell, 1958)

Hendon Aerodrome – A History, David Oliver (Airlife, 1994)

The History of Black Country Aviation, Alec Brew (Alan Sutton, 1993)

History of British Aviation 1908-1914, R. Dallas Brett (Air Research Publications & Kristall Productions. Eightieth Anniversary Edition, 1988)

A History of the Eastbourne Aviation Company 1911-1924, Lou McMahon & Michael Partridge (Eastbourne Local History Society, 2000)

I Kept No Diary, Air Cdr F.R. Banks (Airlife, 1978)

Industry and Air Power – The Expansion of British Aircraft Production, 1935-1941, Sebastian Ritchie (Frank Cass, 1997)

The Jet Aircraft of the World, William Green & Roy Cross (Macdonald, 1955)

Knights of the Air, Peter King (Constable & Co. Ltd, 1989)

Lend-Lease Aircraft of World War II, Arthur Pearcy (Motorbooks International, 1996)

Leysdown – the Cradle of Flight, Brian Slade (Santa-Maria Publications, 1990)

Lion Rampant and Winged, Alan Robertson (Alan Robertson, 1986)

Mach One, Mike Lithgow, (Allan Wingate, 1954)

The Magic of a Name, Harold Nockholds (G.T. Foulis & Co. Ltd 1949)

The Marshall Story, Sir Arthur Marshall (Patrick Stephens Ltd, 1994)

Men with Wings, Wg Cdr H.P. 'Sandy' Powell (Allan Wingate, 1957)

More Tails of the Fifties, Editor: Peter G. Campbell (Cirrus Associates (SW), 1998)

Not much of an Engineer, Sir Stanley Hooker (Airlife, 1984)

Parnall's Aircraft, Ken Wixey (Tempus Publishing, 1998)

Peaceful Fields. Vol.1: The South, J.F. Hamlin (GMS Enterprises, 1996)

Plane Speaking, Bill Gunston (Patrick Stephens Ltd, 1991)

Per Ardua – The Rise of British Air Power 1911-1939, Hilary St George Saunders (Oxford University Press, 1944)

Proud Heritage – A Pictorial History of British Aerospace Aircraft, Phil Coulson (Royal Air Force Benevolent Fund, 1995)

Pure Luck – The Authorized Biography of Sir Thomas Sopwith 1888-1989, Alan Bramson (Patrick Stephens Ltd, 1990)

The Quick and The Dead, W.A. Waterton (Frederick Muller Ltd, 1956)

The Redwing Story, John Lane (Mrs Phyllis Lane, 1992)

Schneider Trophy, The, David Mondey (Robert Hale, 1975)

Sent Flying, A.J. 'Bill' Pegg (Macdonald, 1959)

Shoreham Airport, Sussex, T.M.A. Webb & Dennis L. Bird (Cirrus Associates (SW), 1996)

Shorts Aircraft since 1900, C.H. Barnes (Putnam, 1989)

Slide Rule, Nevil Shute (Readers Union, 1956)

Sopwith – The Man and His Aircraft, Bruce Robertson (Air Review Ltd, 1970)

The Speed Seekers, Thomas G. Foxworth (Macdonald and Jane's, 1975)

The Spider Web, Sqn Ldr T.D. Hallam (Arms & Armour Press (reprint), 1979)

Spirit of Hamble – Folland Aircraft, Derek N. James (Tempus Publishing, 2000)

Spitfire – A Test Pilot's Story, J.K. Quill (John Murray, 1983)

The Spitfire Story, Alfred Price (Arms & Armour Press, second edition, 1995)

Staffordshire and Black Country Airfields, Alec Brew (Chalford Publishing, 1997)

Stirling Wings – The Short Stirling goes to War, Jonathan Falconer (Budding Books, 1995)

The Story of Acton Aerodrome and the Alliance Factory (London Borough of Ealing Library Service with Addenda and Corrigenda, second edition, 1978)

The Story of the British Light Aeroplane, Terence Boughton (John Murray, 1963)

Supermarine Spitfire – 40 Years On, G.N.M. Gingell (RAeS Southampton Branch, 1976)

Tails of the Fifties, Editor: Peter G. Campbell (Cirrus Associates (SW), 1997)

Test Pilot, Nevil Duke (Allan Wingate, 1953)

Test Pilots – The Story of British Test Flying 1903-1984, Don Middleton (Willow Books, 1985)

Testing Time, Constance Babington Smith (Cassell & Co. Ltd, 1961)

That Nothing Failed Them, Air Cdr A.H. Wheeler (G.T. Foulis & Co. Ltd, 1963)

Three Centuries to Concorde, Charles Burnet (Mechanical Engineering Publications Ltd, 1979)

A Time to Fly, Sir Alan Cobham (Shepheard-Walwyn, 1978)

Ultralights – The Early British Classics, Richard Riding (Patrick Stephens Ltd, 1987)

Vapour Trails, Mike Lithgow (Allan Wingate, 1956)

Vickers Aircraft since 1908, C.F. Andrews & E.B. Morgan (Putnam, second edition, 1988)

War in the Air, Edward Smithies (Penguin, 1992)

Westland 50, J.W.R. Taylor & Maurice F. Allward (Ian Allan, 1965)

Westland Aircraft since 1919, Derek N. James (Putnam, 1991)

Wings over Woodley – The Story of Miles Aircraft and the Adwest Group, Julian C. Temple (Aston Publications, 1987)

World Encyclopaedia of Aircraft Manufacturers, Bill Gunston (Patrick Stephens Ltd, 1993)

Other publications:

Flight : 'The First Aero Weekly in the World – A Journal Devoted to the Interests, Practice and Progress of Aerial Locomotion and Transport. Official Organ of The Royal Aero Club of the United Kingdom.'

The Aeroplane: Temple Press Ltd. Editors: C.G. Grey, Thurstan James.

Aeroplane Monthly: IPC Magazines Ltd.

The Aeroplane Spotter: July 1941-December 1945; Temple Press Ltd.

Jane's All the Worlds Aircraft: Published by Samson Low, Jane's Information Group. Reprints by David & Charles Ltd, Collins and Jane's.

Popular Flying: The Magazine of the Popular Flying Association

Royal Air Force Flying Review: 1954-55, 1957-58, 1961-62; Mercury House Publications.

Index

Since this book is based on geographic locations, the entries for place names are listed first.
Please note that only a selection of aircraft types are listed, in particular those types that were most widely contracted to manufacturers across the industry.